REINVENTING CITIES

Equity Planners Tell Their Stories

CONFLICTS IN URBAN AND REGIONAL DEVELOPMENT,
a series edited by
John R. Logan and Todd Swanstrom

Norman Krumholz and Pierre Clavel

REINVENTING CITIES
Equity Planners Tell Their Stories

Temple University Press

Philadelphia

Temple University Press, Philadelphia 19122
Copyright © 1994 by Temple University. All rights reserved
Published 1994
Printed in the United States of America

Library of Congress Cataloging-in-Publication Data
Krumholz, Norman.
   Reinventing cities : equity planners tell their stories / Norman Krumholz and
Pierre Clavel.
       p.   cm.—(Conflicts in urban and regional development)
Includes bibliographical references and index.
ISBN 1-56639-209-8 (cloth : alk. paper). —
ISBN 1-56639-210-1 (pbk. : alk. paper)
       1. City planning—United States.   2. City planners—United States—
Interviews.   3. Urban policy—United States—Case studies. 4. Social justice—
Case studies.   I. Clavel, Pierre.   II. Title.   III. Series.
HT167.K75   1994
307.1′2′0973—dc20   93-42538

We dedicate this book to the memory of *Daniel I. Krumholz*, who died of AIDS in 1990. Dan was a gifted son who loved music and literature and was beginning to make his way as a writer. He is remembered with joy and love.

CONTENTS

PREFACE

This book is about professional urban planners who, in their day-to-day practice, have tried to move resources, political power, and political participation away from the business elites that frequently benefit from public policy and toward the needs of low-income or working-class people of their cities. We call these planners "equity planners" because they seek greater equity among different groups as a result of their work.

This focus on a group of professionals committed to equity also portrays an underreported dimension of urban politics. For decades, academics and journalists have described cities as relentlessly driven to favor the rich over the poor, thus contributing to the unfortunate impoverishment of neighborhoods, neglect of infrastructure, and loss of services. Despite this, from time to time there have been reports of vibrant community movements and neighborhood organizations that are thriving. Here, we describe what we believe to be an underreported set of complementary professional developments.

Most of this book consists of a series of interviews with ordinary planners from every part of the United States—some in planning agencies, some in other departments of government—whose accomplishments have been extraordinary. The interviews come from different cities and different planners; they also reflect different equity planning policy methods from fair share plans for low-income housing to plans for a community-based economic development. We have tried to suggest how these planners thought about their responsibilities, how and why they decided to do what they did, and how they succeeded. We hope our interviews explore some of the inner dimensions of social change, some personal qualities not ordinarily elaborated. We also hope that other urban planners will be inspired by the examples we have selected and "go and do likewise."

The interviewees are white, black, and Hispanic male and female human beings of dimension and flaw, who have tried very hard, often against great odds, to inspire social change. They have reaped some rewards, occasionally achieved great success, and sometimes accepted the costs of failure. Their work and the work of hundreds (we suspect) of other planners like them deserve further analysis, research, and imitation, but we will not get any of this unless their work is brought out into the open, onto urban planning's center stage, and that is our intent here.

Equity planning is particularly important at this time in our history. The past forty years have not been kind to American cities; almost all older industrial cities are losing population and economic investment and are becoming locations of concentrated poverty and unemployment. Much of the population remaining in these cities lives in areas that provide poor educations, have high crime rates, and in every respect offer a sharply lower quality of life than that enjoyed by other Americans.

Local and national leadership, often aided by traditional city planning and redevelopment officials, usually has responded to this crisis by attempts to stimulate new investment, bring the white middle class back to the city, and develop heavily subsidized real estate projects in downtown areas, hoping that the benefits of these efforts will somehow "trickle down" to those in the lower reaches. To an extent, these efforts have succeeded: new offices, hotels, convention centers, and sports stadiums have been built in many cities, physically changing their skylines.

They have not, however, reduced poverty, unemployment, or dependency among their resident populations. They have also left unimproved the neighborhoods of the working class and poor. And they have left virtually untouched the widening economic disparities between central cities and suburbs.

For example, between 1980 and 1990, the rate of increase in employed residents was four times greater in the suburbs than in the central city; unemployment rates in 1990 were significantly higher in cities than suburbs, and the percentage of persons in poverty was more than two-and-one-half times higher in cities. Even in cities where the building boom was strongest in the 1980s, resident poverty and unemployment grew worse by 1990, while economic disparities between city and suburb continued to widen.[1]

In sum, the "trickle down" policy in American cities has produced few, if any, benefits for increasingly destitute resident city people. Instead, it has produced a more and more bifurcated city, split between downtown and other zones of increased affluence and low-income neighborhoods.

An alternative approach to the problems of the central city is equity planning, a reorientation of physical planning that places equity at its heart. Instead of aiming at "trickle down" effects, this policy aims plan and program benefits directly at the deprived residents of the cities. This approach was pioneered by one of the authors of this book in Cleveland in the 1970s; variations of the same theme have since been applied in Chicago, Berkeley, Jersey City,

Boston, and many other cities, some of which are incuded in this book. In these cities, planners have pressed for broadened citizen participation, more open government procedures, fair share plans for public housing, rent control, linkage arrangements, and other programs to aid poor and working-class residents. Other equity planners press for redistribution, but also emphasize a more consciousness-oriented cultural populism aimed at establishing and asserting the rights of blacks, Latinos, and other minorities, as well as trying to bridge issues of gender and sexual preference. The differences between these approaches are elaborated in the Introduction.

The authors of this book, Norman Krumholz, a planning director turned uneasy academic, and Pierre Clavel, a professor and city planner whose research and writing has focused on progressive cities, believe that equity-oriented approaches hold the promise of better policy and program outcomes for the troubled resident populations of our central cities. We hope this book and the personal examples it offers will be of interest to academics and students, but mostly to practicing planners. Some will find reason to dispute the efficacy of the approaches to planning we describe. The most frequent obstacles mentioned are the lack of political support and other factors external to the "professional" role of the city planner. Although institutions and some planning traditions may make it difficult to adopt an equity orientation, and although there is much that is wrong with city politics, the premise here is that the barriers to the achievement of a real equity planning approach are mostly internal. They are internal to the planner's personal approach: what planners need at least as much as technique and ideas are the motivation, the confidence, and the will to try to change prevailing ideas in a direction that is just and useful to the resident populations of their cities. And they are internal to the profession: its ability to incorporate the values these planners adopted, the methods they employed, and the constituencies they cultivated within their everyday, publicly acknowledged practices so that there is support for the personal approaches involved. We hope to fortify both personal will and professional sanction by providing examples, stories, personal accounts of similar professionals who have done just that and who have not only been successful but have sometimes emerged as more fully realized human beings.

Through these personal interviews, we hope the reader will learn

- what it "takes" to be an equity planner;
- how equity planners developed a set of community goals and objectives;
- how they organized and drew attention to their programs;

– how they strategized, seized openings, built coalitions, and exploited opportunities in support of their efforts, and how these efforts varied from city to city;

– how the planners related to the people in the neighborhoods and their advocates and how they tried to maintain that relationship;

– how the equity planners related to mayors and city councils and sometimes sought the support of the business "establishment";

– how the planners changed over time as a result of their work;

– how they dealt with issues of race;

– how they tried and succeeded (or failed) to institutionalize their practice so that it continued under a new regime.

Perhaps we should give more detail. As practitioner and academic, we have been interested in city planning from an equity perspective, that is, a practice that tries to move resources, power, and participation away from elites and emphasizes the needs of the low-income and working-class residents of the community. Part of this has come from Krumholz's experience as director of the Cleveland City Planning Commission from 1969 to 1979. Early on, following a path blazed by many others interested in progressive municipal activities, he and his staff selected the goal of more "choices for those who have few" as a guide for long-range and day-to-day operations, in effect choosing sides in favor of the poor and working-class residents of Cleveland.[2]

The goal shaped the day-to-day work of the planning staff in many ways. For example, consider their work in a long-term negotiation in the 1970s leading to the establishment of the Greater Cleveland Regional Transit Authority (RTA).

Transportation problems are usually defined in terms of rush-hour congestion, automobile access, or the need for off-street parking. The Cleveland planners, led by Janice Cogger and Himanshu Patel, defined Cleveland's most significant transportation problem in a very different way. They saw it as the need to improve the mobility of the transit-dependent population, those families who lacked automobiles and depended on public transportation for their entire mobility around the metropolitan area.

As the planners reasoned, our automotive society has provided enormous mobility for those who have been able to own and use cars, which is to say, most Americans. But as automobiles proliferated and new developments scattered at low densities across our metropolitan regions, ridership on public transit declined, fares increased, and service was cut. For transit-dependent riders, most of whom were poor, elderly, or physically handicapped, there were fewer and fewer destinations they could reach at ever higher fares and longer waiting periods. In effect, they were the people "with fewest choices," since they had been victimized by a national decision to opt for an automotive society. Accordingly, they deserved compensatory consideration and the planner's highest priority.

Over five years of intensive negotiations to establish Cleveland's RTA, speaking first as representatives of a Democratic mayor, Carl B. Stokes, and later of a Republican mayor, Ralph J. Perk, Cleveland's city planners argued their highest-priority goal of improving the mobility of the transit-dependent population. They were beaten back on a number of occasions, but Janice Cogger and other members of the planning staff persevered. The final agreement signed by the Cleveland City Council in 1975 made clear that the planners had made substantial progress toward ensuring that RTA would be responsive to the needs of the transit dependent. The final agreement by the city guaranteed lower fares for the elderly and handicapped, improved service frequencies and route coverage within the city, and offered a low-cost, prenotification, door-to-door service for transit-dependent riders. This was certainly more than the transit dependent would have gotten if Cleveland's city planners had not been ready with clear objectives and the will to fight for them.[3]

Slightly later, Clavel, in part because of the Cleveland efforts, began an extensive survey of similar work. He documented a city real estate program in Hartford, a rent control coalition in Santa Monica, participatory innovations in Berkeley, community economics in Chicago, linkage in Boston, and participatory and redistributive reforms in other places.[4] All this was, or was related to, equity planning in the sense practiced in Cleveland, and, as we suggest in Chapter 1, both the Cleveland experience and that of these other cities relate to an older, if submerged, planning tradition.

We had always felt convinced of the value of what planners and their supporting coalitions had accomplished in Cleveland and elsewhere, but there had also been criticism. The "progressive cities" were said to have little relevance to what went on where politics was more conservative. The central criticism about Cleveland was that what happened there during the 1970s was too idiosyncratic to be useful to urban planners in other cities. This criticism goes something like this: "Well, what happened in Cleveland was very nice, but it resulted from an unlikely set of circumstances—a group of unusual personalities in the planning department, a very poor city with a large poor and working-class population, a group of populist-type politicians locked in an adversarial relationship with the business community. Any of these characteristics is unusual; *all* of them are simply not going to happen again." This argument then takes another tack: "Anyway, practicing city planners are not progressive and bold risk takers but are highly vulnerable civil servants operating in the conservative political environment of their city halls. They are not likely to hold to redistributive ethical principles in the face of contrary political power."

In response to these criticisms, our first thought was to suspect a difference in perspective: were our motives for entering the profession so different from those of our critics that we saw things in a different light? Maybe so, but we both felt our critics were engaging in serious denial of the *facts* we reported. Whatever our own shortcomings of perspective or research method, something interesting was going on in these places, something that needed to see the light of day to a greater extent than previously, before a serious evaluation could begin. A great deal of solid, equity-oriented planning work was taking place all over America that had generally gone unreported and unnoticed. Our first purpose is simply to portray this. Perhaps some planners, reading these chapters, will see the light and move their personal approaches in the directions suggested.

But in addition to the fact of equity planning, there is an interpretation issue. It may be possible to suggest a broadening of the *profession* of city planning to include the essential themes of equity planning within a larger focus. This is the theme of the following chapters. The argument is twofold.

A first point is about constituencies. We want to encourage practicing planners to pay more attention to groups and individuals in their cities who are in need. The interviews in this book argue that the equity-oriented work of city planners can produce tangible benefits for poor and working-class city residents and that openings and opportunities to serve those in need exist daily in normal planning practice in most cities. Moreover, the interviews suggest that a professionally oriented, politically engaged equity planning practice will not only survive in the crucible of city hall but will prosper there. For demographic and other reasons, the constituency for equity planning is a winning coalition.

A second and complementary part of the argument is that equity planners need not be alone as professionals. Although Cleveland planners did many things during the 1970s, we were struck by how alone we both thought the planners were in their efforts. Krumholz put in major efforts advocating his approach to national audiences, but found what he thought was surprisingly little of a similar nature going on in other cities. He was mystified about this. Clavel began researching "progressive cities" in 1980, examining the experiences of Cleveland as well as those of Hartford, Berkeley, Santa Monica, and Burlington, Vermont; and while he found some other examples of planning with redistributive intent, he was struck by the extent to which their experiences remained isolated from one another and peripheral to the mainstream of professional practice. The same thing was true in later work in Chicago and Boston. We never saw why this should be so, and one objective is to show how "mainstream" planners might conceive their work in a more complex way, so as to include and support their equity-oriented colleagues.

The chapters that follow include interviews in nine cities with persons we have identified as carrying on at least some of this new "equity" orientation in their work. Each of the cities or regions in which these planners worked is introduced with a short snapshot that includes the demographics, politics, and economic issues at the time the planner began work. Each chapter is followed by a list of additional readings dealing with the chapter's central issue.

The questions we have posed to our respondents are fundamental. They have to do with how these equity planners think about their work; what makes them tick; how their values and views evolved; what strategies they used to implement their plans; how they related to the mayor, city council, business community, and neighborhoods; and how they obtained and maintained support from these diverse constituencies. The responses of these equity planners, in their own words, make up the body of this book.

We have to add a word about how this book was put together and thank those who helped us. The original idea was Krumholz's. Clavel wrote the first draft of the Introduction and helped by interviewing Mier and Dreier, by doing the original editing of their chapters, and by editing the Vazquez and Stanback interviews. Krumholz did all the other interviews and editing, most of the concluding chapter and Preface, and supervised the snapshots. Jordan Yin, Janet Smith, and Jack Lynch did background research for the snapshots, and Kim McClain helped with the Hartford snapshot. Beatriz Rodriguez did a splendid job of transcribing taped interviews and typing drafts, cheerfully incorporating revisions into the manuscript again and again.

We are grateful for the financial support of the George Gund Foundation and BP America, both of Cleveland. Their research grants came at an opportune moment and were of great assistance. We are also grateful to the following planners who were gracious enough to take the time to provide interviews that do not show up in this book but may in another: Neil Mayer and Eve Bach, Berkeley; Gus Newport, Boston; Patrick Costigan, Mike Siepp, Paul Brophy, and Elva Tillman, Baltimore; Peg Stone, Daly City; Bonnie Turner, Denver; Marla Simpson, New York City; and Chris Warren, Cleveland.

We were helped by initial readings by Todd Swanstrom and William Goldsmith and a review of the Introduction by Anne Clavel. We are also particularly indebted to John Forester, who read the manuscript with care and conscience and made many incisive suggestions. If solecisms persist, it is the consequence of our obtuseness, not of the counsel of our readers.

We want to express special appreciation to our wives, Virginia Krumholz and Anne Clavel, for their patience and unfailing good humor while we struggled with the agonies of composition.

NOTES

1. Larry C. Ledebur and William P. Barnes, *All in It Together* (Washington, D.C.: National League of Cities, 1993); and David Rusk, *Cities without Suburbs* (Washington, D.C.: Woodrow Wilson Center Press, 1993).

2. Norman Krumholz, Janice Cogger, and John H. Linner, "The Cleveland Policy Planning Report," *Journal of the American Institute of Planning* 41, no. 5 (September 1975): 298–304; Norman Krumholz, "A Retrospective View of Equity Planning: Cleveland 1969–1979," *Journal of the American Planning Association,* Spring 1982, 164–173; Norman Krumholz and John Forester, *Making Equity Planning Work* (Philadelphia: Temple University Press, 1990).

3. A more detailed discussion of the Cleveland transit case can be found in Krumholz and Forester, *Making Equity Planning Work,* chap. 8.

4. Pierre Clavel, *The Progressive City* (New Brunswick, N.J.: Rutgers University Press, 1986); and Pierre Clavel and Wim Wiewel, eds., *Harold Washington and the Neighborhoods* (New Brunswick, N.J.: Rutgers University Press, 1991).

REINVENTING CITIES

Equity Planners Tell Their Stories

chapter 1

INTRODUCTION: Professional Support for Equity Planning?

Equity planning means a conscious attempt to devise redistributive policies in favor of the least powerful and to enhance the avenues of participation. For us, it refers to persons working in official capacities for city governments. Equity planners operate somewhat in tension with the equilibrium of politics in most places, and the practice of equity planning differs from that of mainstream (most) city planning professionals. In this chapter we describe how equity planning is different, why it has emerged to the extent it has from a politics and professional practice that, at least on the surface, is markedly different, and we raise the question—to be answered in the chapters that follow—whether equity planning will become a larger part of normal city politics and city planning than it is today.

EQUITY PLANNING DEFINED

As noted in the Preface, Krumholz and his coworkers in Cleveland were among those who publicized "equity planning" in the 1970s, most notably when, in the "Cleveland Policy Plan Report," they defined city policy as "providing choices to those who had few." On many occasions, they took steps to open up city planning issues to larger citizen participation, working closely, if informally, with the fast-growing neighborhood movement of the mid-1970s in that city.[1] Clavel provided a more formal definition in the Introduction to his *The Progressive City,* when he noted city governments that tried to follow participatory and redistributive policy innovations.[2] He found that such cities were committed to doing *both* redistribution and participation but that some did much more of the one than of the other. This led to a diagram where, with participation and redistribution on different axes, cities tried to push out a "frontier" defined by both axes while recognizing that they would do better on one dimension than the other. At times, the one objective would seem to defeat the other. But the places that pushed the frontier farthest were more progressive:

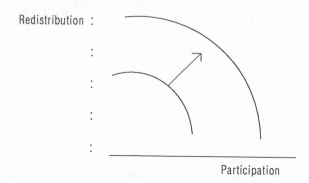

Redistribution :

Participation

It was possible, then, to list "redistributive" innovations and "participatory" ones, and to provide a rough ranking of cities on each dimension. The "progressive" cities did at least some of each. Places such as Berkeley did some remarkable things on the participatory dimension, most notably a "fair representation ordinance" that dramatically opened up participation on citizen boards. Hartford's redistributive initiatives included tax reforms and an informal "linkage" program that charged real estate developers with providing jobs and other concessions to city residents in return for tax breaks, but did much less to open the city to participation. Both places pushed out the frontier compared to most other cities.

Equity planners could be defined as planning for similar ends; in doing so, they created a set of political dilemmas and solutions, a professional practice and way of life that had its own characteristics, whether or not the city moved generally in an equity direction—as in Berkeley or, later, Santa Monica and Chicago—or only partially—as in Cleveland and Jersey City. The dilemma is that if equity planning means a conscious attempt to carry out redistributive policies in favor of the least powerful and enhancing the avenues of participation, it implies that something is wrong with the normal channels of politics: representation through elected mayors and city council members and the tug and shove of local interest groups that seem to work for most people. Why add something that comes into conflict with politics as usual? Why not simply let the elected representatives set goals and the planners carry out those goals? That is what ordinary planners do. They let their ends be decided by politicians or planning boards. Conventional planners basically view themselves as giving their bosses choices—or finding the most efficient means to an end chosen by their bosses, whom they assume represent the people through the democratic process.

Equity planners reject this technical definition of the role of planners. They maintain that planners who seek a better future for their cities and their people must be concerned with ends as well as means. And the end they should be concerned with first is helping the "truly disadvantaged" because, equity planners assume, the existing democratic institutions are biased against the interests of those at the bottom of the social system. That is, equity planners seek downward redistribution, often out ahead of the initiatives of their bosses, the elected politicians.

Second, and perhaps more awkwardly, equity planners seek greater participation and have developed a facility for making participation happen. This is not just a matter of formulating a substantive message that elites and politicians can consider in op-ed pieces and boardrooms. It is a style of sharp interaction, at bottom over issues of class—issues that the traditional political system tends to muffle through technical discussion and political party organization and that scholars have argued are too complex to be handled well, particularly at the local level.[3]

Equity planning is also fraught with issues of race and the problem of "handling" diversity. Here, neither the equity planners nor the traditions of local politics have given an adequate answer. Traditional politics works at access and creates an arena where, on occasion, racially defined groups can bargain for resources by contributing leadership to a system that may work systematically against them. Leadership is thus coopted, while grassroots populations remain, at best, organized in an informal way or outside the loop of politics.[4] The equity planners we have known, as it happens, mostly tend to be white males and females, often representing people of color, but not drawn from these populations. How they manage to function effectively across these lines without contributing to further fractioning of the solidarity of communities of color is one of the great untold stories of urban life—though some of the story is contained in the chapters that follow.

Confounding the efforts of equity planners to solve the problems of cities was the increasing inequality within metropolitan areas, between central city and suburb, and among different central city populations. In the 1980s, it gradually became apparent that inequalities were rooted not only in government policies that planners might conceivably address but in the fundamental processes of the economy, now increasingly stressed by international competition. Thus, manufacturing jobs were shifting out of northeastern and midwestern U.S. cities, not only to rural areas but overseas. Equity planners, in their claims to address these inequalities, were forced to look at their own cities' politics and at the international economy and how the nation would deal with it.

WHY EQUITY PLANNING EMERGED

Equity planning emerged as a necessary function in cities during the 1960s and 1970s, and with particular force in the 1980s. Simply stated, equity planning was necessary because the economics and political coalitions that drove city development and planning in the post–World War II period changed and decayed, and the mainstream planning that serviced city development was no longer adequate to significant segments of city populations—namely, the poor, minorities, and elderly people with few resources who remained trapped in central cities as wealthier people moved out. These remaining city populations, meanwhile, organized a vibrant community life and set of organizations that were able not only to agitate for policies but participate in the delivery of public services. They became an alternative politics, operating alongside the traditional city political organizations and demanding what the equity planners offered.

Changing Economics and Politics Urban politics was powerfully shaped by, and then reinforced, the economic currents after World War II. This created a new period of urban policies at city, state, and national levels that is now ending. The economic currents included expansion of manufacturing driven by consumer demand, itself impelled by metropolitan growth and suburban real estate development. Consumerism and suburban growth benefited huge segments of the public; by the 1960s, the nation had shifted from two-thirds of the population renting to two-thirds owning their homes. That was the mass base of the constituency, but a complex array of groups made it happen; they were the forces that came together in a political coalition. Manufacturers dispersed from central cities to suburbs and sunbelt, while developers created quarters for specialized service and office functions in the cities.[5] Local governments modernized themselves to accommodate these shifts. They implemented urban renewal in the central cities, replacing manufacturing and old housing with office and retail complexes. They built massive suburban expansions to accommodate an outflow of factories and the growing and upwardly mobile working class. They managed much of the construction of the new highways and expressways that linked the suburbs to the central cities and to one another. City and suburban local government employment and spending increased by a huge amount, spurred by intergovernmental funding from new federal agencies. Not just the government agencies but political coalitions emerged in city after city, organized around growth, later known as *growth coalitions*.

One thing that made growth coalitions powerful was that they embodied popular sentiment to such a large extent and mobilized public support so generally. They did not merely combine a set of interests, though this was a necessary condition for success. They also captured the high ground by claiming to represent a public interest. Their ascendance coincided with that of John Kennedy's presidency, with its call to "ask not what your country can do for you, but what you can do for your country" and its assertion that "a rising tide lifts all boats." Kennedy mobilized hopes and faith that government, working with all interest groups, could get the country moving again. For at least a few years, people believed this. The national leadership, in mobilizing such sentiments, was in part following the leadership of innovative city governments that had paved the way for urban renewal and highway construction and had presented a vision for the coordinated development of suburban homeownership along with a fair deal for all in housing and jobs in the inner cities: Philadelphia and New Haven were the most prominent examples. Their programs, refocused at the national level with the rationalism of a Robert MacNamara in the newly modernized Department of Defense and later with the brief promise of Lyndon Johnson's Great Society programs, then percolated down to many other cities, where business and political leadership claimed to solve urban problems of all sorts through the developing instruments of growth.

New Social Movements   A great irony in the modern history of American cities is that, having rebuilt their downtowns and modernized their political and administrative functions through attachment to an emerging powerful growth coalition, that coalition proved relatively unstable and short-lived. By the end of the 1960s, growth policies were creating serious problems. Most obvious were the dislocations caused by the demolitions of urban renewal and highway construction, but deeper demographic and economic shifts occurred as well. Cities emptied out, partly as a result of demolitions, but also because of the incentives from suburban housing construction and the transformation of downtown city cores from manufacturing to office locations. The populations of cities became increasingly minority, aged, and dependent. Growth coalitions were generally identified as business oriented and became the initial focus of opposition by grassroots groups, which emerged in the cities during and after the 1960s. Much of the opposition came to be rooted in neighborhoods, as it was possible to mobilize support among residents who identified with specific locations, around such specific issues as housing, health care, policing, and occasionally jobs.

All these issues could be stated in terms of the relative deprivation of classes, but they had their most dramatic expression through the perception of race. In part there was the moral legitimacy of the civil rights movement, gained through the early 1960s by heroics in the South, to at least some extent a shared achievement of whites as well as blacks, dominated by the nonviolent strategies of Dr. Martin Luther King, Jr. This movement, including Dr. King and other black leaders and movement organizations, had begun turning to northern cities and economic justice issues by 1968. More of a jolt to the nation's white majorities were the riots of the late 1960s and the general agitation from blacks, joined by white liberal allies, that came along at the same time and afterward. Hundreds of community organizations formed, in quick succession in city after city, around protest themes, to some extent aiming for access to power and sometimes along self-development lines. Shortly afterward, but much more prominent by 1970, were white reactions, slowly becoming more organized through the 1970s and after. White neighborhood activism certainly had its economic basis, but race became another prism, for many groups, through which economic issues could most easily be expressed.

The initial response in the 1960s and early 1970s was federal social policies. These included intergovernmental transfers of funds and many new programs, the most well known being the Community Action Programs and Model Cities.[6] These and other programs were the official response to grassroots initiatives that sometimes began as riots and disorder in the 1960s and were inspired, in official circles, by both idealism and fear. What resulted was a tense interaction between neighborhoods and city hall. The new programs sought out, supported, and often coopted these grassroots constituencies. There were struggles between local political organizations and newly emerging grassroots groups, a tension caused by the dissonance between grassroots interests and existing local politics. In the struggle both sides were able to get allies in federal and state governments and elsewhere. Local political organizations tended to win these struggles, but not always and not completely.[7] Local political machines were in a process of transformation in any event by other forces, economic and demographic: a shift from manufacturing based in the central city with a white working-class labor force to a metropolitan pattern with dispersed manufacturing and a suburbanized white working class. Increasingly, the central cities became office headquarters with growing minority and elderly resident populations. Meanwhile, the national employment base was shifting from relatively highly paid manufacturing jobs to low-paid service work. These shifts put stress on the voting base of city political organizations. Cities were losing jobs and their tax base, and populations were becoming more expensive to service. Federal programs were stopgaps, but by the 1970s Republican presidents were laying the groundwork for a retreat from federal involvement in city affairs, a retreat realized finally in the 1980s. All these things reduced the ability of city politicians to reward their supporters and build coalitions capable of implementing city policies.

With the decline of federal funding and the completion of many public works and urban renewal projects, including the removal of much of the white working-class population to suburban locations, much of the basis for growth coalitions was gone. But downtown business, developers, metropolitan papers, and others continued to press for projects, demanding local public subsidy and promising "growth" in various ways; often these were empty promises. This pressure has continued in various guises to the present. It set the stage for renewed grassroots organizations, which grew through the 1970s in response to the continued costs—demolitions, shifts of resources from neighborhood needs to big projects, for example—imposed on them by the growth policies and in the vacuum created by the decreasing effectiveness of political parties and municipal agencies.[8]

By the 1990s, there was essentially a stalemate. Growth coalitions could not pursue projects on anything like the scale suggested by the grandiose plans of the 1950s and 1960s. And the grassroots movements that opposed growth policies had not clearly indicated what direction they would pursue or how far they would go toward developing an alternative coalition or program. In fact, grassroots energy had been spent in two directions, guided by contrasting values, ever since the late 1960s. One of them, identified with the white working class that remained in many cities and that had now established bridgeheads in the suburbs, emphasized a kind of economic populism, which had several facets. There was at least some connection to the civil rights movement, whose leaders were calling for redistribution of national wealth to all the poor, not just minorities, by the end of the 1960s. More notable was the role of a prominent group of organizers trained by Saul Alinsky, who featured a combative style based on down-to-earth neighborhood interests and avoided ideological or political identifications. Alinsky had built ties to minority-based community organizations, but organizations influenced by his approach grew very rapidly in the 1970s, mainly in white working-class neighborhoods. These were supported by religious groups, particularly the Catholic church, which was able to support an economic populism, one that emerged in a famous Bishops' Letter in the 1980s, while avoiding various social issues.[9] These groups gained further from such federal programs as VISTA, created by the Carter administration after 1976.

Since the 1960s, the growth of grassroots neighborhood organizations has been remarkable. Even if block clubs, settlement houses, and neighborhood-based advocacy organizations on the Alinsky model are excluded, the number of community development corporations (CDCs) by the mid-1980s was estimated at anywhere from 3,000 to 5,000.[10] These CDCs ranged in size from the powerful Bedford-Stuyvesant Restoration Corporation, which developed 1,600 housing units, financed commercial centers, and built industrial plants, to single-person operations in some smaller cities. CDC contributions to the infrastructure of low-income neighborhoods across the United States have been substantial. Once seen as tentative, low-budgeted alternative ways to help low-income neighborhoods, CDCs have been increasingly seen as *the* chosen vehicle.[11]

A political version of this populism surfaced by the middle 1970s. The mayor of Cleveland, Dennis Kucinich, was a prominent example. One of his major legacies was a well-reported speech to the National Press Club laying out the principles of economic populism. In addition to an attack on corporate power, Kucinich hoped to unite people across racial lines by emphasizing the economic issues they had in common and avoiding mention of the "social issues" that kept them apart:

> We're uniting poor and working people, both black and white, on economic issues. . . . You may notice that I didn't touch on any of the great debates over social issues. The basis of genuine reform is economic reform. We can solve economic problems if we refuse to be distracted. . . . The substitution of social issues in place of economic issues (far from offering an alternative route to progressive politics) trifles with people's problems: offers false solutions such as the integration of schools which are so bad that you wouldn't want your kids to go to the schools in any case.
>
> Trifling with social issues . . . diminishes the potential of economic issues to rally popular support. The social issues are often divisive and play off against each other the very people who ought to be the beneficiaries of economic reforms. . . . These are the people who have their attention diverted by irrelevant social ideology.[12]

Other elements in the neighborhood and other social movements of the time were at least as important as those reflected in Kucinich's rhetoric. A second version of grassroots populism that emerged from the 1960s placed more emphasis on social issues, more prominently featured African American and Latino interests, and came more directly from the civil rights movement. Later, a more complicated populism developed that sought to create a working-class consciousness that embraced a tolerance for diversity, seeking to include gay and lesbian, feminist, and occasionally environmental activists in coalition. It sought to bridge divisions—race most prominently, but also gender, sexual preference, and other issues. It led eventually to political expression in the "rainbow coalition" support for blacks such as Harold Washington in Chicago and Mel King in Boston, both in 1983, and the national campaigns of Jesse Jackson in 1984 and 1988.[13] The emphasis in this sort of populist program was on process as much as economic advantage. It was, especially, the development of community consciousness and the capacity to share in governing. James Jennings and Mel King defined it in the title of their book, *From Access to Power*. It was a theme that reverberated in the communities of color in particular and that received particular expression in some of the administrators of Harold Washington's Chicago mayoralty of 1983–1987.[14]

By the end of the 1980s, the *technique* of community organizing was moving toward a general appreciation of the multicultural reality of U.S. cities and the methods of interaction necessary to harmonize increasingly diverse populations. School reorganization in Chicago, literacy programs in Baltimore, sensitivity group training, gender-related economic development programs, and AIDS programs in San Francisco and many other places were indications of broad currents beneath the surface of official policy and rhetoric. They were happening despite a relatively conservative surface of urban life, amid fiscal austerity and government rhetoric that remained determinedly "mainstream" and small town. Even the Democrats, electing a president from Arkansas in 1992, kept things low key on the urban front, while easing many of the restrictive policies that had gone on earlier. But these *public* aspects simply masked what was going on outside government circles in most places, and at the local level.

Although a sharp line can be drawn between the two kinds of populism, both organizers and the rank and file will be quick to point out the complex alliances across these divisions. And it may be that economic populism can develop into the rainbow type over time. Concretely, Harold Washington was beginning to make alliances with some of the white ethnic neighborhoods in northwest Chicago before his death in 1987; and Raymond Flynn, while he operated as Boston's mayor with an overtly economic populist program, replete with statements like Kucinich's, was able to work out at least some alliances with "rainbow" organizations in Roxbury.

What is clear, though, is the growth in social organization at the neighborhood level. What began as "advocacy" for a share of the pie for disadvantaged groups in the 1960s became a set of stable organizations with paid staff, capable of delivering a variety of welfare, health, housing, and other services. By the 1980s, city governments were experimenting by simply providing funds they had previously administered themselves to the neighborhood organizations to administer. In Chicago, Harold Washington's administration was supporting hundreds of organizations in this way; dozens of community organizations were involved in housing rehabilitation and new construction in Cleveland and Boston. This was becoming a common practice.[15]

John Mollenkopf provided perhaps the clearest rationale for understanding these developments.[16] The old growth coalition, he wrote, was dead, for the reasons we recounted earlier. The question was whether any other coalition could be created to fill the vacuum. He suggested three alternatives, each with serious problems. One alternative was to revive the "liberal" version: federal largesse delivered through city agencies, supported by the traditional coalition of producers of housing and real estate. That would be hard to do because of the difficulty of running city agencies effectively with few funds, and because the base of the coalition had scattered to the suburbs and sunbelt as a result of its very success in urban renewal and suburbanization in earlier decades. A second alternative was the conservative option: privatize most city functions. This, Mollenkopf thought, would be even harder to implement because of the conflicts it would cause and the protest it would arouse. Some of this began to happen in the 1980s.

Mollenkopf's third option was the community-based coalition. Neighborhood organizations were a definite presence, he observed; the problem would be to harness them with allies, for in the central cities alone they would be too weak to command legislative support. The key would be a broader base from which to work and links to suburban groups, as the suburbs were beginning to feel central city problems.

In other words, there would first have to be a large number of cities in which the politics shifted in the general direction of what community organizations were demanding. It was good to have Harold Washington leading a political movement in Chicago for five years in the middle 1980s, but it would have been better if Chicago had not been so alone. There were a few African American political movements and mayors at the time, and several cities with progressive governments in control, but it would have been better if the numbers could have been higher.

The question of a suburban alliance with central city progressive policies remains in doubt. As William Goldsmith and Edward Blakely have pointed out in an analysis we largely share, the United States, in segregating its poor and middle-class populations in city and suburb, respectively, has also divided its capacity to solve problems in any systematic way.[17] Mollenkopf suggested that suburbs, no longer the white middle-class enclaves stereotyped by analysts in previous decades, might come to share some of the central city perspective on urban problems, and charismatic mayors might find ways to put together multiracial metropolitan coalitions. An optimist might see the beginnings of such developments, but the mass of evidence is against such a picture in the mid-1990s.

Most fundamentally, the economic and demographic evidence suggests a deepening of inequalities on the metropolitan scale, with the causes set in the international economy. Conventional wisdom suggests that the more the inequalities, the more reactionary will be the politics. Faced with the knowledge of these international forces, apathy, rather than a projection of a progressive political future, will be a frequent response.

Against these problems, these improbabilities, we present a scenario that is more hopeful. Viscerally, we cannot listen to the accounts reprinted here and not be impressed by the ingenuity of the planners and other public officials described. What may be occurring is the development of a new public and private capacity to address problems. This does not mean that the nation will use this capacity but that the potential is there. Perhaps more fundamentally, equity planning developed as a government response to community organizing. It was purposive, not simply a set of forces determined by economics. So while we portrayed a swing in urban politics from a regime dominated by the growth ideology to one at least partly responsive to a community movement, what the equity planners represented was a professional and public-sector response to this swing. Its potential to reinforce and direct this swing, should it occur, is what we have to assess.

IS EQUITY PLANNING MORE THAN A PALLIATIVE?

In the present situation of a shaky growth coalition coexisting with a large number of community organizations, there would seem to be a continuing demand for at least some equity planning in most places. But there are alternative scenarios. One of the interesting possibilities is that equity planning may be not only another model for responsible planning but another form of politics. For one thing, equity planning is a way of expressing localized urban interests that would otherwise go completely unrecognized. Without it, poor and working-class neighborhoods would get nothing from the downtown-oriented, "rational" process that is now dominant. But despite the absence of a normal representation apparatus for these constituencies, equity planning may be a way in which citizens may make more human the technical apparatus of urban planning and development. No doubt this diffusion of technical expertise may reduce the capacity to act, but short-term inefficiencies are balanced by a sensitive and adaptive set of policies.

Some of our interviews suggest a slightly more empowered situation of equity planning as a form of politics. In this model, the cities continue getting darker and poorer; more minority mayors and other key politicians are elected to office, but the successful politicians, with a minority, poor, and working-class neighborhood constituency, haven't a clue as to any form of planning and urban economic development other than the traditional growth model. The mayor (or other key political figure) then has to concentrate on big-bang projects (e.g., an airport, stadium, office buildings, hotels) while *talking* a strong neighborhood redistribution game. At the same time, he or she hires and encourages planners to do useful neighborhood things. These are always on a relatively small and underfunded scale. The planners rationalize their support of the big-bang projects and go along. The mayor captures the support of developers and the business community, and the planners protect the mayor's voting constituency. This model is certainly applicable to Cleveland now and may be applicable to some other cities we studied, such as Denver.

The question is, can equity planning be the basis for more than that? Can it move the center of city politics in its direction; can it move the center of the city planning profession? We think it possible that it can. Not only may there be positive changes in city economics and politics along the lines just described, but the experience of the equity planners represents a *response* to economic and political conditions in cities that promises an even more constructive practice in the future.

PROGRESSIVE ROOTS OF NEW PLANNING PRACTICE

What equity planners represent is an elaboration and deepening of professional practice, but one built on past traditions that others may be able to share in the future. Thus, to the picture we presented earlier of a growing community development movement in city politics, equity planners represent a professional response, one that began to move the resources of city halls in the direction of that movement.

Mainstream professional practice in city planning adapted—too well, we think—to the needs of growth coalitions in the 1950s and 1960s. But an alternative practice, one more oriented to equity concerns, has roots as far back as the turn of the century and can find connections to the emerging constituencies of recent decades and the present.

The early history of city planning produced diverse initiatives that have been rediscovered by recent scholarship.[18] These include the "material feminists" who sought housing and community arrangements appropriate to an empowered "woman's sphere"; the work of Patrick Geddes, a Scottish biologist who drew up dozens of town plans in India and elsewhere based on a cooperative model of city evolution; the Regional Planning Association of America, an informal group of housing and regionalist advocates organized by Clarence Stein who sought to build housing to achieve social objectives.[19] There was a discernible doctrine of redistributive regional economics in the agitation of the National Farmer's Alliance in the 1880s and 1980s. Lawrence Veiller, the New York housing reformer, sought to improve slum conditions by establishing standards of ventilation, sanitation, and density. At least the beginnings of an economic planning doctrine surfaced in the work of W.E.B. Du Bois. Populist and radical planning initiatives were certainly unleashed during the New Deal. The public housing movement was one, as was the work of the National Resources Planning Board under Frederic A. Delano and Charles W. Elliott II and the Greenbelt Town program under Rexford G. Tugwell in the Resettlement Administration, and Tugwell's later innovations as the first chairman of New York City's Planning Commission and in Puerto Rico prior to 1946.[20] So was the work of such determined housing reformers as Edith Elmer Wood and Catherine Bauer, who linked housing improvements with planning.

The way in which mainstream planning developed, on the other hand, was very different from equity planning, partly as a result of its striking success in servicing the needs of growth and the growth coalition in the postwar period. Growth advocates required major land-use modifications and the modernization of local governments, and city planners were a big part of both. They typically played lead roles in programming central city redevelopment schemes, highway construction, and suburban development. As a secondary function that expanded through the 1960s and 1970s, they also tried to serve, or at least pacify, large and often victimized poor and working-class populations.

As city economies and government practices changed, and planners became more important in the 1960s, a kind of standard planning practice developed, one that worked and became the prevailing orthodoxy. It had a number of features: a set of values, institutions, a methodology, a constituency. Its values emphasized civic designs that were dramatic in their visual appeal to increasingly middle-class professional clienteles. Earlier city planning value systems that had emphasized small changes responsive to locally generated businesses and the needs of the existing local citizenry received some support, as in historic preservation schemes in such places as Providence and Savannah, but did not usually find a place in the more dramatic urban renewal schemes. The latter were copied in city after city as redevelopment plans spread across the nation. Thoughts of redistribution and participation were pushed to the margin of the profession.

The institutions of planning adapted as well. The original orthodoxy developed in the 1920s was the independent citizen planning commission, tied to a physical planning approach and separated from the political programs of most mayors and certainly the political machines. There was much debate about this institutional arrangement in the 1950s and later, since the independent commission arrangement tended to separate local elite visionaries from those in official power. The alternative, adopted in many places, was a shift of planning functions to a position responsible to the chief executive, and of planning methods focused, not on the master plan and goal setting of independent planning boards, but on an incremental approach in service of the pluralist style of political control. Both changes made it easier for political leaders and city planners to work together and tied the planners to the growth coalition as their new constituency. The drawback, as was to become apparent later, was that no one was thinking about cities' long-term futures in any formal or systematic way. Part of the planning function turned into a public relations operation, with plans produced publicly but in the service of private planning operations and decisions made in camera.[21]

While this orthodox doctrine was becoming established, and mainstream planners were adapting to the needs of growth, another trend was the development of an opposition planning role, often in direct conflict with planners in city hall. In the 1960s Paul Davidoff, Chester Hartman, Herbert Gans, and others invented what they called *advocacy planning*. Planners, they said, did not have to support the "growth machine" but could aid populations and groups victimized by those city policies. By the constraints of their positions, the often limited resources and defensive tactics of their clients, and at times their own choice of strategy, these planners' actions were limited. But they signaled a new diversity. By the 1970s, the American Planning Association's Code of Ethics reflected concern for vulnerable populations: "A planner shall

seek to expand choice and opportunity for all persons, recognizing a special
responsibility to plan for the needs of disadvantaged groups and persons, and
shall urge the alteration of policies, insitutions and decisions which militate
against such objectives." [22]

Many official city policies also included "advocacy" for the poor. There
was a serious question whether an "honest" advocacy was possible when paid
for by the same sources that were causing the problems. Martin and Carolyn
Needleman, in *Guerrillas in the Bureaucracy,* portrayed the internal conflicts
that beset planners in these roles.[23] But the point is that the profession did both
things: advocacy, now supported by public monies, as well as the more dominant attempt to keep feeding growth. James O'Connor, in *The Fiscal Crisis
of the State,* laid out a more general scenario: cities would be forced *both* to
service growth and to serve the poor. The needs of the economy would push
them in the first path, and the need to legitimize the economy by ameliorating
its worst excesses and side effects would cause them to do the second. Many
professionals, he thought, through direct contact with the most affected and
victimized populations, would form bonds with them, thus creating a pressure
for change in cities from within the city administration.[24]

O'Connor's predictions began to be realized. There was an outpouring of
interest in "advocacy planning." Commitments developed in many professions
in the 1960s and 1970s to serve client groups that these professions had themselves expanded in part to serve. There were scores of efforts and a healthy
literature reporting examples both of theorizing in the academy and innovations
in professional practice. A key criticism of advocacy planning as practiced was
that, too often, white middle-class activists sought out indigenous leaders who
most easily related to the dominant culture and its planning process, while
missing the real roots of local need—organizers, not planners. In any case,
much of the discussion was simply an extension of the pluralist doctrine of "incrementalism" that had been infected by the growth-oriented tradition. Perhaps
it was "pluralism with a heart."

Initially, neither the cadres of growth-oriented planners nor the advocates
and "social planners" did much to develop an encompassing core doctrine for
planning. They increased the numbers of people called planners and supported,
indirectly, the explosion of professional schools. But it was a while before the
profession digested its new functions and developed a coherent approach to its
work that could be called equity planning.

By the mid-1970s, professional planners, some of them veterans of the advocacy movement, began to create a body of reports and proposals that sought
to reconstitute city life and politics in fundamental ways. The Cleveland Policy

Plan of the early 1970s was an example. This plan was conceived, not only because professional planners in their city offices had thought through some of the implications of their own contacts with community groups, but also because they and their staffs were in contact with community groups. Sometimes they interchanged jobs and professional commitments with counterparts working as organizers, and they created organizations that thought hard about their work and their communities, wrote about them, and interacted with other groups across the country. Universities also played a role. Professional planning schools took in community organizers and gave them training for jobs in the agencies. There were occasions for deep reflection about the practice of advocacy planning and community organizing in all this.[25] In one notable effort Mel King, a Boston organizer and political figure, established an Urban Fellows program at MIT, with local organizers funded for a year of university training and then moving back into community roles.

The emerging constituencies most likely to support the values and methods listed earlier were the populist grassroots groups. But it was one thing for the constituencies to exist and another for a profession to reach out and establish contact with them. This was difficult to accomplish from city hall. There were many attempts, with planning agencies sending "community planners" out to work with neighborhood groups, but often stumbling, as has been documented in detail. And there was much discussion of the ethics of advocacy planning, particularly the appropriateness of white middle-class planners working in poor black and Latino neighborhoods.[26]

In some cities, too, official relationships with neighborhood groups were formed. In the process, as a corps of planning professionals learned more about the groups in their cities that opposed the growth coalition program, their planning became more populist in tone. Planners began doing what we are calling "equity planning."

But all this fell far short of the emergence of an equity planning practice. The professional organization, the American Planning Association (APA), could encourage a degree of pluralism in its ranks, but the main body of professionals was divided and unable fully to integrate the practices that were emerging. By the 1990s, this was changing somewhat. At the 1993 annual conference in Chicago, 30 to 40 percent of the sessions focused on social equity issues, and the APA commissioned papers on equity topics in such functional areas as health, transportation, and land-use planning. How deep the commitment was among the rank and file had still to be determined, however.

Schools   The emergence of equity planning was reinforced by the development of support systems that went beyond a single city: the professional schools. The city planning profession consists not only of its practitioners but also encompasses a set of support systems: national and international professional associations, a loosely tied network of allied associations and interest groups, and professional training schools. All these institutions grew markedly with the growth of the planning profession. In 1953, fewer than twenty university departments offered graduate degrees in city planning; by 1993, there were over a hundred.[27]

The earliest training programs for planners, usually ensconced in schools of architecture, were devoted to master plans and such regulatory instruments as zoning and subdivision regulations. In the 1960s, however, many of these programs were caught up in the "advocacy" interests of the profession. The schools not only tracked these developments but provided much of the personnel for the advocacy planning movement of the 1960s and 1970s. There were serious outreach operations both within and outside the university structure: in various course projects and in the creation of organizations outside the formal institution, such as Urban Planning Aid in Boston, which used a combination of student volunteers and paid staff, partly supported by government grants, and helped communities fight the extension of expressways through neighborhoods. Associated with schools in other places were consulting operations and government- and foundation-funded projects. Large numbers of graduate students supported these efforts, with faculty support sometimes extending to enthusiastic participation.

University planning departments reflected this experience through the 1970s, reinforced by a generation of scholars who did innovative outreach teaching and wrote extensively.[28] New organizations developed: the Union for Radical Political Economics, Planners Network, a much expanded Association of Collegiate Schools of Planning. Finally, and perhaps most important, a new generation of university outreach programs brought students into contact with grassroots organizations. Notable examples of such institutions were Pratt Institute, the Center for Urban Economic Development at University of Illinois–Chicago, Cleveland State's Center for Neighborhood Development, and the Community Planning Program at the University of Massachusetts–Boston.

Some professional planning schools developed a populist orientation, sometimes of the "rainbow" kind described earlier, in part by relating to and supporting social movements and the politics involved in them. The struggle for a multiracial professional education paralleled the struggle to craft a multiracial populism in the real world of city politics. Many in the planning profession (and others) hoped to educate blacks, Latinos, and other minorities in the profession, at least in proportion to their numbers in the population. For several reasons, this was not achieved. Because blacks and other minorities had not advanced proportionately through the educational system at the college level, there was no change in the racial composition of applications to professional schools, or entering the profession, by the end of the 1980s compared to a decade or two decades earlier.[29]

There may be hope in the *theoretical* development of planning schools. The problem is to avoid the high price of bifurcation between the practice oriented and the more conceptually adventurous students and professors. One can see a connection to populism developing in practice, in an approach that might be called planning-practice-as-theory-building, which has been developed by a number of academic/practitioners who usually operate out of planning schools working directly with communities and produce reports on the work, sometimes collaboratively with the community. The Kennedy-Tilly piece on "Transformative Populism" came out of that approach, pursued at the Community Planning Program at the University of Massachusetts–Boston, which combines currents from urban design and advocacy planning practice with participatory action research currents emerging in the social sciences. This work transcends the community practitioner issues that bothered advocacy planners two decades earlier. Kennedy gave voice to such ideas in a 1992 lecture:

> So here's the central dilemma for the transformative or indigenous planner: finding a balance between assuming that oppressed people fully understand their own oppression and the planner does not, or, conversely, that the planner fully understands the truth (or has research and analysis tools to get at the truth) about people's oppression and that the people do not.[30]

There is support in these thoughts for equity planners. First, they come out of the "advocacy" tradition, which means years of experience in shaping the tools of a profession to the needs of real people in neighborhoods. Second, this idea avoids the early pitfalls of advocacy planning, which tended to favor one side or another of the "central dilemma" Kennedy notes. What is most promising, though, is the way this approach transcends the "redistributive populism" so characteristic of much of the neighborhood movement and lends support to the "rainbow coalitions" that tend to form and occasionally win elections at the local level. Kennedy's statement, if it can be taken as representative of much that is going on in American communities and universities, suggests the possibilities that exist for equity planners: both in the constituencies that operate in urban politics and in the thoughts of professionals who serve these constituencies.

But schools, like the profession, had some distance to go to be fully supportive of an equity planning role. There was not much in the way of coming to terms with advocates of the growth policies still prevalent in many cities. The schools were able to mirror the conflicts in the cities, but not to transcend them.

NOTES

1. "Cleveland Policy Plan Report," Cleveland City Planning Commission, 1974. See also Norman Krumholz, Janice Cogger, and John Linner, "The Cleveland Policy Planning Report," *Journal of the American Institute of Planning* 41, no. 5 (1975); and accompanying Forum articles.

2. Pierre Clavel, *The Progressive City* (New Brunswick, N.J.: Rutgers University Press, 1986).

3. This general point was made most forcefully in Paul Peterson, *City Limits* (Chicago: University of Chicago Press, 1981). An earlier statement that may have influenced many researchers was Theodore Lowi's "American Business, Public Policy, Case Studies, and Political Theory," *World Politics* 16 (1964): 677–715. This view pervades much writing on all sides. For an alternative perspective, we have been impressed by Gerald Frug, "The City as a Legal Concept," *Harvard Law Review* 93, no. 6 (April 1980): 1057–1154.

4. For a general description of how this occurred in Chicago under the political machine that dominated until at least 1983, see Doug Gills, "Chicago Politics and Community Development: A Social Movement Perspective," in *Harold Washington and the Neighborhoods: Progressive City Government in Chicago, 1983–1987*, ed. Pierre Clavel and Wim Wiewel (New Brunswick, N.J.: Rutgers University Press, 1991).

5. On the transformation of the economy as context for shifts in urban political coalitions, the following account generally follows that in John Mollenkopf, *The Contested City* (Princeton: Princeton University Press, 1983). On the diversity of the postwar liberal program, see Benjamin DeMott, "Rediscovering Complexity," *Atlantic Monthly* 262, no. 3 (1988): 67–74. Generally, see Mark Gelfand, *A Nation of Cities: The Federal Government and Urban America, 1933–1965* (New York: Oxford University Press, 1975). Most informative were the essays in Steve Fraser and Gary Gerstle, eds., *The Rise and Fall of the New Deal Order, 1930–1980* (Princeton: Princeton University Press, (1989), pp. 55–84, 185–211 respectively; and Charles Jackson, *The Crabgrass Frontier* (New York: Columbia University Press, 1985).

6. On "new social movements," we have benefited from Carl Boggs, *Social Movements and Political Power: Emerging Forms of Radicalism in the West* (Philadelphia: Temple University Press, 1986); and Manuel Castells, *The City and the Grassroots* (Berkeley: University of California Press, 1983).

7. Katznelson argues that federal programs had the upper hand, thus defusing grassroots authenticity and permanence in the Great Society programs. We are not so sure; we think the tension between grassroots and external and elite influence may have been

productive. See Ira Katznelson, "Was the Great Society a Lost Opportunity?" in Fraser and Gerstle, *Rise and Fall of New Deal Order,* pp. 185–211.

8. On the workings of an ineffective growth coalition, see Todd Swanstrom, *The Crisis of Growth Politics: Cleveland, Kucinich, and the Challenge of Urban Populism* (Philadelphia: Temple University Press, 1985).

9. U.S. Catholic Bishops, *Economic Justice for All: Catholic Social Teaching and the U.S. Economy* (Washington, D.C.: U.S. Catholic Conference, 1986).

10. Neal R. Pierce and Carol F. Steinbach, *Corrective Capitalism* (New York: Ford Foundation, 1987).

11. For a well-documented report on the accomplishments of a national sample of 130 CDCs in 29 cities, see Avis C. Vidal, *Rebuilding Communities* (New York: New School for Social Research, 1992).

12. Kucinich's speech to the National Press Club, Washington, D.C., was reprinted in the *Cleveland Press,* October 3, 1978. A full characterization of this brand of urban populism, in Boston, is laid out in Marie Kennedy and Chris Tilly, with Mauricio Gaston, "Transformative Populism and the Development of a Community of Color," in *The Limits of Activism: Class, Community, and the Politics of Local Mobilization,* ed. Joseph Kling and Prudence Posner, pp. 302–324 (Philadelphia: Temple University Press, 1990).

13. The best characterization may be that of Kennedy and Tilly, "Transformative Populism." See also Mel King, *Chain of Change* (Boston: South End Press, 1979); James Jennings, *The New Black Politics* (Detroit: Wayne State University Press, 1992); and Clavel and Wiewel, *Harold Washington and the Neighborhoods.*

14. James Jennings and Mel King, *From Access to Power: Black Politics in Boston* (Cambridge, Mass.: Schenkman, 1986).

15. Among the best historical overviews of neighborhood movements are Sidney Dillick, *Community Organization for Neighborhood Development—Past and Present* (New York: Women's Press and Morrow, 1953); William Morrow, David Morris, and Karl Hess, *Neighborhood Power* (Boston: Beacon Press, 1975); and Robert Fisher, *Let the People Decide* (Boston: Twayne Publishers, 1984).

16. Mollenkopf, *Contested City.*

17. William W. Goldsmith and Edward J. Blakely, *Separate Societies: Poverty and Inequality in American Cities* (Philadelphia: Temple University Press, 1992).

18. On the early history of U.S. city planning, see Mel Scott, *City Planning* (Berkeley: University of California Press, 1969). On the material feminists, see Dolores Hayden, *The Grand Domestic Revolution* (Cambridge: MIT Press, 1981). Patrick Geddes's more radical ideas about citizen movements are perhaps most accessible in his *Cities in Evolution* (London: Williams and Northgate, 1915); see also Paddy Kitchen's biography, *A Most Unsettling Person* (New York: Saturday Review Press, 1975). On the RPAA, see Carl Sussman, ed., *Planning the Fourth Migration: The Neglected Vision of the Regional Planning Association of America* (Cambridge: MIT Press, 1976); and part of

John Friedmann and Clyde Weaver, *Territory and Function: The Evolution of Regional Planning* (Berkeley: University of California Press, 1979).

19. On public housing, see Jackson, *Crabgrass Frontier*. On populism, see Lawrence Goodwin, *Democratic Promise: The Populist Movement in America* (Oxford: Oxford University Press, 1978).

20. Arthur M. Schlesinger, Jr., *The Coming of the New Deal* (Boston: Houghton Mifflin, 1958).

21. Robert Walker, *The Planning Function in Urban Government* (Chicago: University of Chicago Press, 1940). This was a key argument for shifting planning into the office of the chief executive. On the advisability of incremental methods, see Martin Meyerson, "Building the Middle-Range for Comprehensive Planning," *Journal of the American Institute of Planners* 22, no. 2(1956). Later, Charles Lindblom coined the phrase "incrementalism" as an approach to executive decision making (and the staff work that supported it). This developed into an antiplanning position and, eventually, an antigovernment tack in the 1970s. See Aaron Wildavsky, "If Planning Is Everything, Maybe It's Nothing," *Policy Science* 4, no. 2(1973): 127–153. For a more profound analysis of these issues, see John Dyckman, "Introduction to Readings in the Theory of Planning," ms., ca. 1962; and Alan Altshuler, *The City Planning Process* (Ithaca, N.Y.: Cornell University Press, 1965).

22. Herbert J. Gans, *People and Plans* (New York: Basic Books, 1968); and Paul Davidoff, "Advocacy and Pluralism in Planning," *Journal of the American Institute of Planners* 31 (1965): 331–338. The code of ethics is reported in American Planning Association, "Ethical Principles in Planning," *Planning* 58, no. 3 (1992): 36–38.

23. Martin Needleman and Carolyn Needleman. *Guerrillas in the Bureaucracy: The Community Planning Experiment in the United States*. New York: Wiley, 1974.

24. James O'Connor, *The Fiscal Crisis of the State* (New York: St. Martin's Press, 1973).

25. See Norman Krumholz and John Forester, *Making Equity Planning Work* (Philadelphia: Temple University Press, 1990). One of the best recent interpretative works is Peter Marris, *Meaning and Action* (London: Routledge and Kegan Paul, 1987), which focuses on British cases. See also Needleman and Needleman, *Guerrillas in the Bureaucracy*.

26. Lisa R. Peattie, "Reflections on Advocacy Planning," *Journal of the American Institute of Planners*, March 1968.

27. Jerome Kaufman, "Contemporary Planning Practice: The State of the Art," In *Planning in America: Learning from Turbulence*, ed. David Godschalk (Washington, D.C.: American Institute of Planners, 1974); Frank So and Linda Corby, "Annual ASPO School Survey," *Planning*, January 1974; and Carl V. Patton, "Recent Trends in Graduate Planning Education," *Journal of Planning Education and Research* 8, no. 3 (1989): 215–220. On planning education, see Harvey Perloff, "The Evolution of Planning Education," in Godschalk, *Learning from Turbulence*.

28. Lisa Peattie, Chester Hartman, Ron Schiffman, Bernie Jones, Allan Heskin, Rob Mier, Mel King, Marie Kennedy, and Richard Schramm were outstanding examples.

29. According to Kaufman, by 1968, 128 of about a thousand professional planning degree recipients were black. A more recent estimate can be found in Patton, "Recent Trends in Graduate Planning Education."

30. Marie Kennedy lecture at the MIT Department of Urban Studies and Planning, Cambridge, March 11, 1992.

chapter 2

JERSEY CITY

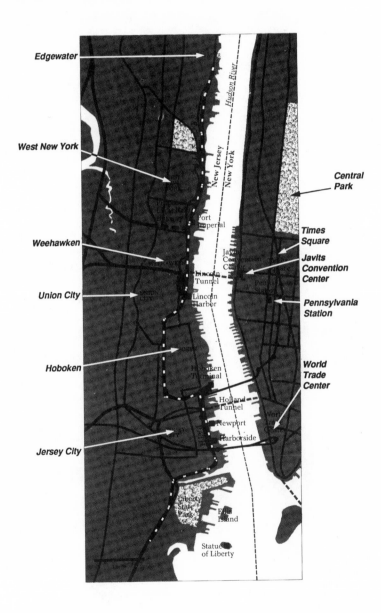

Jersey City and the Hudson River waterfront. Reprinted with permission of Arcorp Properties and thanks to Port Imperial.

SNAPSHOT, 1985

Population Composition for Jersey City, New Jersey, 1970–1990

Demographic	1970	1980	1990
Population	260,545	223,532	228,537
White	202,813	127,699	110,263
Black	54,595	61,954	67,864
Median family income	$9,310	$16,108	$32,785
Percentage poverty	13.7	21.2	18.9

On a clear day, from almost any street in Jersey City leading to the Hudson River, lower Manhattan looms close and large. But from Manhattan, from the twin towers of the World Trade Center, or from Battery Park City, the view is quite different. There, at least until the late 1980s, one looked across the Hudson at the junkpiles, abandoned railroad yards, and rotting docks and warehouses that typified the industrial decline of the New Jersey waterfront.

Then something new began to emerge. Gleaming high-rises, manicured parks, and a forest of cranes on the skyline were rapidly transforming this historic eyesore into one of the most exciting waterfront developments in the nation. The extent of the new development was outlined in a 1987 report by Governor Thomas H. Kean, who identified twenty-two projects on the Hudson from the George Washington Bridge to Jersey City involving 20 million square feet of new office space, 36,000 new apartments, and 100,000 new jobs in an investment package that totaled $10 billion.

What happened during the 1980s was on no one's drawing board a decade earlier. But in the late 1970s, New York City's residential costs began to sky-rocket, and real estate developers discovered that people working in Manhattan would be willing to commute to and from Jersey City in exchange for lower housing costs. The fact that office tenants would be willing to make the same move became clear with the Harborside Financial Center. In this development, two builders paid $25 million in 1982 for an old Jersey City warehouse with 2.5 million square feet of space, renovated it, and sold it in 1987 for $120 million.

In past years, an old waterfront city such as Jersey City in New Jersey constituted one of the nation's largest and most varied manufacturing centers. Thousands of factories made products as diverse as boiler tanks and castor oil and shipped them by rail or water to consumers around the world. In the 1970s, the region's manufacturing complex went into a steep decline accompanied by losses in population. Left behind on the waterfront were old neighborhoods, idle office buildings, docks, and railroad yards—and disproportionate numbers of the poor, minorities, and the elderly.

The Jersey City waterfront remained depressed long after New York City's economic recovery—a revival based not on manufacturing but on finance, communications, and other white-collar, service-sector endeavors—had begun. In Manhattan the boom was so rapid that expansion space was needed. According to developers, New Jersey offered a better alternative than the outlying boroughs of New York City. For example, Samuel J. Lefrak, New York City's most prolific developer, said that land and labor costs in Jersey City were so much less expensive that an apartment built to rent in New York City at $1,250 a month would rent for only $900 in Jersey City. The development boom on the Jersey side of the Hudson River began.

The boom has not been without its problems, however. There is an ongoing, sometimes bitter, controversy on land use, density of development, and parkland versus housing and transportation policy. Currently, the New York Port Authority estimates that 250,000 commuters cross the Hudson River between 6 A.M. and 10 A.M. each day by way of tunnels and bridges. By 1995, the agency expects another 50,000 commuters. With numbers like that, a smooth-running transportation system is regarded as the difference between success and failure. Whether such a transportation system will come into being is still a question.

Of even more concern to the political leadership of Jersey City is the possibility that all the new development on the waterfront will leave their basic problems untouched. They will be left with large populations of poor people in decaying neighborhoods, while others enjoy the benefits of growth and investment. This concern was the chief reason Jersey City elected Anthony Cucci Mayor in 1985. Cucci had charged the previous administration with promoting development with little or no regard for low-income people.

Cucci campaigned on an "open," neighborhood-oriented platform, promising to harness the benefits of development for poor and working-class city residents. His campaign was a world removed from the old-style Jersey City politics epitomized by Frank ("I am the law") Hague, mayor and Democratic "boss" of the city from 1917 to 1947. Hague ran the city like his personal fiefdom.

One of Mayor Cucci's first actions was to appoint Rick Cohen, an urban planner with a history of developing low- and moderate-income housing, director of the city's Department of Housing and Economic Development. On taking office, Cohen found that he and Jersey City had some major housing problems: 7,159 housing units stood vacant and uninhabitable, and the number of rental units had dropped from 63,156 to 58,110 between 1970 and 1980. Rents were rising much faster than the median income of residents, and speculators were driving renters out of their houses and "mothballing" the units to convert them later to condominium use.

Cohen introduced an anticondominium conversion bill and immediately obtained pledges from most of the big developers either to include affordable housing units in their projects or to donate to an affordable housing trust fund. In the $10 billion Newport development, for example, which includes several high-rise apartment buildings, 18 percent of the units were reserved for lower-income people with rents substantially below the average.

Cohen believes that with the right kind of public-regarding urban planning, new developments can serve the needs of developers and upper-income tenants *and* the poor residents of Jersey City. While he concedes that the new jobs opening up on the Jersey City waterfront are most likely going to be similar to the white-collar, service-sector jobs that fueled the recovery of Manhattan in the 1980s, he believes training, job creation, and set-asides will provide many opportunities for Jersey City residents, while linkage arrangements will help provide affordable housing. (Linkage arrangements tie approvals for new developments in "hot" areas to contributions for benefits in "cold" areas, that is, developers are encouraged or mandated to help neighborhood development by contributing to low-income housing trust funds and by training and hiring the unemployed.)

This chapter focuses on how Cohen got his job, how he set out to do the "right kind of planning," and what he learned.

INTERVIEW WITH RICK COHEN

Let me tell you how I got to Jersey City, a story that explains what kind of city it is. I had my own consulting firm for many years, and I was hired by the U.S. Department of Housing and Urban Development (HUD) in 1979 to look at Jersey City because the city had used its Community Development Block Grant (CDBG) money to displace so many families that it was listed as one of HUD's critical cities. HUD was considering removing Jersey City's CDBG allotment. I grew to like the city quite a bit.

Jersey City, home to about a quarter of a million people, is right across the Hudson River from Manhattan. It was one of the "gritty" cities, a very contentious, difficult place, a place where people didn't have a lot of hope that things would ever change. There was a sense that the political machine would always do what it did and that progressive change was an impossibility.

After the HUD contract ended, I stayed active in Jersey City, doing some organizing and some *pro bono* consulting for community groups. In 1985 there was a mayoral election. Surprisingly, Anthony R. Cucci, a pro-tenant candidate, won. I was not part of his campaign; actually, I was barely aware of the election because I was so busy with my national consulting. After the election, I was invited by a couple of housing activists to discuss possible policies that could be pursued in housing and economic development. I wrote a concept paper for them that brought me to the attention of the new mayor. A little while later, when I was in Washington, D.C., doing some consulting, I got a phone call from a newly elected Jersey City council member. He said, "Rick, how would you like to be head of the Department of Housing and Economic Development?" I said, "Not on your life." He asked me to meet with the mayor anyway. The next day, I flew back to Jersey City and walked into a press conference just as the mayor was announcing me as head of HED, which is how I got the job. Later, I suggested to the mayor that I would indeed be willing to take the job if he'd let me carry out a progressive agenda, the agenda for which I thought he had campaigned.

In his campaign the mayor had used concepts that were common in progressive circles. He didn't have that great an understanding of them, but he knew that there was some wisdom in trying to move Jersey City toward social equity. He had used words like *linkage*, even though he didn't quite know how to operationalize it. He had used the term *social justice,* but he didn't quite know how that could be put into practice. Still, he was attempting to set up a framework to try to tackle things. He bought me in and allowed me what I thought was a great deal of latitude.

This was in July 1985. I served as director of Housing and Economic Development for four years to the day because the mayor was not reelected. As a department director, my term was the same as the mayor's, although I also served at the mayor's pleasure. This mayor made sure that all his appointments were very clearly the selections of the city council as well. His theory was that the council's approval would give us a base of support for what we were trying to do. That made some sense.

BACKGROUND

I grew up in Boston in the Orient Heights public housing projects. Even after you've left it, it's hard not to remember what public housing is like. That experience had a formative impact, although what probably took me into this field occurred later, when I went to Boston University. There I worked as part of the War on Poverty in an outfit called Action for Boston Community Development (ABCD).

This was in the late 1960s and early 1970s. ABCD was one of the original "gray area" groups and one of the first antipoverty agencies. I worked in the planning and evaluation section. I worked for a fine man, a planner who had a great impact on me as a professional role model. Charles Sullivan was able to combine solid professional skills with a concern for social justice. My ABCD experience and Sullivan, combined with my having grown up in public housing, were what probably moved me to think as I do.

I went on to other jobs, including running a homeless shelter. When you work with housing 150 homeless people every night, you see what's really happening in society and how inadequately people are being helped. As far back as I can remember, and despite our own lack of resources, my family always cared about people who didn't have much. We felt that caring for others was an appropriate thing to do in life. Working in a homeless shelter seemed proper to me. It was also emotionally exhausting. It's hard to look at your surroundings and not say that these people ought to have breaks, chances, and opportunities as well. The homeless shelter, Boston's ABCD, later working in rural coal-mining towns in Appalachia—it all came together for me. For a while, I even worked on Third World development issues and the impact on the Third World of multinational corporations overseas and at home.

GETTING GOING AS HED DIRECTOR

Early on, I tried to make the process of developing policy as participatory as possible. I did not utilize the typical structure of enunciating a policy and then giving people an opportunity to react. I wanted to avoid this subject–object kind of relationship between the policymaker and the policy swallower. I went through a process of building a coalition of all the people who expressed concern about the condition of the city. Everybody who cared about low-income people, tenants, or social justice was invited to put forward ideas, and my staff and I tried to put meat on the ideas and test the underlying theories. We tried to be a catalyst. Because the only staff I had was inherited from the previous administration, I quickly hired a couple of people I met at these brainstorming sessions. They turned out to be the best possible people to create the right spirit in our office. Our staff tried to look for models in other cities for the ideas that people were generating in these small, informal groups. These weren't formal hearings. We would meet over sandwiches at a little corner restaurant near the courthouse.

To identify these groups and individuals, we relied basically on an informal network that had been involved in the mayor's campaign: people from the tenants' union, from some of the minority-based community organizations, and the few professionals in Jersey City who had taken an active role in fighting for social justice, such as Legal Services attorneys or a church group that had been trying to provide services for the homeless. When they realized that we were serious about reform and were looking for participation, people came to us seemingly out of nowhere. These were people who had been alienated from the political process, who had assumed that Jersey City and its political machine were hopeless.

Given the vicious political infighting that Jersey City was accustomed to, we were somewhat concerned that our openness would allow people into the process who would muck up the works. But we never had to face that problem. In general, the participants all played positive and interesting roles. Not everybody agreed on the issues, not everybody agreed with one another, and some people became critics of the process in the end, but I felt that even the critics were constructive because they added worthwhile ideas.

Having set up this participatory process, we turned to problems and opportunities. Clearly, the problem in Jersey City was a massive housing crisis, caused by the fact that the New York City real estate market had flowed right over the Hudson River and into our backyard. Condominium conversions were displacing thousands of tenants. By my second or third year in office, our city of 80,000 dwelling units was facing 16,000 conversions at prices that lower-income people could not afford. The first thing we had to do was try to stave off the loss of affordable units. We immediately worked to control the speculation that led to condominium conversions, which led to the warehousing of vacant units. Landlords would drive tenants out of their lower-rent buildings and board up or "warehouse" the empty units so that they could convert them later without having to deal with the tenant protections that were in the law. We tried to stop the warehousing of vacant units with an antiwarehousing law. We also tried to establish a price-control ordinance that, like rent control, would fix prices on condominiums. Our thinking was that since rent control was essentially a mechanism for price control, condominium conversions should be subject to price control as well.

Another problem we attacked was the need for more affordable housing units. Public-sector subsidies were shrinking at the same time that a massive development of luxury offices and luxury residential towers was occurring along the waterfront, right on the river. Although construction was just beginning, it was clear that the developers had laid their claims, cut their deals, and carved up the waterfront. Unfortunately, the previous administration had given redevelopment authorizations with virtually no give-backs to the community required. Even though we lacked the legal ability to exact benefits from the developers, we came up with a linkage program. It was an administrative program—it was never adopted by ordinance because of practical realities. Every developer had prepared a redevelopment plan that had been incorporated into his contract with the city, and to amend these redevelopment plans would have meant altering the contracts, which would have created unending litigation. By coming up with an administrative regulation that stated that we expected developers to choose from a variety of options for linkage as an expression of their social responsibility to the city—an expression that would allow the city to provide other incentives to help them market their developments—we would get compliance. Initially the developers screamed and yelled. They started a recall campaign against the mayor, saying behind the scenes that if I were fired, the recall would be stopped. The mayor stood behind me, and the recall never went forward.

The developers then began to cooperate and make contributions to the linkage fund. Actually, we never set up a fund. Instead, we delivered the contributions straight to nonprofit developers of affordable housing, eliminating the potential for any kind of cheating by city officials or politicians. We also helped the process along by giving the nonprofit developers free land. We stopped city auctions of vacant city-owned land. We took every piece of property—vacant land and vacant buildings—that could be potentially salvaged as an affordable housing resource and transferred them at no cost to the nonprofits to be used for affordable housing.

Let me provide a couple of examples of the linkage deals we struck. Colgate Palmolive gave its linkage money to a nonprofit called New Community Corporation, which was doing new construction on vacant city-owned land. Similarly, a developer of luxury condominiums called Portside made a linkage contribution to the YWCA, to which the city had given three buildings with fifty-two units. Not only did the city donate vacant land and vacant buildings, but we provided a subsidy from the CDBG to reduce construction costs by about $15,000 a unit. We marshaled other funds from regional construction agreements, state grants, and the like, further reducing the buyers' burden. In addition, we provided a tax abatement for low-income projects so that carrying costs of the project were low enough to maintain affordability for fifteen or more years. We were trying to say to developers: "Yes, we'll exact this contribution from you, but we're not saying that the burden is yours only. This is a joint effort, and we, the public sector, will do our share as well." By the time I left the department four years later, we had received linkage commitments of $14 million, in addition to facilitating the direct creation of an additional 800 affordable housing units. All in all, nearly 2,000 units were subsidized by the linkage payments and other funds.

THE POLITICS OF LINKAGE

The politics of any city are not pure. Not everything you describe on paper is going to be implemented exactly as you expressed it. The developers certainly had their routes to the mayor. Frequently I would get calls from him, asking, "Why does developer so and so have to pay $1,500 linkage for each of his units? Why can't he pay only $500?" I would answer, "Because everybody else is paying $1,500." The mayor was under constant pressure from those who charged that he was driving development out of Jersey City. I had to help him demonstrate that development remained strong, despite our exactions, and that our exactions were producing other needed development.

Even before we had explored the legality of our linkage program, the mayor gave away the chance of making the linkage requirement mandatory by announcing at a public meeting with the developers that the program would be voluntary, just like passing a plate at church. I immediately jumped up and said, "What the mayor means is mandatory voluntary," implying that if the developer didn't pay the linkage fee, he wouldn't get his permits. From that day forward, my staff referred to the program as the "mandatory voluntary" linkage program.

We made some strategic mistakes with the program in that we failed to encourage the nonprofits to organize in favor of our policies and thus strengthen the mayor's hand. When we came into office, the neighborhood advocacy groups found us so receptive to their ideas that they became somewhat complacent, feeling that the most articulate spokespersons for their perspective were now sitting in city hall. Maybe it would have been more useful to have been seen as the "enemy" so that the progressives would have been banging down our doors to do more.

It's worth noting that our linkage program was never legally challenged. There were legal challenges to our condominium price-control efforts and to our anti-warehousing ordinances. But the concept of linkage was never challenged, probably because we never had an ordinance on the books. As a matter of fact, I asked the developers why they didn't challenge us. They said that they accepted linkage as a cost of doing business and that a legal challenge, which would have required them to stop development while the courts debated this issue, would have been more costly than simply providing the payments and keeping the development moving.

All of us, the developers and the city, were aware of Princeton, New Jersey's mandatory exaction program, which went to court as soon as it was announced. By the time I left the department, the courts still hadn't moved on that case. Everyone recognized that we could fight over the issue and get nothing done on either side or we could work out something that would keep both sides moving forward without delay.

Although they certainly would have preferred not to pay exactions, the developers chose to deal, even though we exacted more than money. We also exacted commitments on first-source hiring (i.e., allowing the city or its agencies to suggest new employees) and infrastructure, or off-site impact, fees. The developers did support the opposing candidate during the next election, but, in general, they were not all that upset with our handling of them. They felt that at least they knew where we stood.

We tried to be fair and professional. We tried to understand their perspectives, and we tried to help them market their products. For example, we helped the developer of the Linpro Building persuade Merrill Lynch to move 2,000 jobs to Jersey City. Our administration encouraged The Limited to make a commitment on an office building at the Newport development. We were successful because we represented the developers' interests with the same professionalism that we represented the interests of the low-income community.

STAFF ISSUES

Let me turn to the essential issue of my staff. It was partially inherited and partially made up of new recruits—and it turned out to be outstanding. When we came in (Jersey City is a tough, nasty, political city), most of the people we inherited were fearful about their jobs. They felt they would be treated the same way their predecessors had been treated: in other words, they would be fired by the new administration. Instead we told them that if they were willing to work for the residents of Jersey City and were willing to represent our standards, ethics, and values, they were welcome to work with us. What occurred was that those people who wanted to do a good job stayed, and over time the people who felt uncomfortable with our political and ethical positions moved on. We also hired new project managers and planners who I thought were the match of any city's in the country. They were really top-notch people committed to doing the right thing. I was always exceptionally confident of my staff's work because even if things didn't turn out correctly, I knew that they were motivated to do their best in terms of social equity.

What we were looking for in the new recruits was a combination of personal commitment to social justice, energy, and planning skills that were sensitive to the needs of poor and working-class people. We didn't have to advertise all that much; most of our recruiting was done through word of mouth. Planners who wanted to do progressive work and who were looking for the kind of environment that supported positive social change came to us. Most of these recruits left when I left, and they've all gone on to fine careers in the public and nonprofit sectors. In addition to planners, I hired attorneys and social workers because I wanted a mix of people who reflected what I thought economic development was all about. We're talking not just about building affordable housing units but also about caring about what happens to the people in the units. This means giving a lot of thought to what legal requirements are necessary to ensure that units stay decent and affordable for fifteen or thirty years.

We had to consider legal and social issues because when you do progressive work in a city, you can encounter active opposition and obstruction from other city departments. This sometimes strident opposition meant that we had to work out programs in great detail and think through possible pitfalls and possible objections. We had to lobby the city council to ensure that the people who had to vote on our projects understood why we were doing certain things, understood the impact of our recommendations, and understood the counterarguments and the reasons the counterarguments should be rejected. We did a great deal of educational work; indeed, we viewed ourselves as educators. We believed that we had to educate ourselves, the city council, the media, and the public in order to create the right kind of environment to support our programs. We were continually sending out what we called "Questions and Answers" memos. These memos, which went to other departments and to the city council, explained why we were doing certain programs, why money was being used in a certain way. We tried to anticipate the questions that might come up. These memos helped to overcome objections from many sources—especially from within city government itself.

Let me give you some examples. Let's say we were proposing to waive fees and costs for a low-income housing development. The Engineering Department would object, since they had no interest in low-income housing. My staff and I would have to argue the case in front of the mayor or at a meeting with the city council. The "Questions and Answers" memos (and lots of other materials) helped explain and support our arguments. Usually there were also objections from The Jersey City Law Department, whose first reaction to most of the innovative approaches we tried to turn into ordinances was that it "can't be done, it's not in the constitution." Our first attempt to write an antiwarehousing ordinance—an ordinance that would penalize developers who warehoused vacant, reusable units—was rejected by the Law Department as illegal. We had to use departments opposed to our objectives that often lined up with the development community. Our chief corporate counsel, for example, referred to the antiwarehousing ordinance in public as the "Landlord Harassment Ordinance." Most of the insiders felt that our progressive movement wouldn't last, that the old guard would soon come back, and that if they were too closely tied to us, they would lose their jobs in the next administration.

Ultimately, we overcame the opposition of our colleagues by internalizing their functions. I hired my own attorneys, who did the necessary legal work to put together the ordinances. After the city's Human Resources Department was unable or declined to provide appropriate support, I hired my own social workers to create in-house programs linking human services and housing. In spite of all this internal friction, the mayor continued to be supportive. From time to time he would call up and bellow at the top of his voice, "You're fired," but he never made good on his threat. Indeed, a joke made the rounds that I had been fired and reinstated three times. Although the mayor wavered on the implementation of our policies because of the intense political pressure he was under—the pressures to favor this or that developer—he never backed down from supporting our overall goals and policies. It was up to us to translate policies into effective programs, to inform and strengthen the mayor, and to take some of the heat. I think he appreciated that, and he never abandoned our program.

INSTITUTIONALIZING CHANGE

Let me turn to some successful and not-so-successful programs. I should point out that some of the things we accomplished didn't last as long as we wanted. Because our linkage program was "mandatory voluntary," we discovered that the administration that followed us did not collect on linkage commitments. They also returned linkage payments, explaining that the developers were being harmed by the declining real estate market. And they took back property that we had given to nonprofit developers. This taught me that you have to plan, not only for the implementation of programs when you are in office, but you have to build in as many protections and supports as possible in anticipation of the likelihood that at some point you will not be there. I guess you might say we didn't give enough thought to institutionalizing some of our accomplishments.

We made an assumption, perhaps naively, that the name Jersey City on our work meant that future administrations would carry out our commitments, just as we had honored the work of the previous administration, even when we didn't like it. We suspected that the linkage program might not be continued, but we assumed that no mayor would ever give back linkage money that had been collected. The next mayor even terminated projects for which we had negotiated a commitment of money from the Casino Reinvestment Development Authority in Atlantic City. We got that money for Jersey City; the next mayor returned it! And I thought that no one in city government ever voluntarily gave back money! I guess you might say we trusted too much that a commitment by the city is a commitment by the city, regardless of who's in office.

Other programs were partial successes. We finally succeeded with our anti-warehousing ordinance, which did a great deal to bring housing units back on the books. We did not, however, succeed as well as we had hoped in slowing down the rate of condominium conversions—in part because the courts overturned our condominium price-control ordinance.

We made a major effort to tackle special needs in housing. There was a large homeless population in Jersey City because of the city's linkage with the New York Port Authority's train system. At the time, Jersey City had the highest rate of AIDS in the United States because of the presence of so many intravenous drug users. Yet there were no residential drug treatment facilities in Jersey City, no AIDS hospices, very little in the way of housing for the chronically or mentally ill or the permanently disabled. When we came into office, there were no homeless shelters in Jersey City. In fact, there were no publicly supported homeless shelters in all of New Jersey.

We created a shelter system for the homeless—not only transitional housing but permanent housing for the homeless through Single Room Occupancy (SRO) units. We got linkage commitments for the SROs, and we even negotiated with the Port Authority to provide money and buildings for SROs. But we didn't do enough political organizing in a timely enough fashion, and we never got the SRO program off the ground. That was quite a disappointment. The AIDS shelter program never got off the ground either, but we did get transitional homeless shelters and other transitional programs operating very successfully. Unfortunately, the succeeding administration didn't have any interest in those programs (this was the same administration that preceded us, an administration that said there were *no* homeless people in Jersey City), and they backed away from our commitments.

LESSONS LEARNED

If I had it all to do over again, I would get more heavily involved in community organizing. Early on and intensely. Our failure to do good community organizing was probably the essential weakness of our program. Maybe I hired all the good community leaders; they were certainly a good percentage of the people we brought to city hall. Whatever the reasons, we weren't effective at community organizing. The tenant movement, for example, relied on *us* to push for various protections. In the previous administration, when they faced opposition at city hall, they had been very active and effective, but when there wasn't any visible opposition, they became complacent, and their complacency was actually more harmful than the previous administration's opposition. As a result, we had wonderful planning programs and wonderful policies, but they lacked community roots deep enough to see them carried on beyond our term in office. As a progressive planner, you can get caught up with what you're doing and come up with unusual and arcane models for doing it. In the process, you forget that it's your ability to articulate policies and gain support for them that's at the root of success. What counts is not how detailed and how well researched and how innovative your programs might be, but how well you organize your political supporters. Teachers and students of equity planning need to remember that.

I earned my master's in planning at the University of Pennsylvania. What was completely missing from my education was a sense of the real world, that is, the political context in which planners must work. I had read a little bit about how planners have to be political in talking with their planning boards and their planning commissioners, which is a very superficial gloss on how you actually design and carry out progressive policies. Students need a thorough understanding of the turbulent social environments that they face as progressive planners because planners who tend to be idealistic tend to idealize their work environments.

Schools of planning might deal with this gap by offering more courses on politics and city hall. I think students also need much more exposure to work "in the trenches." Then they can report back on what it's like to be working not only with bureaucrats but with the people who are advocating progressive policies. In this way, progressive planners can learn to avoid noblesse oblige, an attitude that what we're doing for you people is what we know is best for you. It's quite important for planners to break with that point of view because it can easily lead to the kind of "blaming" that William Ryan wrote about in *Blaming the Victim*.

I'm not talking about merely empowering people, but about helping them understand where they are, how they fit into the scheme of things, and how they can move along in the process and move along the process itself. Mere empowerment sometimes helps people become effective at protecting narrow interests and blocking equitable social change. Our SRO project in Journal Square in Jersey City is a good example. It failed because a local organizing effort helped empower people to organize and coalesce around opposition to the SRO housing. The empowered people were quite reactionary and didn't articulate any values of social equity. So empowerment can be used both positively and negatively.

In Jersey City we saw our role as that of educators as well as administrators. Educators are not dispassionate, value-free people. Indeed, we tried to articulate, describe, and bring home the injustices of what was happening in Jersey City to the people who have the least amount of power. Let's say that a certain community group was advocating a middle-income housing program. Middle-income housing is not a bad thing, but if it hurts the people who have the least resources, then that impact has to be pointed out. Progressive planners have an obligation to identify what is happening to people who are most adversely affected by public and private actions. The failure to do so means that others lose sight of the results of their choices, and low-income people are harmed. It may not be a visible harm, but it is harm nonetheless. Nobody building middle-income housing along the Jersey City waterfront intends to harm anyone, but the fact that in the process low-income people get displaced is certainly harm. The cost of every policy has to be brought to the public's attention, and planners are well positioned to do that.

An important part of this educational process involved our work with the media, who had the ability to support or undercut what we were trying to do. We approached the media with complete openness, seeing them as the key vehicle for education. We shared our documentation, thinking, and analyses with the local newspapers. Their stories didn't always come out the way we hoped, in part because the two newspapers in Jersey City are owned by a pair of conservative chains. It should also be noted that newspapers depend on major developers and businesses for advertising. But we did our best to educate the reporters so that they could ask good, solid, tough questions. We also wrote our own press releases. And we actually provided our background memoranda. We would release these reports and then walk the reporters through them. We'd invite the reporters into our offices for bull sessions to explain what we were trying to do and why.

This approach had mostly positive but some negative results. On the positive side, the reporters trusted us and wrote good stuff about what we were trying to do. The negative side was that we did so much talking that we raised expectations, which had its unfortunate consequences. We came into office in July; because we had had so many conversations with so many reporters, by the end of July the press was writing stories asking, where are Rick's policies? We quickly issued many policy statements in the middle of August, but there were media frustrations at the "delay."

In general, however, I think using the media as an educational tool is more beneficial than not. We discovered that more politicians and laypeople read the newspaper than read our reports. What I learned too late was that even *more* people read letters to the editor than read articles. To the extent that we did any effective political organizing, the process was helped by getting letters to the editors by me and others that talked about our policies.

Finally, the other strategy we used to carry out progressive policies was to look for allies beyond the city borders. We actively sought support from like-minded people elsewhere, and we invited them to Jersey City to share ideas, thoughts, and perspectives. That was very beneficial in terms of reality testing. It also helped us get over our sense of isolation. Particularly in small cities, you can feel very isolated and alone. My staff members would sometimes say that they felt as if they were on a spaceship, with nobody else out there.

We also looked for allies at other levels of government—state, county, and federal—who could provide the support and sustenance we needed. Even though we had a Republican state administration, we found progressives working in the Department of Community Affairs, the Department of Environmental Protection, and the New Jersey Housing and Mortgage Finance Agency. The state people proved to be incredibly responsive to our programs because of the communications we set up and the values we articulated. And we developed a good relationship with federal officials, despite the fact that they worked for the Reagan administration. Many of them were really frustrated with what Reagan was doing and wanted to do a good job in spite of the strictures imposed by his administration. When you develop these kinds of supporting relationships at higher levels of government, it makes your life at the municipal level easier. During our tenure, we received more support from the state for housing than any other city in New Jersey, even though, unfortunately, the mayor and the governor were not political allies. We also did beautifully on economic development.

One last comment. I think it's important for progressive planners to think about the ethnic and racial diversity of their staffs. We made sure that the HED staff reflected the diversity of the people with whom we worked. At the time I was appointed, only one professional project manager at HED was black. By the time I left, more than half of my project managers were members of minority groups. We also gave women major roles of responsibility. We felt that it was important to demonstrate in the way that we ran our shop the same values that informed the policies we were trying to convey to the community. If we couldn't do that internally, it would be very hard to make the case externally.

FURTHER READING: Affordable Housing

Bratt, Rachel G. *Rebuilding a Low-Income Housing Policy.* Philadelphia: Temple University Press, 1989.

Bratt, Rachel G., Chester Hartman, and Ann Meyerson. *Critical Perspectives on Housing.* Philadelphia: Temple University Press, 1986.

Brooks, Mary E. *A Citizens Guide to Creating a Housing Trust Fund.* Washington, D.C.: Center for Community Change, 1989.

Dreier, Peter. "Economic Growth and Economic Justice in Boston." In *Unequal Partnerships,* edited by Gregory Squires. New Brunswick, N.J.: Rutgers University Press, 1989.

Dreier, Peter, and W. Dennis Keating. "The Limits of Localism: Progressive Housing Policies in Boston, 1984–1989." *Urban Affairs Quarterly* 26, no. 2 (1990): 191–216.

National League of Cities. *A Time to Build Up: A Survey of Actions about Housing Policies.* Washington, D.C., 1989.

White, S. Mark. *Affordable Housing: Proactive and Reactive Planning Strategies.* Planning Advisory Service Report No. 441. Washington, D.C.: American Planning Association, 1992.

chapter 3

DAYTON'S MIAMI VALLEY, OHIO

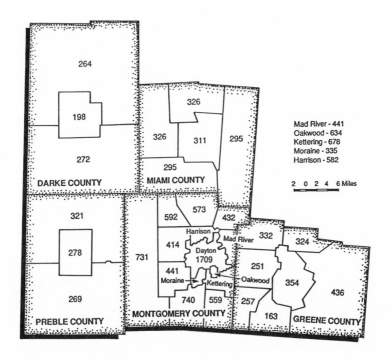

264

198

272

DARKE COUNTY

326

326   311   295

295

MIAMI COUNTY

Mad River - 441
Oakwood - 634
Kettering - 678
Moraine - 335
Harrison - 582

2 0 2 4 6 Miles

321

278

269

PREBLE COUNTY

731

573
592   432

Harrison
414   Mad River   332   324
Dayton
1709

441   251
Moraine   Oakwood
Kettering   354   436

740   559   257
163

MONTGOMERY COUNTY

GREENE COUNTY

Miami Valley Regional Planning Commission Housing Dispersal Plan, by planning units (total units about 14,000). A complete description of the plan can be found in "A Regional Housing Plan," *Planner's Notebook* 1, no. 1, April 1971, American Planning Association, Washington, D.C.

SNAPSHOT, 1970

Population Composition for Dayton, Ohio, 1970–1990

Demographic	1970	1980	1990
Population	243,601	199,321	182,044
White	168,407	122,769	106,258
Black	74,284	74,521	73,595
Median family income	$9,600	$15,202	$24,819
Percentage poverty	14.2	21.0	26.5

In 1970 the white suburbs of Dayton, Ohio, which range from very wealthy to blue collar, agreed to provide housing for low- and moderate-income families despite strong and outspoken opposition by many residents. In what urban planners and national housing experts regarded as a remarkable development, local governing officials on the board of a regional planning agency unanimously approved a Fair Share Housing Plan that would disperse federally subsidized low- and moderate-income housing throughout the five-county area. Similar plans proposed in other areas such as Cleveland were often dismissed without consideration.

The plan, prepared by the Miami Valley Regional Planning Commission (MVRPC), assigned each community a quota or share of 14,000 units, including many public housing units. Many of the planned housing units were constructed over the next four years.

Dayton and its five-county region seemed like an unlikely place to accomplish the difficult feat of distributing low- and moderate-income housing outside the central city into the region. Early on, Dayton's government was known as a model of "teutonic" efficiency. In 1913, under the leadership of National Cash Register President John Patterson, Dayton adopted one of America's earliest city-manager forms of government. For decades afterward, Dayton was known as a city bureaucracy with first-class engineering and managerial skills, but even engineers could not cope with the economic and social problems that emerged in the 1960s.

In 1970 Dayton was an industrial city of 250,000 people within a metropolitan area of 842,000. The five-county Dayton metropolitan area consisted of two largely urbanized counties, while the other three counties were rural in character. About 11 percent of the area's population and 30 percent of the city's population were black. Regional growth followed the typical metropolitan development pattern: major employers began cutting workforces and moving to the suburbs, while the white population suburbanized as well.

As residents of means moved out of the city, the poor stayed or moved in. In addition to the old, dilapidated, and cheap housing that was available, virtually all of the area's 3,350 units of public housing were concentrated within the city limits. As a result, the poor increasingly lived in neighborhoods within the city, largely because they could not afford housing elsewhere. Families that were black as well as poor were further limited by racial discrimination. Large areas of poverty began to develop on Dayton's west side, the concentrations spreading and causing alienation between blacks and whites. In the late 1960s the situation worsened as the cost of housing began to soar, shutting thousands of families out of the housing market.

Thus there was a large demand for subsidized affordable housing of all kinds, from public rental projects to homeownership schemes in which the federal government paid part of the interest on the mortgage. Both nonprofit and private builders were looking for sites for subsidized units, but they were stopped at the city line and limited to certain already impacted neighborhoods in Dayton. According to one observer, commenting on subsidized housing in the suburbs, "If the price is right, the utilities are not available. If the price and utilities are right, the zoning is wrong. If all are right, the neighbors do not want it and the politicians respond."

MVRPC, which had been established in 1964 in response to federal pressure seeking improved coordination in regional grants, approached the housing situation as an essential element in its work program. Regions throughout the United States set up similar agencies. MVRPC's forty-person board was made up of elected officials of the five counties and twenty-nine municipalities in the region. The board hired Dale F. Bertsch in 1964 as the agency's first director.

When he started, Bertsch had no employees and an annual budget of $35,000. He gathered together an impressive staff, including Ann M. Shafor, and began to develop support for regional planning from politicians, businesspersons, and the media. By the time he left MVRPC fifteen years later, his budget totaled $1.3 million (not including another $2.6 million in pass-through money given by the federal government to be used for various federally assisted programs) and his staff numbered 107. In the process, Bertsch also became a national figure, consulted by George Romney, secretary of the Department of

Housing and Urban Development. HUD sent Bertsch around the country to tell other regions the MVRPC story. Their Fair Share Housing Plan was the first and, some say, the most successful plan of its type ever proposed by a regional planning agency. By 1978, 4,510 new low- and moderate-income housing units were scattered outside Dayton and within the five-county region.

Although details of the plan are of interest, the process of achieving public and private support for the adoption and implementation of the Dayton plan is our most important focus in this case. The plan, dropped into an unprepared environment, would probably have stood no chance of survival.

In achieving his program, Bertsch and his staff employed five strategies: being proactive, focusing on the decision-making process, building networks of support, negotiating, and acquiring real power. The following interview explains how he and his staff thought about the issue and strategized and implemented their program.

INTERVIEW WITH DALE F. BERTSCH

I grew up in Sandusky, Ohio. My father was in charge of production for the Sandusky Foundry Machine Co.; ours was a middle- to upper-middle-class family. My mother emigrated from Germany in the early part of the century. I attended Catholic parochial schools in Sandusky through the eighth grade; then I attended Sandusky High, a public high school. I guess I had an uneventful childhood, with the exception of World War II, when people tended to treat our family a little differently because my grandfather and mother spoke German.

I got my first job when I was ten years old, and I've worked ever since. My father and mother emphasized education and the work ethic. Concern for people was built into us by a local parish priest, who held the first religious services for Hispanics and the few black Catholics who lived in Sandusky at the time. I never really recognized social class. I knew there were people who had less than we did because my mother used to feed hobos when they came to the house, and my father hired a lot of neighborhood people when they were out of work during the late 1930s.

We were a very religious family. I served as an altar boy at church, although I don't know that I would necessarily classify myself as overly religious. I was also an Eagle Scout. I didn't think much about minorities because there weren't many blacks in Sandusky. Even so, there was racial discrimination. We learned to swim at Battery Park, where there were two areas, side by side, separated by a rope. The whites swam on one side and the blacks on the other. As a young kid, we used to hang out at the railroad station, which was split in half, with waiting rooms and drinking fountains that said "Negro" and "White." They never took the signs down, although I don't remember their being enforced.

My first real encounter with people of a different color came during high school when I ran track. A number of the athletes on the track team were black. When we traveled to out-of-town track meets, it bothered me that they couldn't stay in the same hotel as the white kids. I went to Kent State University right out of high school, and the same was true there. I remember traveling with a black high-jumper who had been turned away at hotels. I stayed at *his* hotel because it bothered me so much. This was in 1951 or 1952.

Later on, when I was in military service, I was stationed at Camp Polke, Louisiana, with a predominantly black outfit. This was right after the integration of the services began under President Harry Truman's 1948 Executive

Order, and there were only four whites in the whole outfit. Once my wife and I gave a black soldier a ride to Cincinnati on our way home. When we stopped to eat in Kentucky, he insisted that we get him something to take out. My wife and I objected and insisted that we all go into the restaurant together, which we did. The staff wouldn't serve any of us. So I guess you might say I was aware of racial discrimination.

When I graduated from Michigan State University with a degree in planning and landscape architecture, I went to work in Arkansas for Bill Bonner, who was in charge of the University of Arkansas's 701 planning program. The 701 program made federal funds available to support local urban planning efforts. I had planning responsibility for a number of very small towns, including one that I remember really well called Dumas. At the Dumas city limits there was a sign warning blacks not to be caught in town after the sun went down. Only the term they used was "nigger."

I left Arkansas in 1960 partially as a result of my refusal to sign a loyalty oath to the State of Arkansas. I arrived in Arkansas during the summer of the Little Rock school crisis. There was a lot of antiblack sentiment at the time, and many of the planning commissions for which we were preparing 701 plans wanted us to develop plans for segregated schools and parks. I refused to do that. When I left Arkansas, I went to Tulsa, Oklahoma, where I was involved in urban renewal projects, as well as in the preparation of the first fair housing ordinance in Tulsa. About that time, I became involved in civil rights activities, particularly in the South.

My father died in 1963, and I was anxious to get back home to Ohio. I applied for planning jobs in both Youngstown and the city of Lorain, and was rejected. In 1964, I successfully applied for the job as director of the Miami Valley Regional Planning Commission (MVRPC), the first regional planning agency ever in the area. My primary job as the only employee was to design a work program and build a staff to execute it.

EARLY STRUGGLES AT MVRPC

At the time, the board of MVRPC represented three counties: Montgomery, Green, and Miami. Later, Darke and Preble counties became members. At first there were thirty-six citizen members, all appointed, which was very typical of such boards and the enabling legislation in Ohio. Planning tended to be an operation that was placed in the hands of citizen planners. Because the board's responsibilities were fairly fuzzy, board members looked to the staff to recommend a work program. One of the hardest things we had to do was to obtain

701 funding in order to develop our first plan. We had to compete with a separate regional transportation agency and a separate regional open-space agency. There were also a number of other regional agencies with single-function responsibilities, including the Miami Conservancy District and the health-care agency. Over time, each county also developed its own regional or county planning agency. Ohio law tends to encourage competing agencies. It presented some difficult situations for us in the sense that our jurisdiction was the fine line between the counties because each county was independent from us and every activity had to be negotiated.

If MVRPC was ever going to be more than just a "paper" agency set up to meet the minimum mandated federal guidelines, we had to try to develop a board that was more powerful than one limited to appointed citizens. We also had to develop a mission and work program different from the other agencies in the area, all of which were older, better established and funded, and more powerful than MVRPC. We had to be able to compete, to be useful, in order to survive.

One strategy was to get elected officials involved on the MVRPC board; then, we would have greater support from the feds, the people that set the regulations and held most of the money. My second strategy was to try to involve MVRPC in regional planning that was directly or indirectly linked to intergovernmental issues. Therefore, we tried to absorb the regional open-space and transportation agencies primarily because of their functional visibility and their lines of funding. The third strategy was to try to build a fairly broad power base and a work program that provided unique products. For example, most of the other planning agencies lacked comprehensive databases and avoided what we considered to be major policy areas, such as housing. Therefore, ours was a threefold strategy: to develop broad political support; to capture more responsibilities and funding; and to develop a work program that was policy driven.

I tend not to be a strong supporter of the traditional "comprehensive plan" approach to planning. Too many planners spend more time collecting data than formulating and implementing policy. My basic philosophy is that in a democratic society we really don't *plan* futures, we *negotiate* them. In order to have meaning for elected officials, plans and programs have to be policy driven and relatively short-term. Of course, plans ideally should have long-term positive effects, but you've got to be able to hold elected officials accountable for the products. You've also got to be able to provide the elected officials with short-term payoffs. So I tend to be more of an incrementalist than a traditional comprehensive planner. This does not mean that I totally avoid long-term strategies, but the emphasis needs to be on results.

You have to remember that at the time we weren't the A-95 review agency. [This is the regional agency that reviews and comments on the need for and consistency of federal grant applications; such a review was essential before federal money would be released.] There were three groups in our region vying to become the A-95 review agency: the Regional Transportation Coordinating Committee, a new Council of Governments (COG) that the city managers had set up for that purpose, and MVRPC. I prevailed on an old and close friend in Washington, D.C., at the Office of Management and Budget by the name of Bill Brussett to send me a letter saying that MVRPC had been selected the A-95 agency. I used that letter as a vehicle for letting the elected officials know that if they wanted the power of A-95, they had to support MVRPC and, in essence, kill COG. They did kill COG and they helped secure a memorandum of understanding between the Transportation Coordinating Committee and MVRPC defining our areas of responsibility. (That wasn't easy; it was a hard-fought battle between two county commissioners.) The memorandum of understanding gave MVRPC veto power over the Transportation Committee's work program, budget, and personnel. As far as I was concerned, that was good enough.

THE HOUSING PLAN

With that fight behind us, we developed our six-year work program. Part of the program declared that by 1970 we would develop a housing plan—not a *fair share* housing plan, just a housing plan. In 1968 the Federal Housing Act mandated that all regional comprehensive plans prepared with 701 funds must include a housing element, which strengthened our hand, as did the tragic assassinations of Dr. Martin Luther King, Jr., and Robert Kennedy. King's murder caused riots in Dayton and massive fires in the black neighborhoods. A survey taken about that time indicated that the two highest priorities among Dayton's blacks and among low-income people in general were jobs and housing. We seized on the lack of housing opportunities, and with the support of newspaper editor James E. Fain of the *Dayton Daily News* we began to build a coalition supporting regional low-income housing. Letters were sent all over the country trying to find examples of good housing plans from which we might learn, but, unfortunately, most were limited to making a private housing inventory and recommendations concerning the private housing market, which we felt was unresponsive to the needs of those who couldn't afford market-priced housing.

In mid-May 1969, the staff and I began working on our housing plan. We had a number of workshops with our consultant, Richard G. Coleman, Ann M. Shafor, who was head of our housing division, and several other staff members. The workshops were exercises to force us to think about what we wanted in our housing program. Should we focus on market-rate new construction and hope that older units would "trickle down" to the poor? What did we think would be most useful?

Ultimately, we decided to develop a housing plan whose major component would create new housing for poor people in areas within and outside Dayton. Such construction hadn't been undertaken before. We were well aware of the fear and resistance the plan might generate in the suburbs, where many of the residents were afraid that the minute they allowed any subsidized housing in, there would be busloads of black and poor people moving from Dayton and overwhelming their communities. Something had to be done to quiet that fear, otherwise our plan could not be implemented. Implementation is the most important part of planning.

To make the plan adoptable and to make it politically acceptable, we said, "If you give us a commitment to accept some low- and moderate-income housing, we will not allow your community to be inundated by these projects." We pledged that the commission would use the A-95 review process not only as a lever to open the suburbs but also as a clamp. We promised to reject any applications that went beyond a community's "fair share" of subsidized housing, as set out in the plan. The MVRPC commissioners seemed to agree.

In the spring of 1970, one year after beginning our work, we unveiled the MVRPC "Housing Dispersal Plan" at a regional housing conference with more than 350 attendees. It was called a "dispersal plan," but a *New York Times* reporter named John Herbers later called it a regional fair share housing plan, and that name stuck. The plan called for a total of 14,100 units, many of them public housing, to be built in the region over the coming four years. The plan divided the five-county area, including the city of Dayton, into fifty-three "planning units," each of which was assigned a quota of subsidized housing under a mathematical formula that took into account the amount of existing housing for low-income families, population density, and other factors. Kettering, for example, a middle-income incorporated suburb south of Dayton, with a population close to 70,000, was assigned 650 units over the four-year period. The staff and MVRPC commission members pointed out that under the plan, no neighborhood would be overrun with the poor, and new public housing would be built only in small, scattered-site projects.

In July 1970 the MVRPC board held an open hearing on the housing plan and directed the staff to present the draft that summer to as many communities as possible. We were to come back in the fall with a report and then the board would consider action. There were fifty-four public hearings that summer, many in suburban locations or Dayton neighborhoods in which there were no blacks or low-income people. The meetings were extremely heated affairs. We went through a difficult—no, a *hellish*—summer. At some of the hearings the police were put on notice to escort staff in and out of town. Community members recited the Constitution, and the John Birch Society caused no end of trouble. There were guns present at some of our meetings. There were times when I wasn't sure that, once I turned the key to my car, there would be anything left to drive out of the parking lot. With that kind of emotion and pressure, it was clear that we would need to win the support of a key group of politicians on our board.

Thomas A. Cloud, a county commissioner and chairperson of our board, said he would support our plan if it was designed to include policy items that could be removed by amendment without weakening the plan. We complied, deliberately designing expendable policy items, things that we knew were going to attract the public's eye and would please and gratify people if removed. For example, our plan specified that, should a community fail to adopt the fair share housing plan, MVRPC would have preemptory zoning power, that is, we could override the community's zoning laws. Now we knew that such power is not legal in Ohio. The provision attracted tremendous attention, so much so that it became the focus of hate rhetoric. We also placed some items out of context and deliberately jumbled the plan. The net result was that when the plan came up for vote before the MVRPC board in September 1970, there were a whole series of predetermined amendments from the floor. Staff objected to many of these amendments, even though we knew that they were going to be passed. Ultimately, the board struck all the items that were expendable, but the plan did not change in any fundamental way. The elected officials came off as both strongly supportive of the housing plan and yet sensitive to the wishes of the people. They approved the regional plan by a 26–0 vote. The members of the board went one step further. They directed me to send the plan to those members not attending, notifying them that their vote would be counted as no unless they returned a yes vote within a week. Remarkably, every absentee responded in favor of the plan. It was really an act of courage, for neither I nor the state nor HUD had anything to offer these elected officials to influence their votes!

STRATEGIES FOR PLAN SUPPORT

George Romney, the secretary of Housing and Urban Development, came to visit MVRPC in January 1971, after reading about our fair share plan in the *New York Times*. Romney wanted to know how we had pulled it off. We asked a large group of members of the local power structure and the core politicians on the MVRPC board to lunch at the Wilbur and Orville Wright House in Dayton. Romney put the question to them, and they explained that they had voted yes because it was the right thing to do. They had also been convinced by the logic of the plan and the supporting materials the MVRPC staff put together.

One key element was a slide talk that portrayed those affected by poor housing. It was less than half an hour in length and could be used on television. We wanted viewers to understand that the term "poor people" was not synonymous with black, but people just like them. We used this show to kick off every suburban hearing. The message was clear: if you are going to go against the plan, you are going to be turning your backs on people like your parents, your postal workers, the teachers in your schools, the custodians, the people who pick up your garbage. One teacher stood up at one of the public hearings and said to a person who was objecting to the plan, "You're willing to turn your child over to us eight hours a day to teach, yet you're not permitting me to live in your community." A number of these people were planted at meetings to make sure that both sides were heard. For example, before a meeting in Miamisburg that had to be moved from city hall to the school auditorium because so many people were expected, the mayor called me and said, "Look, we're going to be lynched. We're going to have to turn your plan down, unless you can make sure that some people can speak eloquently in favor of this thing." The Dayton Community Action Program agency recruited two busloads of people. The plants were there early, and took the front seats. The people speaking against the plan were in the back and in the balcony, so the people who spoke first were in favor of the plan. Although there were some blacks in this group, most were white.

In general, supporters of the plan included the community's elite, the newspapers, television stations, and most of the politicians. Those who opposed it tended to be of three groups. Many professional city planners fought it from the standpoint that MVRPC should not become involved in social issues, as this was not a proper role for a regional planning commission, nor was that the intention of the enabling legislation. They argued that equity issues such as fair share housing were not regional issues and should be limited to the local jurisdiction involved. We took the position that the terms *region* and *community* were much broader than that, that when the legislation referred to community, it meant the broader community of the entire region, not individual communities.

Second, many professional city managers argued against the plan, claiming that we were violating home rule, of which they saw themselves as guardians. The third group arguing against the plan was made up of school superintendents who said that we were overburdening them with families who would contribute little to the property tax base that supported the educational needs of the children of these newcomers.

In addition to opposition that had status in the community, several racist organizations, such as the John Birch Society, the Committee to Restore the Constitution, and the Ku Klux Klan, fought the plan. They were easy to deal with because their members could be baited at public hearings. When making presentations and answering questions, we would attempt to say things that would irritate these people. They would invariably respond with racist statements that would disgust the uncommitted people who didn't know a great deal about the issue or were undecided, but wouldn't identify with racists.

The black leadership was, I think, generally supportive of our fair share plan. Jesse Jackson, with whom I discussed the plan in the early 1970s, said that what we were really trying to do was destroy the base of black political power. But Dayton state representative C. J. McLin, a power in black political circles, answered that argument in an article in *City Magazine*. McLin said: "I don't expect my constitutents to jump into buses and move to the suburbs, much as the suburbs worry about that. But I want them to have the opportunity to move if they so choose."

You can generally expect about 20 percent of the people to be against these kinds of programs, simply because they attack what they consider to be their prerogatives. On the other hand, about 5 to 10 percent of the people will be strongly in favor of such a program simply because it's "liberal" and it's good. It's interesting to note that, in most cases, these are people who are not going to be affected by the plan, such as the League of Women Voters and other do-gooders. It's the middle group, the "undecided," that we had to convince. I wanted 51 percent of the population to indicate support; I could not care less about the other 49 percent. Favorable media coverage was a key; we were helped enormously by Jim Fain of the *Dayton Daily News*, who editorialized against any politician who spoke out against the plan. Fain was so effective that he was nominated for a Pulitzer prize for the newspaper's coverage of the housing plan. There wasn't a single issue in the Dayton area that summer that received more press coverage than housing. I should also note that my staff was terrific. I had handpicked all the staff, both for their intellectual ability and their commitment to planning. Of course, there were times during the process that staff questions arose, and I encouraged them. My method of management is to document thoroughly both sides of an issue and allow for full discussion. But in this case, the entire staff of twenty or twenty-five people was supportive of our approach to the issue.

Staff support and solidarity were really important because we were under so much pressure. We received bomb threats at the office and at home. Many of us had to request unlisted home phone numbers because of harassing calls. If my daughters, who were in their teens at the time, or my wife answered the phone, the caller would say, "We're going to make sure that the first nigger that comes into our neighborhood rapes you." During July and August, when the public hearings were ongoing, the police watched our home. When school began in September, the children were monitored by the police. But no one followed through on threats of major violence.

BUILDING SUPPORT FOR EQUITY

I'd like to return to the crucial task of building support for such ideas as our fair share housing plan. In 1964, when I joined MVRPC, there was no regional constituency for affordable housing or anything else. There were county planning commissions and municipal planning commissions that had little to do with one another. Regional issues were handed by single-purpose functional agencies: regional water control was with the Conservancy District, transportation was with the Transportation Coordinating Committee, open space with the Open Space Committee, and so on.

We made a deliberate point of trying to create public understanding and support for regional planning and regional issues. About four times a year we were invited to speak to the Area Progress Council, a group of about a hundred corporate presidents, in order to keep them advised of our work. In the first year and a half that I was at MVRPC, I may have spent five evenings at home, including holidays and weekends. I ate dinner and most breakfasts with newspaper editors, business owners, civic leaders, chamber of commerce people, city managers, and elected officials, so I got to know people and they got to know me. I shared my vision of the region's future. I tried to find out what they needed and what I might build into my work program to help them. As a result, we gained a number of strong supporters, such as Marvin Perk, head of the Dayton Chamber of Commerce; C. Paul Tipps, who became Democratic state chairman; Tom Tepin, Phil Donohue, Erma Bombeck, and Jim Fain of the media; Gordon Price, a highly visible Episcopal priest—the list goes on and on.

Over the next three to four years, MVRPC delivered on its commitments, every one of them. When we conducted surveys as part of our planning, I religiously made a point of asking politicians what questions could be included to give them better insights into the issues, in order to make the survey more useful to them. Our basic position was that if you need information and you can't find it, come to MVRPC, and we'll get it for you. We developed all kinds of databanks. One member of the power structure never bought a site for development without talking to MVRPC people about it beforehand. It was market work that we did free of charge, but when we needed seed money to build a fair share housing project in Fairborne, that person gave us $17,000. When I told him I couldn't ensure his being paid back, he said that, if it was a successful project, he'd get his money back from the feds. If it was not successful—well, at least he'd tried.

We also helped community groups. MVRPC staff people were assigned to Dayton neighborhoods, despite the objections of some in the city of Dayton, in order to build neighborhood support for our work. We provided MVRPC staff support to the NAACP's school desegregation effort. Glenn Thompson, the father of open-space planning in the Miami Valley, agreed to encourage actions that would fold the open-space agency into MVRPC, subject to a number of considerations. He wanted us to help develop the scenic river legislation for the State of Ohio. That legislation was developed and given to the Ohio Department of Natural Resources for introduction to the general assembly. Our local legislators supported the bill and pushed it through the legislature. Glenn Thompson got the scenic river designation he wanted. It was called the Little Miami River Scenic River.

All these things built support, but they usually involved a quid pro quo. There were times when MVRPC narrowed its agenda and eliminated items from its work program or put them off entirely in order to maintain support. But all these efforts to build a regional constituency meant that when we went forward with the implementation of our plans, the necessary support was there. We also received help from people with the federal government. To implement our housing plan, we needed to have a housing component added to the A-95 review, which would provide the power to review and comment on all housing proposals in the five-county region. At first, getting the feds to agree was tough. Copies of our plan were sent to Carlos Campbell at HUD. No luck! At the time, I was working with the National Committee Against Discrimination (NCAD) and made a point of asking to get NCAD to intercede with HUD; they did, but to no avail. Then one day I happened to have lunch with John Herbers of the *New York Times*. I told Herbers the story of our housing plan and the rulings that we needed from the feds to implement it. His story ran in the *New York Times* in December.

The morning after its publication, Undersecretary Sam Jackson of HUD called to ask me to come to Washington and explain what we needed to implement the housing plan. On the plane to Washington, I put together a list of six things that I hoped to accomplish. First, I said we needed supplemental 701 money in order to continue intensive planning on the fair share housing program. Second, we wanted Sections 237 and 236 (of the Housing Act of 1968) subsidized housing commitments and some supplemental rehab money earmarked for our public housing authority—just for MVRPC, on a noncompetitive basis. These commitments for subsidized housing units would help us produce what we promised in the plan. Third, we wanted to be able to control housing approvals from the two FHA regional offices—Cincinnati and Columbus. We didn't want FHA undercutting the plan. Fourth, we wanted HUD's support in requesting that housing be added to the A-95 review process. Fifth, we wanted HUD to make fair share housing a requirement for the continued 701 funding of regional agencies like MVRPC. Sixth, we wanted to be able to use the A-95 process broadly as a vehicle to demand compliance with federal policies and programs. We wanted to be able to turn down an application for transportation funds, say, if the applicant community had not adopted a fair share housing plan. This would be key to getting the leverage needed.

About a week after meeting with a group of HUD officials and Romney, we received a letter from HUD saying that we had gotten our wish list. A line of credit of some $15 million in supplemental appropriations for housing was sent to assist the Miami Valley region. FHA would no longer withhold approval of housing units in our communities for local community reasons after MVRPC had approved them. We also received supplemental 701 funds, called Special Studies Money, to the tune of $150,000 the first year and $200,000 a year for the next three years. And Secretary Romney put me on the road, talking to regions all across the country about regional fair share housing plans. In the spring of 1971, I was also the lead witness before the U.S. Civil Rights Commission, where I argued for regional fair share housing and a regional approach to equity issues. Romney also began to build into his own speeches support for the fair share housing concept. In an interesting sidelight, Romney closely followed the next local election of officials on the MVRPC board. The day after the November 1971 election, he called and asked for the results. He was tickled to hear that all our board members had been reelected.

Although the A-95 process does not actually contain veto power over grant-in-aid proposals, we used our A-95 review as a negotiating tool to force compliance with fair share. Let me give you an example. Fairborn wanted a public swimming pool, and Zenia wanted a park. When we met with the county commissioners in Green County, we told them, "You haven't adopted the fair share housing plan." They said, "Our delegate on MVRPC voted for it." I suggested that should they go further and take action adopting the fair share housing plan; then the HUD funds could be delivered. The county commissioners adopted the plan in the restroom during a break in their meeting. A letter was sent to HUD requesting the money, and a commitment for both projects was received within thirty days. That kind of collaboration between the feds and MVRPC continued for a few years, until the beginning of Nixon's second term as president. George Romney left HUD around that time, and his successors, James Lynn and Carla Hills, did not share Romney's commitment to our program. Without the feds, there began to be some problems. Revenue sharing and block grants hurt MVRPC by widening local powers. They began to do away with our ability to function on a discretionary basis, to link the federal funds for parks, highway projects, water and sewer plants, and the like to adoption of affordable housing plans. When the feds put all these formerly categorical programs into a block grant and gave it back to the municipalities with no strings attached, we began to lose leverage.

Certainly the lack of strong support on the part of the second Nixon administration and the housing moratorium it imposed (because of alleged corruption and "runaway" costs) hurt us. Municipalities began to tell us that they couldn't adopt our fair share plans even if they wanted to because there weren't any subsidized housing units available. The communities in our region began to doubt our clout and whether we could or could not deliver. When I left MVRPC in 1979, the director who took my place, John Vining from metropolitan Atlanta, came in with a clear message to change MVRPC's direction. The people who interviewed him wanted the agency to become less involved with housing and social issues and more involved in economic development.

RETROSPECTIVE ASSESSMENT

You know, it might be worthwhile to speculate about why, in the annals of city and regional planning, more open housing or fair share housing schemes similar to the one at MVRPC have not been adopted by other regional planning agencies. It may be that we had a number of things going for us. One was certainly the local housing market: we had a very low vacancy rate in the Dayton area and a high demand for housing. Many union workers were out of work, so when we talked about the need for housing for low-income people, we were able to relate that to people like you and me.

Also, the timing was right: our housing plan followed on the heels of the riots of the 1960s. A lot of good people were looking for answers; we tried to supply some of them. We had strong support from civil rights groups. We also had a lot of business support. We argued that housing for low-income people is good business—for example, we pointed out that when you build a house for low-income people, it requires a refrigerator, stove, and bathroom fixtures just like a high-income house—and the business community clearly recognized that argument. We did a study that showed that every house built creates or maintains two and a half jobs. That looked like new jobs from the labor standpoint. We had such strong business community support and labor support because it was nurtured by the staff. We aimed at building coalitions; one of our housing projects was supported by the Black Panthers and a Vietnam veterans organization. In the same way, our plan and the leadership of our board were able to command support from HUD and other federal agencies. Once we demonstrated we could and would lead, other responsibilities—physical and social—began coming our way, along with the funding to support them.

I'd contrast my leadership approach with that of the person who replaced me as executive director in 1979. Whereas I expanded funding and responsibilities, he began dumping MVRPC programs in the name of "good management." They asked Jim Fain what he thought about the contrasting approaches, and Fain said, "Give me leadership over management any day. Dale never worried about costs. He never worried about where the money was coming from. He felt that if something needed to be done, where the money would come from was a secondary consideration."

When I came to Miami Valley in 1964, one of the first things I did was to sign a letter of resignation without dating it. I gave it to every chairman I ever had, saying, "When you can't get along with me, you date the letter and turn it over to the media."

I think most people and most communities have a deep social consciousness. I think planners have to build on that sense of social responsibility, devise ways of making it strong, and then be able to deliver products to it. I think that planners tend to get bogged down too much in planning, in data gathering and the like, and lose sight of implementation. I think there are enough bureaucrats to go around. I tried to empower constituencies that didn't have a bureaucracy to serve them. In most cases, that's poor folks, central city folks. In the meantime, you have to do transportation, waste water, open-space planning, although I would say from 60 to 80 percent of my time during the 1970s was spent on issues of housing and other social programs.

In retrospect, I'd do it all again, especially the move to convert the MVRPC board from a group of builders and planning-oriented citizens-at-large to elected officials. The politicians gave us legitimacy and clout; without them, we'd have gone nowhere.

FURTHER READING: Fair Share Plans for Low-Income Housing

Atlas, John, and Peter Dreier. "Grassroots Strategies for the Housing Crisis: A National Agenda." *Social Policy* 19, no. 3 (1989): 25–38.

Baer, William C. "The Evolution of Local and Regional Housing Studies." *Journal of the American Planning Association* 52, no. 2 (1986): 172–184.

Cleveland City Planning Commission. "A Fair Share Plan for Public Housing in Cuyahoga County." Cleveland Planning Commission, Cleveland, 1971.

Downs, Anthony. *Opening Up the Suburbs: An Urban Strategy for America.* New Haven: Yale University Press, 1973.

Dreier, Peter. "Community-Based Housing: A Progressive Approach to a New Federal Housing." *Social Policy* 18, no. 2 (1987): 18–22.

Dukakis, Michael. "States Take a Fresh Look at Housing." *Journal of State Government* 60, no. 3 (1987): 95–97.

Franklin, Herbert, David Falk, and Arthur Levin. *In Zoning: A Guide for Policy-Makers on Inclusionary Land Use Programs.* Washington, D.C.: Potomac Institute, 1974.

Hughes, Mark Alan, and Peter M. VanDoren. "Social Policy through Land Reform: New Jersey's Mount Laurel Controversy." *Political Science Quarterly* 105, no. 1 (1990): 97–111.

Hula, Richard C. "Rediscovering Housing Policy." *Urban Affairs Quarterly* 26, no. 2 (1990): 313–319.

Listokin, David. *Fair Share Housing Allocation.* New Brunswick, N.J.: Center for Urban Policy Research, Rutgers University, 1976.

Mallach, Alan. *Inclusionary Housing Programs: Policies and Practices.* New Brunswick, N.J.: Center for Urban Policy Research, Rutgers University, 1984.

Miami Valley Regional Planning Commission. "A Regional Housing Plan." *Planners Notebook* 1, no. 1 (1971). American Planning Association, Washington, D.C.

chapter 4

CHICAGO

State Street, Chicago, 1992. Photo used by permission of the American Planning Association.

SNAPSHOT, 1983

Population Composition for Chicago, Illinois, 1970–1990

Demographic	1970	1980	1990
Population	3,366,957	3,005,061	2,783,726
White	2,207,767	1,490,214	1,263,524
Black	1,102,620	1,197,000	1,087,711
Median family income	$10,242	$18,775	$30,707
Percentage poverty	14.5	20.3	21.6

In November 1983 Harold Washington was elected mayor of Chicago, ushering in a new era of progressive city government. As the city's first black mayor (1983–1987), he led a successful multiracial coalition and introduced reforms that signaled the end of the Richard J. Daley political machine. Washington's administration promoted a progressive neighborhood and economic development agenda. One of the partners in this progressive reform movement was Robert Mier, Washington's appointee as commissioner of economic development. Under Rob Mier's direction, the Department of Economic Development (DED) pursued a new city economic policy—one based on participation, redistribution, and racial equality.

Robert Mier arrived in Chicago in 1975 to teach community development and planning at University of Illinois at Chicago (UIC), and in 1978 he founded the UIC Center for Urban Economic Development (CUED). Previously, Mier had served in Vietnam as an advisor to the South Vietnamese navy and was later involved in antiwar and community development movements in Oakland and St. Louis. Mier was also a founding member of the Community Workshop on Economic Development (CWED), whose policy statement on community development provided many ideas for the Washington campaign platform. Subsequently, Mier was deeply involved with Washington's campaign and helped put together the campaign's economic development agenda. Mier joined the Washington administration in 1983.

The Washington administration walked into a city whose postwar economic and political development had been guided by the powerful Democratic Daley political machine (1955–1976). Daley favored downtown development and middle-class concerns over the well-being of minorities and the working class. Furthermore, Chicago had been negatively affected by structural changes in the U.S. economy. Reconciling the pattern of uneven development to meet the needs of those with few opportunities presented a challenge for Mier's department.

During the postwar era, Chicago experienced a loss of population and jobs caused by suburbanization and the decline of manufacturing. From 1950 to 1985, Chicago's population fell by 25 percent to 2,880,000. More drastically, between 1947 and 1982, the number of manufacturing jobs in the city plummeted from 668,000 to 277,000. The city appeared to be on the rebound in the early 1980s when a downtown building boom led to $4.5 billion in private investment. But these developments were of benefit mostly to white-collar professionals living in high-rise lakefront apartment buildings and suburban commuters, not working-class Chicago residents. In spite of billions in investment, the result was an increase of only 18,000 jobs, most of them in the high-skill service sector.

Washington campaigned on the ideas of neighborhood-based economic development and a broad concern for social justice, promising a new, more equitable pattern of development. It was Mier's job to translate these ideas into a formal development plan. The document that came about was "Chicago Works Together: The 1984 Development Plan" (CWT). CWT was a policy plan that stated five broad goals: job development, neighborhood development, balanced growth, efficiency, and a state legislative commitment. It also articulated more than forty-five specific development policies. Based on these policies, the plan proposed more than 200 specific projects that were to be implemented. The 1984 document was critically acclaimed and has been described as "the strongest indication thus far that American cities are willing to harness economic development for their disadvantaged residents."

Although Mier and his colleagues had created a thoughtful plan, they still faced the challenge of implementing it. The Department of Economic Development would face obstacles presented not just by business and political concerns but also by many of the carryover bureaucrats in city hall. Mier inherited a department whose staff, programs, and everyday operations were not well suited to deliver on the Washington agenda. Staff had to be retrained, there was too little money, there were disagreements on planning strategy, the media were hostile, and new programs were difficult to get up and running. In addition, Mier found that altering Chicago city government to become more responsive toward neighborhood needs was a greater task than winning the election or developing the CWT plan. While Mier and his division heads worked to redefine the administrative culture of the DED, they experienced overt and covert political opposition within their ranks. Kari Moe, a DED division head, described the process of reorganization as "fighting a war with someone else's army."

The demands of business and industry also presented many challenges for Mier and his department. Washington's administration was under political pressure to continue to deliver downtown development programs. Completely dismissing media-supported private development initiatives was sure to lead to accusations of government incompetence. Large-scale development challenges included the World's Fair, the Navy Pier, building the Central Public Library, negotiating with the Chicago Cubs and Playskool, and addressing demands for new stadiums by the White Sox and Chicago Bears. Although some of these issues were addressed in the 1984 development plan, others were new. As new issues arose, the DED used the policies and fundamental ideas stated in the 1984 plan as the rational basis for evaluating specific proposals and developments. Although many struggles were lost and some goals were not fully realized, Mier remarked, "Our involvement with large-scale projects convinces us that it is both necessary and possible for a progressive local government to undertake them."

What follows is Rob Mier's account of his personal background and his story of attempting to balance development between downtown and the neighborhoods in a progressive city government in Chicago. Mier's account is followed by that of Arturo Vazquez, later director of Mayor Sawyer's Office of Employment and Training, and Kari Moe, a key administrative aide for Harold Washington, who in 1993 was chief of staff for U.S. Senator Paul Wellman. These three discuss some of the same issues from somewhat different perspectives.

INTERVIEW WITH ROBERT MIER

I came to Chicago in 1975 to teach at the University of Illinois at Chicago (UIC). Two experiences in my life had engaged me with neighborhood organizations as vehicles for change, Vietnam and its aftermath, and a research project I was involved with late in graduate school.

I came back from Vietnam in 1968 with my head turned around. I was still in the military, but I wanted to engage in protest. I lived at the time in Richmond, a largely black community north of Berkeley, in the San Francisco East Bay. The antiwar movement was headquartered on the campus at Berkeley. There also was a strong civil rights–oriented neighborhood organizing movement in the area, especially in Oakland with the Black Panthers. Richmond was a natural place for a neighborhood organization to form, one that became an expression of some counterculture values, antiwar values, and empowerment values. I found a personal closeness in neighborhood organizing that enabled contradictions to get on the table to be struggled with. We were not dealing with abstract issues; we were dealing with the struggles of the world in the context of our daily lives. For example, my neighbors and I could understand what the war was doing to us because we were dealing with an aspect of it right before us. We had a chemical factory across the street that we believed was producing defoliants. But it was also an employment base for our largely black community. We had to struggle with that contradiction.

When I got out of the navy, I moved back to St. Louis and got involved in another very active community. The issue in that community was racial change and gentrification. Again I found community organization a good vehicle for dealing with a lot of the larger struggles. At that point I was working as an engineer. What I found I was bringing to those community situations was certain technical skills, but I wanted more, wanted to broaden myself, wanted to understand more about politics and political economy. So I went to planning school at Cornell.

My first couple of years there I was always finding ways to raise issues in my courses from my community perspective and from these sets of experiences. Until that point my technical focus was more on housing. That's what I had done as an engineer: I'd built housing. Then when I was at Cornell working with Tom Vietorisz and Bill Goldsmith, I began to focus on the role that employment played in many of the basic social struggles that I previously had defined other ways: as housing issues or empowerment issues or antiwar issues. I began to reinterpret many of them from the perspective of employment.

For my last two years of graduate school, I moved to New York City to work with Tom Vietorisz and Ben Harrison on a large research project focusing on the urban consequences of subemployment. The project had a prominent place in the rich debate at that time about dual labor markets—a concept that for me became an important linkage between neighborhood and society.

So, these two experiences—Vietnam and my subsequent involvement in community building and the research project—developed in me a *trust* in neighborhood organization and a passionate focus on employment, and laid the foundation for my next two decades.

UIC AND CUED

When I first interviewed at UIC in 1975, I brought a clear economic development orientation. The UIC planning program was brand new, and they wanted me to teach and work in this area. The curriculum was flexible, with lots of room for experimentation, and I took advantage of it. In a relatively short time after arriving in Chicago, I was enmeshed in an extended community development network. I was involving students through courses in the solving of a variety of community problems so that the academy and community had begun to develop a way of relating to one another.

The best higher educational experience I ever had was a field workshop that concluded our two-year masters' program. We used to put students, in groups of five or six, in a year-long community problem-solving situation. They had to find their own problem. One faculty member would be the advisor to each group, going through the year working with the group. My groups always seemed to find community economic development problems. Building on this experience, I started the Center for Urban Economic Development (UICUED) in 1978 with a major grant from the U.S. Economic Development Administration. The thing that UIC had to offer, compared to our competitors, was a real connection with community economic development organizations. They not only were starting to grow in number and quality, but many of the early organizations had my former students involved with them.

UICUED tried to do things in a somewhat participatory way. I found as soon as I began to get involved in community after I came back from Vietnam that I had as much to learn as I had to contribute. So I never had pretensions that I had the solutions for problems, that I even knew what the problems were. I never imposed my definition of problems or my will on the solutions, but tried to engage my students and the community organization people we were working with. That's something that enabled me to maintain a continuing relationship with my students after they graduated. So it became clearer as time went on that that participatory process was very important to community formation and development. I hoped that I was not taking power from the organizations or using the organization as a basis for my own personal power.

I tried to set the tone for this by making sure everything we did internally at UICUED had a participatory nature. Within UICUED we began consciously to experiment with ways of self-management and participatory decision making. I think this orientation also had its roots in my Vietnam experience.

I saw my share of big shots going home in body bags; so I developed this philosophy that everybody is equal and there are some great equalizers out there to remind us. In fact, if anything, the people who stayed connected with their fellow men were better able to survive than those who put themselves up on a pedestal. From the time I came back from Vietnam, from that day forward, I've never been impressed with big shots. All people are equal, and all need each other.

GENERATIVE METAPHORS: THE NEIGHBORHOOD AGENDA AND CWED

My most rewarding experiences as a planner came in working for Harold Washington and then, after Washington died in 1987, for Eugene Sawyer. This was from 1983 to 1989. The economic policies we developed seemed to many like a new departure. But in fact they developed from the efforts, the thinking, and actions of many individuals and groups in Chicago over two decades. By 1982, when Art Vazquez and others put together the plank on which Washington campaigned, a large number of community-based organizations were engaging in what they perceived as community economic development. They had a clear sense of what they wanted to do and what they thought city government needed to do to promote their efforts.

These neighborhood organizations were much more proactive than reactive. By the late 1970s, Chicago had seen the emergence of some important policy and communications networks: the Rehab Network, CANDO, the Task Force on Black Political Empowerment. These were forums for discussion across communities that hadn't existed before. Support groups also had emerged and were capable of deepening and sharpening the dialogue that was occurring within the networks of community organizations. UICUED played that role. So, to a degree, did the Center for Neighborhood Technology. The Urban League was active: this period was probably the peak of the Urban League's policy research work.

And then out of the sharpened community dialogue came the broadened utilization of a set of what I call generative metaphors, ways to talk about what we were about that constituted a broader and deeper understanding—an inspirational, interactive language. Some of the metaphors were a bit misleading, but they were enormously helpful as organizing devices. For example, there was a common perception of the political terrain being downtown *versus* the neighborhoods. This metaphor inspired the notion of community empowerment, community planning—people were saying that we've got to take control and do the planning for ourselves. The language and dialogue emphasized a real focus on city hall. The notion of needing to reform government was in everybody's daily lexicon, and people were able to tick off examples of either why government needed to be reformed or what could happen if government was reformed. And, finally, the rhetoric incorporated the language of the civil rights movement—fair share, equal opportunity, fairness.

So, by 1982, the city was populated with community development groups. They spoke an integrating language. They had a strong sense of self-confidence and to a degree self-sufficiency. They had a strong animus against city hall. One of the catalytic things that happened at this time was that enterprise zones came onto the agenda, at the state level, and some of us decided to respond to it. This was the beginning of CWED—the Community Workshop on Economic Development.

The concept of CWED came out of one of those purely serendipitous situations. I was playing a facilitator role at this meeting of community leaders to discuss enterprise zones. There were about 300 people there, and it got heated. I realized in the midst of the session that, with a nudge, the process could go in an unanticipated direction. The initial mood in the room was a feeling of tremendous pressure to work with enterprise zones because people were really fired up about enterprise zones—Reagan had all this momentum going, people felt like they ought to give it a chance. Alternatively, there was a mood among some to reject it out of hand. Attendees loved it or hated it. That was a pretty provocative tension.

I led the debate down the path in the middle to accept the fact that the tension existed and to exploit it for our own community purposes. Inspired by some catalytic floor work by Art Vazquez, I was able to draw out of that meeting a commitment to seek a new public policy that would facilitate our community work. They accepted out of Reagan the fact there was a need for a strong, community-directed public policy; they rejected his particular one. What the zones brought to the table was a desire to refocus policy on community, that you weren't talking about an urban policy but about a community policy.

From this meeting emerged a core group of around twenty organizations that could pull out maybe a hundred people for a meeting, although most of the working sessions had about twenty-five. This group became the nucleus of CWED. I think this group sensed, early on, that it had an opportunity to develop and promote some sort of a breakthrough strategy. The culmination was the actual CWED platform: economic development meant jobs, not real estate projects; there should be balance in city investments between downtown and the neighborhoods; and neighborhood organizations should be a part of the decision and delivery systems for city economic development policy.

The whole effort to put together CWED as a statewide organization was based on a confidence that the agenda could, via the 1982 governor's campaign, be forced onto the political terrain. So there was a belief that it was time to get political on a scale that Chicago community groups had never tried before. This effort was seen as a big step. It succeeded in that it pulled together a statewide platform. It failed in terms of political organizing because we got it together too late to do anything—I remember having some meetings on how we were going to feed this into gubernatorial debates around the state and things like that, but we never got to that place.

WORKING FOR THE CITY

Meanwhile, the Harold Washington mayoralty campaign was getting under way, and many of us, led by Kari Moe, joined his research and policy group. The CWED platform helped frame and articulate a set of expectations and goals for what the city could do once it came under the control of a progressive administration. We thought the city could take direct community development block-grant dollars and infrastructure dollars and direct more of those dollars into neighborhoods. We also expected that we could mount a pretty good business retention program that involved community-based organizations interacting with businesses that felt that city hall had ignored them—that played into the formation of chamber of commerce–oriented and industrial development groups. We felt we could foster a different sort of relationship with those businesses, ones that coincidentally constituted the majority of the employment base in the city.

We thought the government could think of development as not only real estate development but could also develop the ability to address the needs of manufacturing, to take a more diverse sectorial approach to development in the city. We wanted to see a more focused use of the city's loan dollars and purchasing dollars. And we thought we could, through the mayor, help change the terms of the debate about what are appropriate state and national policies that have an impact on city economic development. Putting jobs on the agenda was our thrust, especially jobs for the most needy.

There is one last policy item that was important, and we failed miserably on it. From the outset, we saw the need to bring some sort of coherence between education, employment training, and development. It was codified in Washington's platform by the notion of merging the departments of economic development and employment and training. But beyond that, we saw the mayor taking on the public education bureaucracy and relating education to development. For a lot of reasons, this agenda got overwhelmed by the day-to-day realities and didn't surface again until Washington's second term.

A couple of important things made me decide to go into the government after the election. It seemed to me that as the campaign unfolded, economic development became one of the central substantive issues. Now obviously the campaign was fought on several levels. At its heart and soul the campaign was totally about race: keep the black man out of city hall or get control of city hall. But at another level there was additional substance to it that was important to broadening the black coalition. The substantive elements of the campaign focused on human values, civil rights, and jobs for the needy. The development agenda played an important role in bringing progressive whites and Latinos in, although it was not the only thing. To the extent that people talked substance beyond civil rights, it seems to me that economic development became the major substantive component of the campaign.

That was precipitated by the first television debate, which was on economic development. Suddenly Harold Washington burst on the scene, and people realized that he was a serious and substantial candidate. He was charismatic; furthermore, his ideas about development were in marked contrast to those of his opponents. He had ideas he drew upon, and they were different.

I had started out in the campaign coordinating his economic development issue group, and I ended up being on a committee that oversaw all the issue groups. I ended up writing the neighborhood plank as well as doing some editing on the other planks. So the things emerging out in the economic development issue area were also being driven into some other issue statements, yielding more coherence across broad functional areas. These and other papers got put together as the *Washington Papers*—really an elaboration of the CWED platform—as a campaign document.

Three or four weeks before the general election, Kari Moe got plucked out of the issues office and plopped into the car with Washington to be his substantive aide as he traveled from stop to stop, briefing him. She was able to use this over and over again to reinforce the uniqueness of his platform: "Here you are stopping at this point and here are some of the themes that are emerging and you can address them here." Along with others from the group, I was cranking out issue one-pagers daily on "the mayor's going here and here's what it means to that spot," and Kari was riding in the car and weaving them in.

Washington's performance on the campaign trail was extraordinary. I felt that in the campaign we fed him some raw material, and he took it to a level that was beyond my imagination. When I say he could take it beyond my imagination, we had a plank that we thought really touched the soul of the people the mayor was speaking to because it had come out of them, but his contact with that soul was much deeper. It was apparent to me that he was able to put it into a perspective that was much richer than even my decade of experience in Chicago would have enabled me to do. I couldn't put my finger on what it was at the time. But it didn't take me long after I actually began to work with him to understand it. He could take a current issue and put it into a thirty-year historical perspective that saw that issue in the context of the struggle for black political empowerment, the struggle for community empowerment, for civil rights, human rights, fairness, labor, and good government. He had this thirty-year history at his fingertips and could relate any current issue to that. In making these historical connections, he was touching in a very fine-grained way on what people were responding to, what they were looking for, who the key actors were, the bases that had to be touched, and so forth.

This ability to take our more or less technical contribution to another level is a really important, very significant part of the history of who Harold Washington was. This was because of the way in which the establishment media and the political opposition tried to package him as a charismatic speaker whose victory was somewhat of a fluke. No one in the establishment addressed the content of what he really thought.

After the primary, the business community rallied behind the mayor, and he had to figure out what the hell to do with these folks. So he created a huge transition apparatus in which everybody who wanted to help could be on the transition team. This transition apparatus in the development area involved people who had been disconnected from the campaign, disconnected from the movement that launched the campaign. It was dominated by business leadership. They came at it as if this man had no ideas, and their job was to fill his brain. One thing that just surprised the heck out of me was that nobody involved in the shaping of the economic development agenda in the campaign was brought onto the transition team. And the transition team started to go off in a totally different direction.

Five days before the actual election, a group of us who had been working on economic development issues decided that in terms of issue formulation the campaign was over and we should spend the next five days out on the streets ringing doorbells. But we agreed to meet the day after the election because there was another battle to be fought, to be sure that the mayor implemented what he had campaigned on. So we went out and rang doorbells for five days and then literally the day after the election, after being up all night celebrating and everything, we met again. And we started right then and there the battle to keep him on track for what he had campaigned for. And that's when we wrote our own transition report. We did that over the next five or six days.

Right away, it was clear that Kari Moe was moving from the car right into the mayor's office. We would have an ally there. And it also became clear to us that we had to try and get someone who was sympathetic to what we were doing appointed commissioner of economic development. Somewhere in that period, with the encouragement of the issues group, I decided to make a push for it. So we were out in the streets during the month after the election, sitting down with key people who were long-time confidants of the mayor. I remember making the rounds of people that either I knew or Kari pointed out to me as "this is someone the mayor has listened to for years—you ought to go talk to him"— and going and helping these people understand the evolution of the ideas that the mayor had campaigned on, where they came from, and juxtaposing it against what was beginning to crop up in the business community.

PLANNING IN DED

In the end I became commissioner of economic development. The first time I went in to meet Harold Washington, the chemistry was there. The first time I sat down, it was clear to me that we were of like mind. In fact, he almost hired me on the spot. I remember he scrambled all over the place to try to find his chief of staff to bring him into the office, but couldn't find him. He rescheduled our meeting and closed the deal a month later.

I took office in August 1983 and set about the business of evaluating what I had. I knew the department I was taking over as well as any incoming department head because I had worked with the staff for so many years. I knew the people well. But I had to go through a process of putting together a team and making some organizational changes. The main planning we did involved the Chicago Works Together plan, and perhaps a set of big projects that play off against and in some tension with the overall plan, which emphasized small-scale development.

The Subcabinet and the Chicago Works Together Plan   Toward the end of 1983, two main events occurred: the creation of the development subcabinet and the launching of a development plan. As soon as I came in, Bill Ware, the mayor's chief of staff, told me he wanted me to pull together the development departments. I don't know when we actually started. I know when we really moved into high gear was when we set up to do the development plan, which has been known as Chicago Works Together (cwt). I woke up one morning to hear on the news that the mayor had announced that he was going to be releasing a development plan in about sixty days. So I went to his office that morning and asked, "What's this development plan you were talking about?" He got this sheepish smile on his face that he got when he knew he had you. He said, "I figured you'd fill in the blanks."

We cranked into high gear. We had sixty days to produce a development plan, which became a great device to whip the rest of the departments into line. I remember bringing the subcabinet together in my office and basically handing them the *Washington Papers,* and saying, you know, contrary to what you may believe, the *Washington Papers* is the Bible. None of the other subcabinet members had come out of the campaign. Some were old guard carryovers—Tom Kapsalis in aviation, Jerry Butler in public works—some were new people that had been brought in—Brenda Gaines in housing, Liz Hollander in planning, Maria Gerda in MET—but none of them had been involved in the campaign, and none of them knew really what the Mayor was all about. When I handed them the *Washington Papers* and said this is the Bible, it created a lot of consternation, and we spent a long time grappling with that and helping them understand that it really was the Bible.

The question anytime you do a plan like that is, What purpose does it serve? I think, at a minimum, if you codify what you're all about and what you want to do, then you are more likely to have people understand it and buy into it and operate as if that is the game plan. The development plan was conceptually a direct successor to the CWED platform, and of course the *Washington Papers* and a lot of its language then got picked up in some of the strategic plans that other local development organizations were doing. We required some of the neighborhood groups we funded to do strategic plans and in many cases these strategic plans—without our prodding—became reflections of cwt. So I think the more you take the language out of the plan and imbed it in other things, the more you're creating a structure of sorts within which planning and development can occur.

That's lesson number one. Number two, of course, is it was a great team-building exercise that operated on a number of levels. We got the commissioners thinking more alike. It created the reason for us to get together regularly and that's something that kept on going until the mayor's death. Even more important, it created an opportunity for our staffs to work together across departmental boundaries, and the relationships that developed there and the teamwork development became a powerful resource.

Third, it also was an occasion to broaden the external constituency base. Kari Moe, for example, who was chief of staff of the development subcabinet at that time and was well connected with external constituencies, was running the interdepartmental staff doing the development plan. Doing the plan helped some of these staff people, who saw themselves as professionals and didn't pay much attention to external constituencies, develop new contacts. And so it also helped open up government. Washington was trying thousands of different ways to open up government; this became another way.

In summary, the CWT plan became an important reference point throughout my time at city hall even after Washington died. It became a reference point for Sawyer and even, to a degree, Mayor Daley. So it was quite a guidebook.

World's Fair and Navy Pier   I think these two projects were both important because we always had this struggle, this tension between large projects and the small-scale, organic ones. Further, we had cast the die by positioning ourselves as skeptics about large projects.

An early high point was the World's Fair. It kicked into gear immediately; it became one of the first things that challenged the rest of the subcabinet to take the *Washington Papers* seriously. There were wide-ranging views about how the World's Fair should be approached. Some in the subcabinet who were carryovers believed in it—Kapsalis and Butler—and some newcomers believed in it—Liz Hollander—and they were really somewhat unquestioning and uncritical of the whole thing. To be confronted then with the *Washington Papers,* the plank that basically said the challenge is to shape the mayor's approach to the World's Fair out of this framework, was really a provocative process.

Our handling of the World's Fair was a signal statement. The fair was a thing the "movers and shakers" wanted more than anything; therefore it was most important that we open up the process for looking at the World's Fair. It was most important that the way we judged the World's Fair was compatible with the principles we were stating in the development plan, that there was consistency between the development plan and our actions toward the World's Fair. This became the point of departure for all approaches to big projects. From that time on, the growth coalition would say about us that we're probably going to be *opposed* to a big project unless they could make an extraordinary case as to why we shouldn't be. I suspect the usual mentality in government is *behind* the big projects unless there's an extraordinary case made as to why they shouldn't be. The whole burden of proof had shifted. The burden of proof was now on the elite as opposed to the people. It was on the elite to make their case, as opposed to the burden of proof on citizens for why we shouldn't. That difference is enormously important.

I think, if anything, running the World's Fair through the screen of the development plan reaffirmed to us the sensibility of the *Washington Papers*.

The other thing that happened early on that also became a vehicle for pushing the agenda was the Navy Pier. The pier development was under the responsibility of Butler and it was floundering, so the mayor dropped the whole thing on me. The Navy Pier was important because at the same time we were throwing up roadblocks in front of the World's Fair, we were engaged with this other large project, the Navy Pier. It was important to be really aggressive about the Navy Pier precisely so that we wouldn't be typecast as knee-jerk opponents to every large project. We didn't want to wear the jacket of nay-sayers, so we really asked ourselves, in the context of the Navy Pier, was it possible to do a big project in a way that reflected what we were all about and to help achieve our goals. We also chose the pier for this approach because it was being promoted by the Rouse Company, and the company's managers had a reputation for being flexible. They would go a long way toward helping cities meet some of their affirmative hiring and purchasing goals, so we really pushed the Navy Pier project and tried to impose some of our development standards on them. We went way beyond the usual targeting of purchasing, hiring, and minority entrepreneurship to get them to drive some of this thinking down to the tenants. For example, the Rouse Company agreed to put some of our purchasing requirements in tenants' leases, something that they hadn't done anywhere else. And we also got them to agree to try and help us work on neighborhood projects. As they negotiated with national franchises to locate on Navy Pier, we wanted them to require those franchises to open up some neighborhood sites as well. We also wanted the Rouse Company itself to look at taking on a neighborhood project. Essentially the neighborhoods of the city at that time were redlined for most national franchises; they've since been opened up.

All this was built into the Navy Pier negotiations. That's why the council opposition killed it; they didn't want to see us doing all that stuff. But I think it would have been a really significant project. It happened several times in my tenure that the most significant projects generated enormous political conflict: the Bears stadium was killed in the Illinois General Assembly and the conservative Republican leader in the state senate was quoted as saying that if we pass this bill, we're setting a dangerous precedent for all state public works projects.

WERE OUR ACTIONS AD HOC OR AGENDA DRIVEN?

People have asked whether our actions were ad hoc. On the one hand, there was a clear sense of what we wanted to do. There was the sense that jobs were the bottom line and that local economic development was going to march to a different drummer. But then once you get in there, how do you make this mean something in the day-to-day operation of a department? We worked it through as we went, and it multiplied a thousand fold into the range of things with which the mayor was involved. It was this micro level at which there appeared to be a lot of "winging it."

Basically I don't think ad hoc versus agenda is the right question. The question is how does an agenda and operating ad hoc go hand in hand. On a day-to-day management basis, there was a continual tension between the agenda and the particularities of the situation we were in. There was a constant interplay. For example, the development plan had some fairly clear principles in mind, one of which was that "jobs are the bottom line." In any particular development, we had to figure out what "jobs are the bottom line" meant. In figuring it out, our whole understanding of that goal of jobs was reshaped. It was a constant interplay, a dialectic tension, between a malleable structure imposed by the development plan—the agenda, the game plan—and the particularities of our day-to-day work. So there was always a tension. I think it's important to see "agenda" and "project" as existing in this dialectic tension because it was not the case of the structure being all "window dressing." It's easy, almost glib, to interpret it that way. I think the tension between structure and day-to-day actions was real, alive, and palpable and something I personally thought about every single day. I'd get up in the morning generally, go for a run or a swim, something to start my day, and use that as a moment to think and feel this tension. "Here's the stuff I'm facing today; what in the world does it mean given this context within which I'm operating, this game plan." It was always there.

It was enormously difficult to concentrate on this, constantly putting little pieces into this larger puzzle, over four or five years. By the time I moved to the mayor's office, I was dealing with literally a couple of hundred discreet activities every single day: phone calls, letters, decisions. They ranged from something I could dispose of in thirty seconds to something that would take two hours. On any given day I might have one or two hour-long issues and then I'd have lots of tiny ones. I always thought I had a good mind for detail and could pretty much keep it all filed away in the recesses of my brain, but as time went on, it became more and more difficult, a constant struggle not only to remember something but to put it into context and keep those connections going. It just was an enormous challenge, especially as I got deeper into it and literally got more tired, physically tired. That's why it was always important to keep in shape. But as I got more tired, it was a lot harder. By the time my six years were up, I was really exhausted. It was an enormously difficult task. I learned to use staff more efficiently. I learned to manage my time, I learned recordkeeping, I dabbled in some computer programs but I never mastered them. It was really tough—the tension between agenda and action.

LEADERSHIP, PLANNING, AND TRAINING FOR PLANNING

I think that the questions of the role of leadership and the importance of race are the areas where I changed the most in my six years at city hall. When I came in, I did not believe in the importance of leadership. I felt the leadership was a group characteristic, and I really considered Harold Washington an aberration. It was clear to me that Washington's election was the result of an enormous and vibrant group process and the charisma of an individual who could lift it and elevate it. So I had right before my eyes the evidence that leadership was important. But I was still reluctant to place an importance on leadership beyond that provided by the mayor. Some of my staff, people like Kari, used to get really irritated with me because I would not be a more forceful leader. They wanted me to go out and be highly visible, and to be much more aggressive in the bureaucracy, be a bureaucratic infighter. I thought I was visible enough. I felt I was a good bureaucratic infighter, but they wanted more.

But I felt that these were team things. So, for every four opportunities I had to be visible publicly, I would shove *them* out on three of them. When they wanted me to be more aggressive in forging changes in the bureaucracy, I made them forge linkages. It was mandatory for my senior staff to go out to lunch at least once a month with someone from another department and start building linkages across departments.

So I was resisting this leadership mantle, even though the deeper we got into it, the more I realized that yes, in fact, I was playing a major leadership role in many of the successful community-based efforts. I was caught in this tension of a group process and the leadership of an individual. Where there was no individual leadership, the group process was less effective. And as I just described, by the time of Washington's death, I finally was fully able to accept the importance of leadership, including my own.

Some other things are important. I think the dynamics of race in this country is the most powerful force confronting, shaping who can and should do planning. It is the central issue facing planners, and it's got to be confronted in every aspect of the daily work, daily life, of planning. Planners have to focus attention on it. I think a lot of planning is attention shaping. Plans shape people's attention. So planners have consciously to admit that they are confronting race. I never go into a room without being aware of the racial composition of the room. At a lecture I gave yesterday, I was absolutely, totally aware that there was one black and no Hispanics in that room and that about half the attendees were women. It is automatic. Every work situation I'm in, I'm aware of race and gender. I think it is absolutely essential for planners both to preach the message on race and to practice what they preach. They must do everything in their power to shape and mold every work situation they're in so that it becomes an occasion for people to challenge their racial stereotypes and learn to interact across racial boundaries.

One lesson on this I learned from Washington. He used to insist on final personal approval on every board or commission, task group, or ad hoc working group that we created, even if it were a departmental-level advisory body. His concern was not who the people were on that group. He wanted to know that the work group was a microcosm of society. He was concerned about the race, gender, class, and life experience mixes of these groups. He wanted the participants to be forced to consider their differences and their stereotypes. He took every occasion to do that, and I think that's just absolutely essential.

Another lesson, less important than leadership and race, is to be constantly aware of the dialectic tension around community empowerment. Community empowerment is at once liberating and a very conservative and racist force. I constantly remind my student at UIC that the first community organization that formed in Chicago was the Hyde Park Conservation and Protection Association, which was created to lobby for racially exclusive covenants in land titles in Hyde Park, home of the University of Chicago. So an awful lot of community empowerment is a conservative "keep the folks out" force. And so social justice and community are not the same thing. A lot of times, people get careless and say community is good, community is more just, but it just isn't so. I think attacking social justice issues at the community level is an extraordinarily effective way to attack, but they have to be attacked.

For me, planners need to be much more skilled in communication than in analysis. They need to appreciate the beauty of listening to people as opposed to telling people what they think is right. I think that planners have really gotten away from this because they use the public meeting as a crutch and assume that the meeting is a vehicle for group participation in problem solving. They get away from it because the technology available to planners makes it more and more possible for an individual planner working alone to do a wider variety of tasks involved in putting together a plan. There's an organizational tendency that's manifest in a personal tendency for the profession to become more individualistic. Most planning curriculums do not train planners at group process and communications skills.

The final lesson is to have greater faith in intuition, to respect doubt. The more certain planners are, the more scared I am of them. It's the ones who are really scared of what they're doing and have a lot of doubts that probably are on the cutting edge of things. To be afraid to plunge into messy situations is to be afraid of failure. If you're afraid of failure and afraid of doubt, chances are you're reducing the problem you're dealing with to something that is both manageable and irrelevant. Well, it's funny—occasionally I teach courses that require numerical analysis. For example, I teach a development finance course where people have to learn spreadsheets. I have to teach students the joy of problem solving with a pencil. To me, the essence of problem solving with a pencil is making mistakes and being able to erase them. You learn by making mistakes, and it's OK. The most intimidating thing in the world is to work in pen and ink because you can't erase your mistakes, therefore it makes you risk aversive. Or to work on a computer where it's easy to assume you're immune from mistakes. I encourage students not to be afraid of mistakes, to enjoy learning from mistakes, and that's tough to do.

INTERVIEW WITH ARTURO VAZQUEZ

I was born on the south side of Chicago in a house just about three-quarters of a block from the entrance to U.S. Steel. I grew up in a steelworker's family. My father was very much involved with the union. He was not an organizer, but he supported the organizing work that was being done at the Carnegie plant; this was back in 1934. I grew up in South Chicago and throughout my early life, everybody that I grew up with was in a family that was involved in steel. Everyone in South Chicago worked in the mills, and I grew up with that kind of background. When I finished high school, I intended to work in the mills. I was a musician, and I was going to play music on weekends—like the rest of my buddies. I did in fact go to work in the mills off and on for about three years.

It is a long story about how I went from being a mill worker in the steel industry to being part of the Harold Washington administration in the 1980s. I managed by accidentally being at the right place at the right time to get to Northwestern University on a music scholarship. I went to school up in Evanston; I guess it was 1953 when I enrolled. I graduated in 1959, ending up with a B.A. degree, with a major in philosophy and a history and literature of religions kind of background. After that, I got drafted into the army. In the army, I was in the Fifth Army Band. I continued being a musician. When I came out, I began looking for work.

Through a fluke, I started working with the city of Chicago in youth work. This was in the first Daley administration, with a guy named Charlie Livermore, who was setting up the Commission on Youth Welfare. During my college career I had done a lot of work volunteering with youth in churches, so I got into really trying to work with kids, poor kids. I worked in the Daley administration for about five years, from 1961 to the beginning of 1966. This was of course the time of the civil rights movement in Chicago. Two things happened to me about this time. One was that I broke with the administration on the issue of police brutality in Latino communities.

I was working in a Puerto Rican community for the commission. There was tension between Mexicans and Puerto Ricans in those early days. I never really identified totally with the Puerto Rican community; but, I guess, a larger Latino identity was very much in order for me at that point. Also, from a professional standpoint we were supposed to be dealing with the problems affecting communities and youth, so I actively intervened. I saw it as part of my professional responsibility and began to deal with the issue of police brutality, and it led to a break with the city administration when politics got into the way of resolving the issue.

The police department didn't respond in reasonable ways. They tried to whitewash a number of police brutality incidents. And then a local alderman, who was very powerful at that time, a guy named Tom Keane, also intervened and stopped the work that I was doing to try to bring it out into the open.

My break with the administration was important politically for me, and then a riot broke out in the Puerto Rican community and I got involved. I wrote an article detailing the background of incidents of police brutality that led up to that particular riot. That caused a further break with my previous friends in city government, as well as the fact that I also alienated a lot of the people in the police department that I had worked with previously. That was an important part of my development.

So I broke with the administration at that point and began working with a group called the Community Renewal Society in Chicago, with a really good guy named Don Benedict, who had been doing work trying to get the corporate structure to begin responding to the needs of low-income communities, particularly black communities.

The second thing that occurred was that, as a member of the Community Renewal Society, I was sent out to the first major national demonstration that Cesar Chavez organized in support of the farm workers' movement. I participated in the march that ended in Sacramento. Previously, I had been an observer and supporter of the civil rights movement, but it didn't get under my skin. I was neither white nor black, but the march from Delano to Sacramento really did a job on me. When I came back, I was useless for about three months. Because up until that point, I had been totally upwardly mobile. From that point on, I began to look for alternative ways to find a way to work and make some changes, to reconcile my new feeling of identification and commitment with some kind of a life career.

I never had any problems with my Mexican identity; my parents came from Texas. My grandmother had crossed the border with my father in 1913. My father and mother came to Chicago in 1929. My grandmother was a product of the generation of the revolution in Mexico and had taught me and my brother an awful lot about that and our identity with the revolution and our Indian–Mexican background. So I never had a problem with that. But I had lost touch. Delano revived it.

The Community Renewal Society offered me the opportunity to work this stuff out; sort of like the beginning point. The trip to Delano to be part of the march with the delegation from the Illinois Council of Churches started it. I came back and continued to work with them, and they gave me support to work with local community organizations around the city, Latino community organizations, and social service agencies, to begin moving them toward community development activities. So there was a vehicle to begin doing positive work and that involved, from a planning perspective, to begin understanding what the needs were in local communities: looking at resources and trying to shape investments that the society was putting into those communities to leverage other resources to move people toward community development activities.

The Community Renewal Society also provided me with an opportunity to support the growth of community organizations in Latino communities. At that time, there just weren't any. Through the Renewal Society we supported the first group that began to emerge in the Puerto Rican community after the riots, the Spanish Action Committee (SAC), and in the Mexican community, the ALAS organization. One group that we organized I was very much a part of putting together—the first middle-class, civil rights Latino group composed of young entrepreneurs and professionals of all nationalities. I can't remember what the name was, but it was the first one that really began trying to deal with Latin American issues from a political perspective by negotiating with the political structure.

I worked with the Community Renewal Society for about three years and then a job opened up in an agency called the Neighborhood Service Organization, in 1969, in the Mexican community of Pilsen on Chicago's near southwest side. The job opened up as a result of the work that I had been doing, and the community organization I had been working with in that area asked me to apply to become the executive director of the agency. I did and went in and began trying to create a model for how social service agencies, traditional settlement houses, could move into a community development mode.

We began building community development. Our efforts were to begin putting people together, decentralizing agency programs to allow people in the community to take part in the agency, begin developing leadership and shaping the use of resources. Up until that point, the agency was what I called a colonizing instrument. It was controlled by outside people. It was a Presbyterian–United Church of Christ organization, and most of the people on the board were from suburban churches that contributed money and supported that kind of work. They were well-intentioned people, but they were still people who were not really sensitive to what was going on in the community. What we did was decentralize the programs, develop local community program boards, and give them staff and resources. These boards began calling the shots on the programs. The other thing that I did was to get rid of all the Masters of Social Work and let community-resident staff run the show together with the local program boards. That of course, led to conflict, and after a while the board left. We began developing a new board—a community board.

The other thing that happened was that we began developing a youth structure. After two years, the agency was no longer called the Neighborhood Service Organization, it was called Casa Aztlan. It developed a totally Mexican identity and was well into the community development mode. Out of that agency came a new youth agency—El Centro de la Causa. A babysitting co-op became a day-care center. We developed a free health center, part of Chicago's health center movement, all under their own boards. We really moved the whole thing into a community development mode.

The kind of work we were doing inevitably led to the development of a political movement on the West Side. Leadership developed, additional resources were brought into the community, constituencies were created, and organizing around concrete and serious issues took place. The existing political machine leader and their allies in the Mexican community were unresponsive. From the base of the new, young community leadership we put together an independent political movement and developed an alliance with the black community on the West Side of Chicago. Eventually we jointly ran people for office against the machine.

But before that, before we got into electoral politics, we were doing politics by coalition building. I had been involved with putting together a citywide effort, along with a guy named Slim Coleman from Uptown, Nancy Jefferson (who just died, and who was my role model) from the West Side, Bob Lucas on the South Side, and Mecca Sorrentini from the northwestern Puerto Rican community, putting together stuff that called into question Chicago's use of federal monies for urban development work. This first effort (1975) was called the Chicago Coalition to Stop the Plan 21. The city was concentrating monies into areas that were already driven by market forces, instead of putting resources into low- and moderate-income neighborhoods.

So we were developing citywide coalitions across communities, across racial lines, and moving forward to try to have an impact on the city's policies. In 1977 we put together the first major community coalition meeting actually to develop a political platform and neighborhood political agenda. In 1978 two people ran on that political agenda. One in Uptown—Helen Schiller, who later became, and still is, an alderman—and a person on the West Side who didn't make it. In 1979–1981 we put together another coalition that began challeng-

ing the city's overall economic development program. We forced Jane Byrne—
the mayor in 1980 who preceded Harold Washington—to appoint community
people to the Overall Economic Development Program Committee, required
by the EDA, through a court suit. Again we had six people—Latins, blacks,
and whites—who were appointed to it as part of the coalition that challenged
the city's policies on the use of federal funds.

So we ran our own political slate, in effect. This was the late 1970s going
into the 1980s. From 1980 to 1983, we put together two more coalition efforts.
One was the Community Workshop on Economic Development (CWED) that
challenged, at the state level, the new enterprise zone programs that the governor was putting into operation. Then, at the city level, CWED challenged
the city's economic development policies again. The basic idea was to use
resources to stimulate areas having difficulty rather than put them into areas
that were already market driven. Rob Mier was very much involved in the
CWED effort. Then in 1981, with this background in coalition building, we put
together the coalition called "The Chicago 1993 Committee" that began challenging the downtown growth coalition's proposed World's Fair. We worked
very hard at fighting the fair and finally succeeded in stopping it after Harold
Washington took office.

That was the background, that was hundreds of people across Chicago's
neighborhoods laying the groundwork for Harold's campaign. The CWED
effort, which I chaired, developed an economic development platform that
many organizations worked on and that became a major part of the Harold
Washington agenda for economic development in the city. That's how we got
into it. When I say we, I pay tribute to Chicago's neighborhood organizations and my compañeros in Pilsen in an organization that I headed up called
the Pilsen Housing and Business Alliance that was a cornerstone in the later
coalitions. We actually did a lot of voter registration together with other Pilsen
organizations, manned precincts; we did an awful lot in our community in
developing votes for Harold.

GOING INTO THE GOVERNMENT

That's pretty much how I got into the political arena. When Harold Washington got elected, we then went into action to see if we could get Rob Mier
into being commissioner for economic development. We were successful, and
Rob started to put together the economic development department. He looked
around and began pulling people together that he thought could help him do the
job. He talked to me about coming to work for the department in the capacity

of deputy commissioner in charge of the division that was essentially business services and the marketing arm of the department's programs. After looking at it, I decided that I would go ahead and do it because it also had within the division responsibility for the department's community development block-grant program of grants to local organizations. The budget for that program was somewhere around $400,000. But I agreed to accept responsibility for that division.

There was a major problem: we inherited a workforce that had been largely identified with past administrations. I had worked with city government for five and a half years, and I think that gave me a different perspective on who worked for government. My experience was that there were some damn good people there. There are always good people in city government—but there were also some hacks and of course the patronage appointees. When I agreed to take the job, I had a pretty good idea of who was in the division and felt there were some possibilities for working in that division. But there was a problem because you couldn't bring in your own people. Just prior to the mayor's taking office, the Byrne administration had made several thousand "temporary employees" permanent, giving them civil service protection. Also, a federal judge had issued a decree protecting city workers from political firings. Out of a workforce of 40,000 employees, the mayor had discretionary hiring powers over 900 positions. So when I walked into the division, I came in alone; I couldn't even bring in a secretary. I had to deal with it myself.

Fortunately, I didn't have to deal with people who were more committed to the kind of traditional economic development efforts focusing on downtown development; that was Rob's responsibility. He was able to bring in some good people to take responsibility for reworking those divisions and turning them around. He replaced the first deputy who had been primarily responsible for downtown planning. He put Rosalyn Paswell in the first deputy position. Roz was a person who was really progressive, who was committed to keeping industry in the city. She had come to work for the Byrne administration from out of town. She was brought in because of her reputation and abilities and was somebody we could work with. Mier effectively replaced that layer of previous appointees who had carried out the policies the neighborhood movement had been challenging. The rest of the people in the department were essentially civil service and just followed the direction of the office.

BUSINESS RETENTION PROGRAM

Let me say one more word about my background. I had gotten involved in a lot of antiwar stuff. I started off with a mere protest on the war from an ethical perspective, but very rapidly got into a left perspective on it. So when I came back into city government, I was no friend of capitalism. I had real mixed feelings about what we had to do. The major responsibility of the division was to begin dealing with business services across the city. That is, with a sector of capital—small businesses and manufacturing communities—that had been shut out of the development process by previous administrations. Looking at it as an organizer and now a representative of the mayor, we had some very strong responsibilities to that sector, to begin working with them to make sure that they were going to be able to continue in business in the city, to keep and expand the job base, tax base, and so forth. That was of course a major problem we encountered, particularly the manufacturing base in Chicago, which had been so neglected. Daley had completely ignored that sector. Recent studies show that in the 1960s and 1970s—throughout the 1970s—Chicago probably lost more jobs to suburbanization and out-of-state relocations than almost any other city in the country.

It was very rapid job loss. This was not just a question of "market forces," it was an action of neglect by the city to try to keep manufacturing jobs in Chicago. Mayor Daley had turned the city over to the downtown growth coalition. That went on through the 1960s and accelerated through the 1970s. Neighborhoods and neighborhood businesses were forgotten. You had people out there who were really hurting, who saw themselves struggling against the tide, doing business in Chicago but increasingly looking toward the suburbs or out of the country. There was also the problem of shakedowns. You had inspectors going out there, from the Inspectional Services Department. There were scandals almost every other week about somebody being caught taking money, shaking down a business for money under threat of losing a license. The business community lacked confidence in the city.

Another major problem was that a whole lot of promises had been made to community-based organizations about their role in performing economic development. Rob and I had been part of that whole process. Another problem, from an administration point of view, was that we didn't have a workforce in city hall that we could depend on in terms of delivering the goods. Those were three major things we had to deal with.

A fourth problem was from our own perspective: the need to create a participatory model for economic development activities. Just before coming to the administration, I participated in a conference in Florence, Italy, on decentralization, and it was a real eye opener for me. In Italy there is a public law that authorizes cities with more than 400,000 people to decentralize their polity. In Florence and other cities in Italy they had actually gone through a decentralization process where you had locally elected councils in neighborhood areas. The city budget was distributed to these neighborhood areas by formula, and the neighborhood councils had discretionary powers to spend within the budget categories. You had local people making decisions on how to spend lire. This was not merely a bureaucratic decentralization device but a democratization of city services. It was a real eye opener for me to see how local people were spending dollars for health care and infrastructure and were involving people in the neighborhoods doing health-care work, work on the streets, restoration of buildings. So when I went to work for the city, that model got stuck in my head—the fact of decentralization, democratic decentralization.

The political problem was that we couldn't get it through the city council. This was "council wars" time. During the transition process there had been a lot of talk about creating neighborhood planning areas and having local groups become the planning boards. But it was impossible in the political climate unleashed after Harold Washington took office. The question then was how do we begin dealing with the problem of creating participatory models and achieving decentralization.

The program we inherited was a grants program from CDBG funds. It was called Technical Assistance to Business Groups. It had been used by the Byrne administration for getting money to groups around the city that were going to help her reelection. We took that program and began to expand its concept and funding. The vehicle we saw for doing what we wanted to do was the contract mechanism.

We developed some very specific aims that we turned into the "boilerplate" for the contracts under this program. Initially, we divided the groups from across the city that applied for this program into three categories and later created a fourth: beginning groups (level 1), middle groups with some experience (level 2) and advanced groups (level 3). The fourth category were groups involved in industrial work, which we set up as a program called the Local Industrial Retention Initiative. We assigned specific objectives to each one of these groups in order to be able to create and improve their capacity. We then got organizations like the Center for Urban Economic Development at the University of Illinois (UICUED) on contract to provide capacity-building services to these groups. We also assigned specific territories to them. So what we were doing with the program over the four-year period we were working at it was de facto creating a decentralization model.

We did this under contract. Internally, in order to remove the city's staff from calling on businesses, we pulled back staff members from the field, because prior to this, it was very politicized calling. The business community had a lack of confidence in them. What we did under contract was to give the business-calling function on behalf of city government to local groups. Every local group had a business constituency and businessmen on their boards, as well as a neighborhood constituency. So at the grassroots level they would call on businesses and find out what the businesses wanted and needed and help them get it.

What we did after we pulled back our staff was to reorganize it to create a more efficient city business services follow-up mechanism. All referrals for city services that could not be handled at the ward level (we made sure all organizations had contact with their ward supervisors) were sent to the department. We computerized the whole operation for processing purposes; we were then responsible for making sure that the city delivered and had a fast turnaround for all service requests that came in.

So we created a division of labor with the groups being contracted to provide specific services and evealuated on the basis of their success in meeting their goals. They had the responsibility of marketing city services and program products to the constituencies and referring requests for service, and our responsibility as a division for field services was to process these requests to the proper division in the department, or to other city departments, and do the follow-up to make sure that the turnaround time was short.

This was quite a successful program—and it is still in operation today. It has been carried on by the current administration. The present policymakers don't understand the program as well as we did, but the staff we developed to manage it is still in place and is working to keep the program going. So we managed to institutionalize the program.

I think that by doing those two things we were able to work on a major problem with business confidence in Chicago: making sure that the business calling was done and that business groups in fact had some control through a role with the local groups and a contract with the city. The legal mechanism of the contract was central to all this, and was a negotiated relationship. We pulled our staff out so that there would be no political taint to the work being done, we professionalized our staff so that we could provide the follow-through, we developed some mutual accountability on a contractual basis. We gave a role in economic development to local organizations that we had worked with a as a constituency, and funding that role, providing resources. We were also creating a philosophy in government through creating capacity in these groups and giving them funds according to their capacity. The key for me was that we were de facto decentralizing and making these organizations partners with government.

It was grassroots economic development in a most fundamental way. It provided local organizations with a chance to shape investments in their areas. A special projects category of grant, which I didn't mention before, gave cBos the opportunity to develop community-owned businesses, like a laundromat, a construction group, and the rest. Overall, I think the program was enormously successful.

Many additional groups developed in response to this, and I think the quality of work—that is to say the technical work that was being done in the neighborhoods—was improved as a result of our program. When I went in, we had fewer than twenty groups in the Technical Assistance to Business Groups program. When I left, we had about 113. The budget, when I came in, was less than $400,000. When I left, we had over $3 million of grant monies. All of it came out of the Community Development Block Grant.

During this whole period, the program I managed was the only program, I believe, that grew significantly in the entire city budget. There was a conscious tactic that I used in increasing allocations. I knew that key alderman favored certain groups. So, in my budget, which was sent to the budget office, I would keep these groups at lower budget recommendations than groups that were not favored, knowing that they would be increased in the council negotiations. So I ended up with more total dollars in the program. I came out of the budget fights with my budget going higher and higher.

What I am particularly proud of is creating a "bureaucracy," in the good sense of the word, actually organizing the department so that it could function. When I walked into the division, for example, out of thirty-five staff people, only two had rank; everybody else was at the same level. There was no structure, no hierarchy; so there was no accountability. Some staff members had been given jobs they didn't know anything about. Standard operating procedures didn't fit the policies, and so people were disorganized; it resulted in low morale. Some of those people had been with the city for a long time and saw themselves as professionals, but they had no role. Others were political patronage people who were just sitting on their butts doing nothing. What we did was to create some hierarchy, and we developed some accountability—actually began to professionalize and structure the department so that we could function in the way we wanted to.

I think that was the reason we were able to develop the loyalty of people who had been loyal to the former administration or committed political patronage appointees. We actually converted to our progressive point of view the people we inherited from less progressive, or even regressive, administrations that preceded us. I think the approach came from the mayor. There was an understanding that the holdover people did what they did because there were no alternatives. You gave everybody a chance, and if they responded, you worked with them; if they didn't respond, you got rid of them. We would tell them, "Look, this is a new day. We have specific responsibilities. The contract is going to be shaped this way. You either perform or you don't perform, but you all get the same chance." Groups located in wards of alderman unfriendly to the mayor were given the same chance as any other groups—it was a question whether they would work for the city of Chicago on a professional basis. That's the way the mayor wanted it, and that's the way it worked.

Were we effective? I think there were some key elements to that question involving equity and efficiency. We called it the three *E*s: "efficiency, effectiveness, and equity." Those were the three major goals we were striving for, but the question is, "How do you do that?" Because sometimes people think that equity is contradictory to efficiency or effectiveness. Our perspective coming out of the neighborhood movement was that there is a hell of a lot of talent out there. If they have their "fair share," given an opportunity, responsibility, and the time to develop, they'll get the job done.

We addressed the equity question by bringing all those organizations into the planning mechanisms. We had the first major one occur of course prior to the administration, and that was through the CWED organization. We had a large number of CBOs participating in putting together that platform. The second major effort occurred during the Washington administration by bringing more than 400 activists, community development people, together to do the Chicago Works Together plan—a planning session that took six or seven months to plan and finally ended with a day-long session with 400 activists turning out and evaluating the plan and coming out with a new twist on it. Incidentally, almost everybody got sick that day because the chicken salad sandwiches were tainted. I hope there's not a lesson there. We almost wiped out the whole neighborhood movement!

And then there's the question of effectiveness with respect to the goals you're trying to achieve. For us, the question was revitalizing industry and commerce in the neighborhoods to achieve a balanced growth for the city. If we could address the equity question, by providing training to increase the planning, administrative, and technical capacity of the neighborhood organizations, effectiveness in terms of achieving our goals for the city and its neighborhoods would follow. I think we took a giant step in that direction against tremendous political odds, but remember we only had four years to make an impact after many years of neglect and a political culture that is deeply ingrained in Chicago. Of course, there is the larger issue of the regional, national, and international economy that had an impact on Chicago; but we started.

Another aspect of efficiency could be looked at in terms of whether providing city economic and business development services is best done by a local development organization as opposed to city government paying a staff person to do it. We thought that the monies we provided also leveraged private monies, foundation grants, and so on. It was also more efficient because they were able to address the needs at a much closer level, and more rapidly, than we could do it from a centralized operation.

Were we effective in the short run? Sure, we greatly increased the number of companies called on, the number and total dollar amount of loans to Chicago companies, through the delegation of city responsibilities to neighborhood business organizations. In 1986 the city bottomed out in loss of industrial firms, with more business births than deaths for the first time in years. Did the mayor take credit for that? You know he did. But a major accomplishment was the organization of the manufacturing community through a program that put the retention of the city's industrial base squarely up front as a political issue.

We also had a role in building minority business participation. We did a hell of a lot as a department in promoting and stimulating the growth of minority business: through set-asides, capacity building, technical assistance, through the way in which contracts were broken up to permit minority subcontractors to perform for primes.

Our department was proactive in terms of freedom of information. That was most important. My division was responsible for setting up workshops and conferences, training our delegate agencies in city policies and procedures, clueing them in on how to access information and services, how to apply for city loans and funds, making sure that they knew how all relevant departments carried out city policies. When we got through, many organizations out there knew as much about how city government operated as we did. We tried to make it transparent, to demystify it.

Those are things that I'm proudest of, having been a small part of it. But the last word has got to give credit to Harold Washington, the man, the mayor, who so easily made the vision of the neighborhood movement part of his larger vision of making democracy work in a multiracial, multiethnic city. He hungered for it. That's why we all worked like hell for him.

INTERVIEW WITH KARI MOE

I grew up in a military family (U.S. Air Force). When my parents were asked what they did for a living, they never said, "We work for the government." They rarely even said, "We work for the air force." The language that they always used was, "We are in the service." This is the one phrase that characterizes the core values of my upbringing. Mom and Dad were patriotic about World War II, and they saw their lives as dedicated to public service. They were very proud of this and instilled a sense of commitment to the larger community, or nation, in me and my sister.

Additional family influences also shaped my ethics and values. Both of my grandmothers were teachers in tough parts of the country, Montana and northern Minnesota. They had a strong commitment to education and had lived in communities where cooperation was essential. My mother was a social worker in a very poor county in northern Minnesota in the 1940s. I grew up hearing her talk about families coping with all sorts of hardships, not the least of which was trying to eke out an existence in remote locations. And so the stories that I grew up with were of Scandinavian ancestors who settled in Minnesota and North Dakota, of grandfathers and fathers who were soldiers, and of women who were teachers and social workers.

The Vietnam war and civil rights movement also served to politicize me when I was fairly young. My father was assigned to a military base in northern Thailand during the Vietnam war in 1967. I was fourteen and a freshman in high school at the time, and so the war entered my life at a time when few of my civilian friends knew much about it. He left for a year. In those days communications technology was rather primitive—especially compared to the AT&T phone centers set up for Persian Gulf troops. My father mailed a small reel-to-reel tape recorder from Bangkok, and we sent tapes back and forth for a year. I may have talked to him once on the telephone. My sister was older and went off to college shortly after Dad went to Vietnam. She soon became involved in campus politics.

My father returned to the United States in April 1968, shortly after the assassination of Dr. Martin Luther King, Jr. My mother and I were living in northern Michigan, but on my dad's return, we were assigned to an air force base near a small town in central South Carolina, not too far from Orangeburg. The nearby town still had segregated schools, and I remember filling out my "freedom of choice" form at the school office. All the base kids went to the one local integrated school outside of town. The town still had white and colored entrance signs in 1968. My mother was concerned about my adjustment to moving there from Michigan, so she signed my sister and me up to do volunteer work at community programs in and around the town where the air force base was located. My sister worked at a Head Start program, and I spent my mornings teaching kids how to swim. They were all African American kids in a day camp who were not welcome in swimming pools in the town. They were bused out to the air force base so they could swim.

I spent my afternoons that summer with my church youth group at a rural community center where I was right in the middle of very hard-core rural poverty. We took food and clothing to families surviving in shocking living conditions. I was fifteen and confronted with children living in ways that seemed intolerable and inexplicable to me. Between the Vietnam war and direct exposure to southern poverty and racism, my perspective was permanently altered.

Soon after his return from Thailand, my dad retired from the service and went to work for Xerox Corporation in Rochester, New York. We moved from South Carolina to New York midway through my junior year of high school. I became very active in high school and church youth activities. I helped organize some Vietnam war teach-ins, worked on hunger marches, and visited alternative schools in the inner city of Rochester. I had a Lutheran pastor, a journalism teacher, and a couple of social studies teachers who were talking about values and provided models for the unfolding politization that started for me in 1967.

I went to college at Carleton College in Northfield, Minnesota, partly out of a homing instinct. At that point we had moved so much that I wanted to be close to my grandparents and extended family. Minnesota served as an anchoring location for me. In general, I wanted to study social issues. I was really concerned with poverty and injustice. The teacher who spoke most directly to my concerns was a political science professor, Paul Wellstone. [In 1993, Wellstone was the junior senator from Minnesota.] He taught the politics of poverty and all the urban policy and politics courses, so that is what I ended up focusing on. In addition, he involved his students in community organizing projects in rural Minnesota. I graduated with a degree in urban studies with a focus on urban history and sociology.

INVOLVEMENT IN CHICAGO

I first went to Chicago in 1972 as a college junior—we later affectionately called it the McGovern semester. I attended a Carleton College off-campus program, the Chicago Urban Studies program. This program was an intensive work–study experience that was run by faculty committed to experiential education and political training. They wanted to train organizers and people dedicated to community service. My work in Chicago that semester recalled my 1968 South Carolina summer, but in an urban setting. I was significantly influenced by the teachers I met there—Hal Baron, Ingrid Christiansen, Jody Kretzman, and Walt Reiner. Exactly a decade later, in the fall of 1982, Hal Baron hired me to be the research director of the mayoral campaign of Congressman Harold Washington.

I graduated from Carleton College in 1974. I wanted to be in Chicago out of desire to go beyond my studies and understand the city from the inside out. At this time I did not have specific career goals—I wanted, quite simply, to be of service. During my last couple of weeks at Carleton, I received a job offer from a children's agency in Chicago where I had worked the previous summer. My acceptance of this job launched me on a six-year period, 1974 to 1980, of doing youth work. I spent three years as a counselor in a halfway house for juvenile delinquent teenage girls who were wards of the state. I spent the next three years teaching English, history, and social studies in a community-based alternative school for young adults who had dropped out of high school in the Uptown neighborhood of Chicago.

I saw everything during this period. I accompanied overdosed kids to emergency rooms and held them down while their stomachs got pumped. I went out in the middle of the night to bail kids out of jail. I visited my kids in mental hospitals and juvenile jails. I helped kids find places to live after being burned out of apartments. I knew kids who'd been shot and knifed. I took the rage from kids intended for their absent or abusive parents. I painstakingly built relationships with eighteen years olds who had been told they were stupid, just to get them to agree to read aloud to me. I was an advocate for my kids with the police department and the welfare department, with hospitals and with schools. I saw the world through the eyes of young people who had been rejected, kicked out, and told they weren't going to make it. I interacted with every dimension of the social service system from the point of view of "clients" of those systems. As a companion to this work, I also became involved in community organizing activities related to neighborhood development funding, housing conditions, and so on.

When I was teaching (1977–1980), I started going to night school at the University of Illinois, Chicago (UIC). That's where I met Rob Mier, who later became my boss in the city of Chicago. I went to UIC because it was clear to me that the kids I was teaching, even if they were successful in school, didn't really have many future jobs to look forward to, especially if they had to stay in the city. Putting all this energy into teaching them how to read wasn't going to keep them motivated, wasn't going to keep them out of jail, wasn't going to have them not be killed, if they didn't see decent jobs with a living wage in their future. I wanted to spend some time thinking about poverty, economic development, job creation, and employment and training. I wanted to think in policy terms about what we could and should be doing differently as a nation so that these kids wouldn't be facing wasted lives for themselves and their children. I felt like I was in a constant process of helping to fix these broken kids, and helping them to envision a future that they couldn't see.

During the course of my studies at UIC, Rob Mier suggested that I think about going to school full-time. It was proving too hard to juggle full-time teaching, crisis intervention, and studying. I decided to go to MIT because I wanted to study with Bennett Harrison, who was doing research on deindustrialization and teaching about economic development and employment and training policy. While at MIT, I stayed in contact with friends and colleagues in Chicago. During my first year, I got a research assistantship with the Boston Neighborhood Network and started doing action-oriented research for different Boston neighborhood organizations. I went back to Chicago the summer between my first and second year in the master's program and worked in a small urban planning consulting firm and helped write a community plan and Urban Development Action Grant applications.

I was focused on the question, Where are the jobs of the future going to come from, especially for folks at the bottom? In addition to hard-core unemployment, I also wanted to understand the problem of plant shutdowns and permanent layoffs of industrial workers. At a conference on this subject, I met a women named Melva Meacham, who had been an assembly-line worker at a Hiram Walker bottling plant in Peoria, Illinois. She had led an unsuccessful attempt to avert the shutdown and then fought for services for the workers there. Inspired by Melva, I decided to do a study of plant closings in Illinois for my MIT master's thesis. I was particularly interested in community- and labor-sponsored responses to plant shutdowns and the implications of these experiences for public policy. I visited several industrial centers in the state and conducted interviews with employment and training staff, union representatives, unemployed workers, and others. I looked particularly at a program that was sponsored by the state AFL-CIO, which provided adjustment assistance, job training, and job placement services to dislocated workers.

I left MIT and returned to Chicago to be co-director of a newly organized network of community economic development organizations, called the Community Workshop on Economic Development (CWED). It was a network of about twenty groups that had come together to analyze and critique the enterprise zone concept, being touted as *the* urban revitalization policy of the 1980s. The groups were clear about their criticisms regarding the limitations of enterprise zones. But they also wanted to advance an alternative vision of neighborhood development policy. [Both Rob Mier and Arturo Vazquez were founding members of CWED.]

CWED was just getting off the ground. Our first task was to organize a statewide conference of community organizations and community development corporations and generate a community development platform that we were going to advocate in the upcoming mayor's and governor's races. Several groups met over a weekend in Peoria, Illinois, and left with a surprising degree of consensus about a policy platform for neighborhoods.

Chicago was in political ferment that summer of 1982 with the boycott of Chicago-fest and talk of several black candidates who could mount a serious campaign for mayor. By September the CWED platform had been completed and ratified. I started raising money to turn this ad hoc, statewide network into an ongoing organization.

We were close to being funded when Hal Baron called me during the first few days of November. Baron said, "My good friend Harold Washington is thinking of running for mayor of Chicago and wants me to advise him on policy issues. I told him I wanted to hire a full-time research and issues director. Do you want to do it?" I jumped at the chance. He told me to send over my résumé so he could show it to Congressman Washington. About ten days later I started working on my first speech for Washington—a critique of the Byrne budget that became his first major speech after his announcement. It turned out to be one of the most challenging and exhilarating opportunities of my life.

For six months, from November to April, I worked, along with thousands of enthusiastic volunteers, seven days per week—virtually nonstop. I remember solving problems during my sleep. Along with Hal and a campaign policy advisory committee, we organized citywide issue teams that advised Washington on urban policy issues and wrote the individual policy papers that later became the core platform document—the *Washington Papers*. We put together a group of staff and volunteers that wrote speeches, did the daily briefing book, did opposition research, and provided debate preparation. It is important to note that Washington made the decision personally to place a lot of emphasis on policy in the campaign and to develop policy positions in a highly participatory fashion that required a lot of resources to manage. He wanted people involved; he wanted different points of view; and he wanted to build constituencies for the tough governing challenge that he felt sure he would face.

I was most fortunate to be pulled from the office during the final weeks of the general election campaign and assigned to the car that traveled with Washington as he campaigned around Chicago. My job was to brief him for each upcoming event. I remember being so worried that I would make a mistake with some fact about the unemployment rate or crime statistics. The campaign had become ugly with the racial taunts of the opposition. Harold went strongly on the offensive about reform. He knew he was going to win.

INSIDE THE WASHINGTON ADMINISTRATION

In May I joined the mayor's office as an assistant to the mayor. In those early months, this meant special projects. I was first called over to set up the mayor's daily briefing operation with former Mayor Byrne's press staff. They were all still there, except for her press secretary. My next main project was to reconstruct the boards and commissions files—Byrne had left nothing—and start to set up the process for mayoral appointments. I have been quoted as saying that going into city hall and trying to get things done was like fighting a war with someone else's army. This metaphor remained true throughout my tenure, but had its origins in these early days when I could name every person who had joined the administration with the mayor. This was a government, mind you, with more than 40,000 employees.

By the fall, the basic mayor's office organization was in place, and I wanted to play a role in implementing that part of the agenda I had helped to shape— the economic development agenda. By then Rob Mier was the commissioner of the city's Department of Economic Development (DED). He and I proposed to the mayor that I would transfer from the Mayor's Office to DED to set up a new division in the department, called Research and Development (R&D). We wanted a unit that could play a strong innovation function—evaluate existing programs, design new programs, do policy research and strategic planning, and keep the mayor's constituencies involved in the agenda they had helped create. All my efforts were focused on wanting to implement the policy direction articulated by the mayor during his campaign—neighborhood investment, balance between commercial and industrial development, affirmative action, small business development, and jobs. We also wanted to be vocal and effective advocates for cities at the state and federal levels.

It proved to be an extremely useful organizational decision by Rob. When Mayor Washington called on him during the winter of 1984 to pull together all the development departments to draft an economic development plan, he had the organizational capacity to respond. In addition to being deputy com-missioner of R&D, I became chief of staff for the development subcabinet, the formal grouping of all the development departments. This was the role in which I coordinated the planning and writing of the Chicago Works Together plan. In addition to the CWT plan, R&D started several new research and planning initiatives while I was there. I should note that the R&D unit also provided Rob with the ability for quick responses needed by the administration, in addition to the planning, program development, and interdepartmental coordination functions we performed.

In 1984 the mayor hired a deputy chief of staff, Ernest Barefield. One of Barefield's main jobs was to try to rationalize Washington's approach to gov-erning and decision making. This included getting on top of our strengths and weaknesses. Barefield saw the development subcabinet as a model that groups of similar departments should adopt. Ernie set up a committee in 1985 called the Mayor's Policy Advisory Committee whose mission it was to assess the progress on the mayor's agenda at that point and recommend "mid-course" corrections to the mayor. We all felt that we didn't have sufficient control of the government. Because of my knowledge of the *Washington Papers* and other campaign commitments, my experience with CWT and with the development subcabinet, I became heavily involved in this effort to think about reform and effectiveness from a governmentwide perspective. Many policy-oriented plan-ners in the administration were, over time, promoted to take on more general management responsibilities because there was such a big need for people with management skills who also understood Harold's agenda.

As a result of this analysis, the mayor decided to make a series of changes. I became an assistant to the mayor for community services, overseeing a group of departments including the Departments of Health, Human Services, Aging and Disability, Information and Inquiry, the Chicago Public Library, and the commissions on Women and Human Relations. Harold brought me to the Mayor's Office to replicate the work we had done with the development depart-ments. This proved to be enormously difficult for several reasons that illustrate the kinds of problems faced by a progressive mayor.

First, this group of community services departments was much more dis-parate in mission and in the leadership styles of the commissioners than the development departments. The Human Services Department was very focused on a major gang-intervention initiative and emergency programs such as shel-ter beds and heat shut-offs and food programs. The Health Department was facing unprecedented demands on their services to address AIDS, infant mortality, substance abuse, and the recurrence of tuberculosis. The Chicago Public Library was trying to build a new central library, in what would become one of the main large development projects of the Washington administration. Within all these departments, key parts of the mayor's constituency—Hispanic and African American community organizations—were arguing among themselves and with the city about the distribution of limited resources. As the liaison to the mayor's advocacy commissions—for women, veterans, Asian Americans, and gays and lesbians, I spent an enormous amount of time helping these folks get a hearing in the less responsive quarters of Harold's government. The mayor held several cabinet meetings during this period, and I remember him admonishing department heads repeatedly to work with their middle managers to get them on board with the mayor's agenda.

I want to emphasize that Harold really cared about governing well—in addition to caring about politics. In fact, he saw the them as integrally related. This conviction affected how we defined our mission as public administrators and explains the "improvement" theme that emerges when the former Washington aides reflect on their work. We believed, with Harold, that the public deserved well-managed city government. After all, this was one of his campaign promises. For him, well-managed meant the fiscal, programmatic, and political dimensions. I remember him giving a talk to the Mayor's Policy Council during one of our midterm strategic planning sessions. At that point he was being given high marks for his fiscal management of city government—he had brought the deficit under control; he was modernizing financial management; he had improved the city's bond rating. He told us that he was pleased with what we had done so far—but that it wasn't good enough. People still needed decent streets, housing, good schools, and accessible health clinics. Moreover, they needed to know what we were doing and to be involved. He wanted them involved in city government. Getting our financial house in order was a necessary but insufficient first step.

ACCOMPLISHMENTS

I must add a general caveat to my answer to the question, "What did we accomplish?" which is that the accomplishments need to be viewed in the context of the obstacles we faced. We tried to get things done in the face of council wars and enormous internal bureaucratic inertia. We were feeling the cutbacks of the Reagan years, especially in such areas as housing and community development. The Chicago job mix was being adversely affected by the globalization of the economy. We took over a government that had not kept pace with information technology and that still bore the cultural attributes of a patronage system. Finally, many of us were relatively inexperienced public managers. Independents, progressives, minorities, and women had never been welcome in city employment. So while the mayor had a cadre of experienced political and legislative staff and friends, he did not bring a set of ready managers into his political network.

But every day we set out to change things according to Washington's vision of a government that would be more open, more fair, more effective, more fiscally sound, and one that would provide more opportunities to individuals left out over the decades. As I mentioned earlier, we were incredibly focused on doing things better—both large and small things. For example, I would coach receptionists about how they were Harold's voice—people who had never felt welcome calling city hall before were now calling. If department heads sent over letters for the mayor's signature that were too bureaucratic, I would send them back.

One of the main things we did was to start to spend money differently. I should add that we had discretion only over a relatively small proportion of the budget. Expenditures for police, fire, streets, and sanitation were largely locked in and represented the vast majority of the budget. Within the realms where we had discretion, Community Development Block Grants, for example, we significantly increased the amount of money going to community-based organizations and really developed strong partnerships with them for service delivery of everything from housing services to youth counseling in neighborhoods. I feel very proud of the concrete redirection of resources. Both Mier and Vazquez discuss our efforts to ensure that our neighborhood-based partners provided good services.

The neighborhood infrastructure program is another example of redirection of capital expenditures caused by a very strong neighborhood focus. Harold did the first significant neighborhood infrastructure bond issue that had been done in twenty-five years. We aimed capital improvement dollars at neighborhoods. Neighborhood industrial retention was also a factor in prioritizing capital expenditures. Actually being able to redirect some spending was an important accomplishment.

The Chicago Works Together (CWT) plan illustrates a couple of other points about how we were trying to do things differently. First, by settling on five policy priorities, we were trying to focus the limited resources of the development departments. We also wanted a way for other departments in government to think about how their activities could support the mayor's development goals. Further, the listing of projects and programs throughout the plan would provide a way that the public could hold the mayor accountable. The policy framework of Chicago Works Together guided the bulk of our subsequent decisions.

Other departments of city government, even some in the development sub-cabinet, bought into CWT, but the commitment was uneven. The neighborhood infrastructure program, for example, required the enthusiastic participation of the public works department and administrative agencies like law and purchasing. Because of a short construction season, they needed to develop an expedited implementation scheme. But these agencies weren't prepared either by motivation or by bureaucratic organization to be able to follow through quickly enough. Eventually, the management of the neighborhood bond issue was assigned to an assistant in the Mayor's Office who set up a SWAT team and literally gave orders to the department heads. This is an example of having to go around the bureaucracy to deliver something that we were committed to.

Community participation was another policy commitment of the mayor's where the delivery by departments was uneven. Commitment to the goal varied, as did skill in execution. For example, shifting to social services for a minute, the commissioner of the Department of Human Services was very committed to community participation in the development of policy initiatives. She developed a gang-intervention program that included several community hearings throughout the city, a citywide advisory board, and individual neighborhood advisory structures. There were other initiatives where the department heads did not develop genuine involvement of people.

The affirmative action accomplishments—both in economic development and in other departments that I saw—were significant. Harold's senior management really did reflect the racial and ethnic profile of the city. City government went from about 10 percent of executive positions being held by women to 40 percent of senior management jobs—cabinet jobs—being held by women by the end of Harold's term. It was dramatic! Significant progress was also made in regular civil service jobs for women and minorities. For example, for the first time there was a program set up to recruit, train, and prepare women to go through the rigorous test to get into the fire department. Significant commitment to get women into nontraditional jobs in the departments of streets and sanitation is another example.

A few other accomplishments bear mentioning. The mayor supported reinventing government even before the term was in vogue. There were several initiatives in the category for managing more effectively, having to do with computer systems, purchasing processes, accounting procedures, and the like. He also set new standards in freedom of information and ethics.

REACTION

The reaction was evident as early as Mayor Washington's inaugural address. The mayor delivered an aggressive reform speech—including an elucidation of the Byrne budget deficit and a restatement that "we will not do business as usual." This speech was later blamed by the political pundits as the triggering event for council wars. Immediately after Harold was elected, the Democratic party regulars set out to thwart him at almost every move you can imagine. One of my favorite examples is the comment of a well-known alderman when the mayor was trying to get his neighborhood infrastructure program passed through the city council. The alderman was quoted as saying that he would rather vote against money for his neighborhood than vote for a good program that the mayor would get credit for. In what became known as the "hostage crisis," the city council refused to move on the mayor's nominees to important boards and commissions. Eventually the *Chicago Tribune* and interest groups howled enough that the logjam started to break. Nevertheless, there were more than fifty names stalled when the opposition was called on the carpet. In his third year, the mayor won a council majority through some victories in local special elections. It wasn't until this victory and subsequent council reorganization that the mayor was able to overcome this chronic opposition.

It is worth noting that the mayor was under significant pressure from several sources—the media, the business community, the regular Democratic party leadership, and even some of his own allies to "make peace" with the council opposition. He was not prepared to sell out his base or compromise on his agenda so quickly. He had a combination of courage and political acumen when the stakes were high that was unsurpassed. Harold was mentally prepared to fight for what he believed in and hold out for the best deal—skills he developed as a legislator.

The council also wanted to make sure that Harold wasn't successful in delivering big projects. For example, Jane Byrne (the previous mayor) had started negotiating a contract with the Rouse Corporation to redevelop Navy Pier. The contract had not been completed when Washington was elected, but Rouse was committed to the project. Rob Mier renegotiated the contract to include some of the mayor's policy goals—affirmative action in jobs and business opportunities. This was another example of our attempt to drive equity principles into the deals we were making. But the deal got shut down in the city council committee, and Navy Pier sat empty for the duration of Harold Washington's term.

The business community wanted the Navy Pier deal, but they did not jump into the fray on the mayor's side. That was pretty typical—it was more lack of support from business than it was an outright attack.

The media were another source of consternation for the mayor. In the beginning they operated within a framework that assumed the mayor's agenda was to develop a black machine. The mayor always felt that his reform accomplishments were not given sufficient coverage. City reporters covered politics, but less about governing. Black businesspersons receiving city contracts were routinely described as "friends" of the mayor. This example in particular would prompt the mayor to ask the media if they assumed that every black business owner in Chicago was his friend. He was particularly outraged one day when one of the major dailies reported that the mayor had been weeping at a speech the night before, when he had in fact been sweating and mopping his brow. He publicly observed the lack of minority representation in the ranks of political journalists. Over time, Harold won over many individual reporters with his humor and incisive repartee at press conferences.

Perhaps the most difficult negative reactions we had to deal with personally came from within the mayor's political base. For those of us in the development departments, many of our friends were neighborhood leaders who wanted to be supportive, but who were also critical. It was hard to "agree to disagree" and not take the criticism personally. We wanted the outside critics to understand the difficulty of the task we were facing. We had enough opposition in the city council and elsewhere—we wanted support and advocacy from our political allies. Another strain of tension ran along racial lines. Some African Americans felt that Harold was being too inclusive of Hispanics and whites. This issue was constantly present in decisions about the schedule, about appointments to permanent and ad hoc boards, about hiring, about funding. I remember having a disagreement early on with a manager at DED about whether or not women business owners warranted any special attention or resources. He argued that they weren't disadvantaged and would unfairly detract from other minority business development efforts.

EVALUATION OF ACHIEVEMENTS

I think that the work we did in the Washington administration actually produced meaningful improvements in the lives of the people we were trying to serve, even though the numbers were limited. The improvements came in different layers or different dimensions. At the individual level, there were the people who benefited directly through the affirmative action hiring, promotion, and training policies of the administration. A set of people now have capacities and opportunities they probably wouldn't have had without Harold. Their lives have been concretely enhanced.

This would also be true of the small businesses that got a foot in the door and were able either to start or to grow their businesses because of the mayor's expanded commitment to minority procurement and small business procurement through provisions we designed and implemented. People also benefited in the community organizations that got contracts to provide city services. There were specific additional opportunities for people who were working in those organizations and the people they served. There were also the neighborhoods that received infrastructure dollars. There is another set of examples about people and programs and neighborhoods that had positive things happen and resources allocated because of specific decisions made by Harold and carried out by the administration. Beyond additional resources, several new programs were started by the Washington administration, many of which continue to exist.

Another set of beneficiaries were people brought to the table for the first time to participate in policymaking and decision making. They gained new and different access to city hall. Citizens also gained access to information about how the government worked by using the freedom-of-information Executive Order that Harold signed. We also constantly held neighborhood forums and budget hearings that provided additional opportunities for sharing views and information.

Such openness may be normal in other cities, but it was a dramatic shift from past practice in Chicago. We took some criticism for having a committee on everything because we were constantly bringing folks to the table to talk with us about how to do things, but lots of people in Chicago now have a better understanding of city hall, the budget process, and general information than they would have otherwise developed. I think that in the process we helped create better advocates—and we were advocates for people who would not have been at the table otherwise.

Another dimension of Harold's accomplishments has to do with stories that got invented and told and the ways he shifted the terms of debate. One of the things that Harold loved to talk about was how the eyes of young African American children would light up when he would visit them in the streets and in schools. He loved kids and he loved being around them, and he loved the idea that he had created for them the possibility that there could be a black mayor in Chicago. He created for them a different sense of their own possibilities. And that was an important dimension of his leadership and one he wanted to underscore for the young African American children throughout the city. It was something he was very much aware of.

Another theme of Harold's stories was the vitality of cities and the importance of championing them. He had a speech cadence about being born at Cook County Hospital, going to Chicago public schools, growing up on Chicago's streets. After embellishing the images, he would proclaim, "I love this city." He was the most visible mayor to decry Reagan's war on the cities. Advocacy of cities and the folks he loved in them were his drumbeat. He intended to raise his national profile on these issues in his second term. It is truly a loss to the nation's cities that this dream was not realized.

Race—with the dual theme of racial pride and the need for multiethnic understanding and political coalition—was an issue Harold talked about often and authoritatively. I hesitate to comment on these issues because his understanding of race and power was profound. But these issues are so central to the meaning of his tenure in city hall—and to our lives as planners working for him—that this theme must be included in any discussion of his legacy. Harold, in his daily interactions and public speeches, exuded pride in being African American. This awareness and pride was unambiguous, and he transmitted this message of pride everywhere he went. His presence as Mayor sent a dramatic message about the role of African American leadership and presence in Chicago—quite significant in one of the most racially polarized cities in America.

But Harold also truly was the mayor for all Chicago, in addition to being the mayor for black Chicago. Through the duration of his mayoralty, I listened as he worked to develop the imagery of the city's diverse people needing to learn to live together. I heard the mosaic speech, or the tapestry speech, or the wer're-all-in-this-together speech countless times, but it never failed to bring tears to my eyes. Harold, from his staff appointments, to the young political leaders he mentored, to the exhausting schedule he kept—lived this theme of respect for distinctiveness and diversity. He did his utmost to preach this vision from pulpits in every corner of the city. One measure of his success was Mayor Daley's description, shortly after his inauguration in 1989, of his newly appointed Cabinet as a "rainbow."

TEACHING EQUITY PLANNERS

I'd like to see a reinvigoration of planning and other public service careers. We need students in the next generation to be committed to public service. We need more equity planners who understand that their practice has to grapple with values in addition to statistics. Teachers could help by doing a few things.

One is really to engage students around their values, what they care about and what they want to do with their lives. It is the kind of thing that Paul Wellstone used to do with his classes. In a class on urban poverty, for example, he would ask us to write about how choices in our own lives could have an effect on the poverty problem. Or what did we believe personally, given knowledge about hungry children in America—how did that affect us? He pushed us to confront injustice. Too many professors seemed to think that there was virtue in disengagement. Wellstone's approach was challenging and life changing for me. He took our personal choices seriously and drove home the point about a connection between what was going on in the world and choices that we would make.

Teachers could challenge the conventional wisdom that one person can't make a difference. Granted, it is very tough to be teaching a commitment to public service, and a commitment to cities, at a time when public service and government have been under attack from the president of the United States for more than a decade. It is hard to convince young people that public service is worthwhile work while it is being publicly denigrated. How is it that being a public health nurse is so much less valued than being a marine? As a nation, as citizens, we should combat this attack on service. Teachers should engage students in critical thinking about their cynicism and figure out how to move beyond it.

Talking about success stories would help overcome frustration about making a difference. These stories can remind people that underneath the history of those with formal power is a history of ordinary people being very creative with nothing and really creating new opportunities and making things happen in their communities by force of their own vision and tenacity—just working together on concrete things that they care about. Students should know about success stories of individuals, of community organizations, of stopping negative things, and of making good things happen. They should also know about success stories of government agencies and legislatures passing positive laws—in addition to all the negative stories they hear.

I would like to see planning schools provide students, in a more concrete way, with more of the skills that they need to take on the battles that they will encounter with the newspapers and battles with entrenched bureaucrats. When you do the kind of work that we do, you are fighting constantly, always swimming upstream. First, you must have your values intact so that you remember on the bad days why you keep doing the work. Second, being effective requires a heck of a lot of skills. I ended up learning on the firing line and, luckily, I had a lot of good teachers. But I wish that there had been a part of my planning curriculum that focused on implementation. Teachers should be saying, OK, you have this great idea, now how are you going to get this done? What is everything that could go wrong, and how are you going to deal with it? Who is going to oppose you, and what strategies and tactics are they going to employ? How are ou going to build alliances with people who don't see things the same way that you do but who can be useful for this fight?

We all need some victories to keep going, and you can't achieve them on your own. So it would be helpful to have more courses on how to implement equity planning ideas.

Whenever I talk to students about my Chicago city government experience, and now I would add the same thing about my experience working for a reformer in the U.S. Senate, I tell them that I continue to believe in the ability of each of us to make a positive difference, through public service—in the lives of individuals or in the life of a community, on up through the nation. I continue to believe this in the face of an ever-deepening understanding about the difficulty of getting positive things done.

FURTHER READINGS: Neighborhood Economic Development

Benick, Marc, Jr., and Mary Lou Egan. *Business Development in the Inner City: Enterprise with Community Links.* New York: Community Development Research Center, 1991.

Clavel, Pierre, and Wim Wiewel, eds. *Harold Washington and the Neighborhoods: Progressive City Government in Chicago, 1983–1987.* New Brunswick, N.J.: Rutgers University Press, 1991.

Mayer, Neil S. *Neighborhood Organizations and Community Development: Making Revitalization Work.* Washington, D.C.: Urban Institute, 1989.

Mier, Robert, Robert Giloth, Kari J. Moe, et al. *Social Justice and Local Development Policy.* Newbury Park, Calif.: Sage, 1993.

Mier, Robert, Kari J. Moe, and Irene Sherr. "Strategic Planning and the Pursuit of Reform: Economic Development and Equity." In *The State and Local Industrial Policy Questions,* edited by Harvey Goldstein. Chicago: American Planning Association Press, 1987.

Shifman, Ronald, and Susan Motley. *Comprehensive and Integrative Planning for Community Development*. New York: Community Development Research Center, 1990.

Twentieth Century Fund Task Force on Affordable Housing. *More Housing, More Fairly*. New York: Twentieth Century Fund Press, 1991.

Wiewel, Wim, and Robert Mier. *Analyzing Neighborhood Retail Opportunities: A Guide for Carrying Out a Preliminary Market Study*. Planning Advisory Service Report No. 358. Chicago: American Planning Association, 1981.

chapter 5

PORTLAND, OREGON

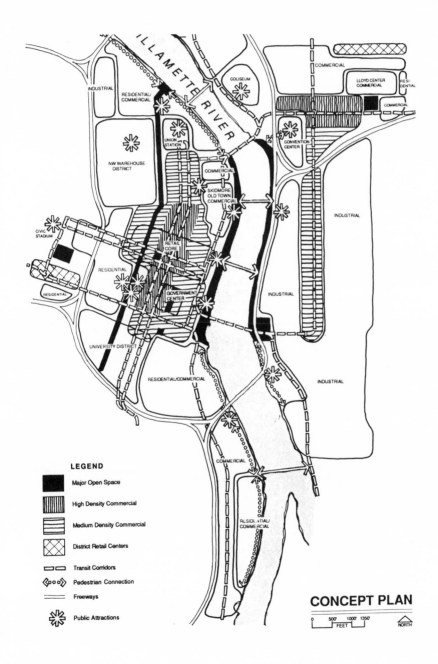

LEGEND

Major Open Space

High Density Commercial

Medium Density Commercial

District Retail Centers

Transit Corridors

Pedestrian Connection

Freeways

Public Attractions

CONCEPT PLAN

0   500'   1000' 1350'
FEET

NORTH

SNAPSHOT, 1985

Population Composition for Portland, Oregon, 1970–1990

Demographic	1970	1980	1990
Population	382,059	365,051	437,319
White	352,076	315,754	370,135
Black	21,572	27,720	33,530
Median family income	$9,794	$19,493	$32,424
Percentage poverty	12.9	9.8	14.5

Portland, Oregon, is home to about 450,000 people, about one-third of the metropolitan area's total population of 1.3 million. Most people regard the city as well kept, charming, and picturesque, although a bit soggy. Portland is often praised for its parks. The city, which calls itself the "City of Roses," contains the International Rose Test Gardens and Forest Park, a 4,800-acre nature preserve and hiking area. It also contains elegant fountains; small, human-scale development; and a population that is seen as laid-back yet unusually keen on the environment and on planning.

The city has become a paragon of healthy urban development at a time when most American cities find themselves mired in seemingly intractable problems. While it is by no means immune to the suburbanization that has sapped the vitality of many cities, Portland's core—especially the downtown—has become more attractive and popular than ever.

Part of the reason for this is careful downtown planning, which mandated the inventive and attractive use of public outdoor gathering places, including Pioneer Courthouse Square and the frontage along the Willamette River, lined for more than a mile by Tom McCall Waterfront Park. Oregon is a state that mandates comprehensive planning and zoning for all communities, and Portland is considered a leader in these. The latest central city plan was adopted just as the city was recovering from the economic downturn of the early 1980s and was built on earlier plans for the central area, although with considerably more citizen involvement.

The Portland Central City Plan was approved unanimously by the city council in March 1988, after about four years of preparation. The new plan cost $1.6 million, all of which came out of the city's general fund. The current plan is a revision of an earlier plan for Portland's downtown. The 1972 plan covered only the west side of the Willamette River, while the 1988 plan involves a much larger land area on both sides of the river.

As with the 1972 plan, the new downtown plan represents one of the broadest-known attempts at citizen involvement in urban planning. The plan is also unusual in that it includes a number of social welfare elements, an example of which is Single Room Occupancy (SRO) housing for low-income individuals. To protect the central area's 2,000 SRO units, the plan allows a transfer of development rights from SRO sites to other projects. Another popular provision of the plan gives developers a density bonus if they spend 1 percent of their total construction cost on public art.

The Portland Central City Plan was initiated by City Commissioner Margaret Strachan in 1984. Under the Portland system, each of the city's four commissioners oversees several departments. During her time on the city commission, Strachan administered the city bureaus of transporation, building, human services, and city planning.

Strachan, a lay planner as well as former neighborhood organizer, had been staff coordinator for six neighborhood groups in northwest Portland. She believed that planning for downtown should encompass several nearby neighborhoods including several across the Willamette River. She also believed that the planning process should involve as many citizens as possible and that they, as active participants, without the extensive oversight of the planning agency, could develop an ideal "people's" plan.

Accordingly, Strachan set up a fifteen-member volunteer citizen steering committee and hired a small professional staff to develop the plan with a minimum of assistance from the formal city planning department.[1] Over three and a half years, the steering committee set up other subcommittees ultimately involving 108 people, hired consultants, and produced 65 research reports and a general plan in draft form.

Strachan was defeated for reelection in 1986. The city's new public works commissioner, Earl Blumenauer, directed the completion of the plan under the leadership of chief planner Michael Harrison of the Portland Bureau of Planning. Harrison, with a small professional staff of planners, reviewed the research reports and the draft plan and produced a review draft of the final 130-page plan, which was adopted by the city council two years later. The Portland Central City Plan raises questions about the proper mix of citizen involvement and professional oversight in urban plan preparation.

In this chapter, Margaret Strachan (who won a Distinguished Leadership Award in 1988 from the American Planning Association) talks about involving more than 100,000 citizen volunteers in the discussions and "visioning" that led to the final plan. Strachan speaks of a sense of common purpose, an easy communication among Portland's leaders, and a long-standing conviction that Oregonians should conserve the good life even at the sacrifice of some self-interest. As she says, "When over 100,000 people have input into a plan, it must be more representative of the public interest."

INTERVIEW WITH MARGARET STRACHAN

I was raised on a ranch where everybody worked really hard, and that background taught me that if you put in your hours, you will take out the goodies, so to speak. My aunt was an agricultural extension agent, and while that work is different from city planning in many ways, it was also similar in that she did a lot of things to get people involved, to give them a chance to shine in their own work. I suppose that those things were important in shaping me, as well as my first memories of political arguments at home about how to make things be fair.

I do not have formal training in city planning. After I had my children, I went back to school and studied English literature. I had originally thought that I would like to study philosophy, but my father was paying for my tuition and didn't think a woman needed a degree in philosophy, so I got one in English literature and taught for a while. I also did a lot of volunteer work. When I came to Portland in 1973, the first job I had was working in a neighborhood office. I ended up working for six neighborhood groups.

Around the time I arrived, the city had decided, under Mayor Neil Goldschmidt (1972–1979), that it wanted to recognize and fund neighborhoods. I worked as a volunteer to help define the criteria for recognition. One was nonexclusivity. In other words, anyone who lived in the neighborhood, owned property in the neighborhood, or worked in the neighborhood could belong to the neighborhood organization. Two, the groups could charge no dues. They could ask for donations and have fund raisers, but they couldn't require dues. The idea was to get broad participation. Neil Goldschmidt really believed in that concept, as did the feds. In those days nearly all federal dollars required a citizen-participation component. Neil and his staff realized that they were wasting money building a citizen-participation component into various city programs and decided to design a citizen-participation process as part of city policy and structure. Then, when federal money was available, Portland would have an inside track in terms of citizen participation.

I worked in the neighborhoods for five years. The first neighborhood development plan recognized by the city was prepared by one of the groups with which I worked. Portland's planning director at that time was Ernie Bonner. Even when it made things uncomfortable, Ernie was a firm believer in citizen participation, and, in fact, he still is active with citizens' groups in the city.

Ernie was very helpful in the drive toward neighborhood recognition, as was Mary Pedersen, who pushed for including a neighborhood needs assessment in the city budget process. The city finally accepted that idea, although not without a lot of pushing from the neighborhoods. Some of the commissioners kept complaining, "We're funding the revolution." Keep in mind this was right after the demonstrations of the 1960s.

After I had worked as the primary paid staff person in neighborhood offices for five years, I began to feel I should move on. A neighborhood coordinator who stayed in that position too long began to have too much power, not because the person was deliberately trying to take control, but because he or she had all the information. People would come to me and ask, "What happened here?" and "What happened there?" I was worried that the neighborhoods would get lazy. Whether you mean to or not, when you've got power over the information, you begin to do all the shaping.

Then I went to work for Mike Linberg, who was on the city commission. I worked for Mike for about a year and began to think: "Hell, I can do this." During that time, the city passed an ordinance requiring that vacancies on the commission had to be filled by election, not by appointment. This was a fortunate development because I would never have been appointed. I was viewed as too pushy. When a vacancy occurred, I ran for the commission along with sixteen other people. I called on all my neighborhood organizing skills and my contacts with neighborhood volunteers throughout the city, and after spending half a year on the election, I won a seat on the commission in 1980.

Portland has a commission form of government and that means that the commissioners have direct administrative responsibility for certain bureaus. I didn't run for commissioner of planning. Commissioners have to run at large, and the mayor has the power to appoint them to various bureaus. At the time, Frank Ivancie was mayor, and he did not particularly trust neighborhoods. He felt that they were "a bad idea whose time has come." So he didn't give me the planning bureau.[2] As I had expressed interest in housing during my campaign, he gave me the Bureau of Building and the Office of Housing. I was assigned to some other bureaus, too, but my major assignments allowed me to reorganize how the city dealt with building permits. When I came on board, it could take as long as six weeks to two months to get a building permit for a single-family house. We cut that to five working days. If you had a more complicated project, say one that required zoning changes, we asked you to come in for advance meetings with all the bureaus, which could advise you about the need to work with neighborhood associations. Out of the Office of Housing, I launched a campaign for a central city plan by saying, "Look, we're not getting the housing we need." Frank Ivancie was basically forced to move ahead with a central city plan.

After I'd been in office three years, Ivancie was defeated by Bud Clark. Interestingly enough, Bud had served on the boards of two different neighborhood groups with which I had worked. He knew that I was interested in planning, so he gave me the Planning Bureau. At that point, I moved the central city plan back into the Planning Bureau.

TOOLING UP FOR PLANNING

I was really fortunate to be in a city like Portland, which had a history of good planning, especially when it came to downtown development. When I started looking around, it was clear that housing was all that was left to do downtown. We asked ourselves, "Where do you find room for housing in the central city close to downtown?" We began looking at the industrial southeast and northwest. Did it make sense to build housing there? There was a significant amount of land around the railroad station that was no longer used. It was a logical place to look at for expanding the city.

Also, I had felt for a long time that the river had been a divider instead of a focal point. While businesses were located along the river because of their need for water transporation or in some cases because it feels like a park, most new development tended to stay on the old, or west, side of the river. You also had the issue of what to do with the Lloyd Center area on the east side. At that time the Lloyd Corporation held the largest amount of central city property under the control of a single firm. A lot of it was underdeveloped. The Lloyd Corporation was a privately held corporation, and family members were getting old; the question was how to plan so that the eventual development of all that land adds to the success of the city. How can we manage growth so that downtown and Lloyd Center are not competing with one another but the central city of Portland is competing successfully with the suburbs?

I took all these questions to my personal staff, which consisted of ten people. My executive assistant was a former Legal Aid attorney. Some of the others were neighborhood activists. In addition, I asked about nine or ten folks for whom I had respect—some of whom were in design, some in planning, some in other businesses, some in government, but all of them were neighborhood people—to advise me on how to move ahead with the plan. How are we going to sell it, not just to the city council, so they'll give us the money that we need, but to the public. I have seen plan after plan formulated and then, when it went to public hearings, shot down or watered down or so completely changed that in some instances it was worse than no plan at all because it had lost all cohesiveness. We decided that in order for the entire city to feel that down-town was theirs (you'd meet people who said they hadn't been downtown in twenty years), we would take the plan to the citizens and involve them in the process all the way along. Identifying problems was the first task. We had to keep explaining to some people that even though totally contradictory ideas were coming in, that was OK. We wanted everybody to understand that we had heard what they said and that we were going to try as our next step to resolve those conflicts and move ahead with the plan.

Besides the more formalized hearings and discussions, we set up citizen committees around issues. There was a housing committee, a social service committee, one for parks and education and so on. A second set of committees was to be geographically based. That group of committees did not function quite so well as the first group. Eventually its members moved on to the issue committees. Then we did some programming on cable television. We also did programs in classrooms with fifth and sixth graders because they understood about parks and zoos and all the fun things there are to do. We felt that we would pull a lot of people in through the involvement of their children. We re-cruited a teacher to go around to the schools with triangles of plastic on which he encouraged kids to draw. Then he put them all together and used a wind machine to blow the assemblage up into a hugh geodesic dome. Inside this dome, we set up maps and questionnaires and interactive computer programs, all about the central city plan. They could see at what stage we were in the plan and what some of our ideas were. A lot of kids said to their parents, "My picture's on the dome downtown, and I want to go see it." We supplied paper and colored pencils and pens, on which people could write ideas. That was another way of involving people. Each of our issue committees also did their own outreach.

We did almost eight or nine months of planning for citizen involvement in the plan. The citizens' involvement committee was also open to the public. In addition to discussing how we were going to involve people, we considered how we were going to take all the ideas generated and assemble a cohesive, do-able plan. We came up with what we called the "reiterated planning process," in which we kept narrowing ideas down and going back to their originators and asking if we were still on track. We ended up taking some important issues that we couldn't really deal with in the plan and setting them aside, to be dealt with outside the framework of the plan. We tried very hard not to include anything in our plan that would prevent the future implementation of the set-aside ideas, such as removing the freeway on the other side of the river, which I would still dearly love to do.

We encountered plenty of opposition, of course. I'm not saying it all came from the business community, but that was part of it. It was almost a matter of personality. While I don't like to make generalizations, generally the opposition came from men; I think men tend to deal less well with what they perceive to be confusion. I've got to tell you that using volunteers means that there's going to be lots of confusion. You just have to have faith that you're going to be able to keep moving forward and keep getting consensus from folks. When I say consensus, I mean something different from approval. I mean that people say, "This isn't the best thing, but I recognize that it's probably the best that we're going to get at this time." So people buy in, reserving the right to be able to come back and say, "I want more housing," or, "I want better bicycle paths," or whatever their issue might be.

I kept trying to bring the critics back into the process by pointing to the fact that earlier planning based on citizen participation had been successful, such as the original downtown plan and plans that had been successful in revitalizing some of Portland's neighborhoods. I also pointed out that many of the proposals would end up on the ballot at some point. In fact, part of what we were doing was giving people ownership so that they might in fact vote favorably on future bond issues.

I also did a lot of work with the media. We had information sessions at which we handed out packets. I had some really long discussions with the editors who dealt with city issues at the *Oregonian*. One of the fears of the business community and the newspaper was that we would put all development on hold until the plan was done. Since there were some pretty good projects under way in the city, we were not trying to stave off some disastrous development, so we were able to say that we had no intention of holding things up. We pretty much lived up to our word, although there may have been a few projects where we suggested that it might be to the developer's advantage to wait a bit.

I want to state again that we benefited from some good previous planning. The original downtown plan does a step-down from the tall buildings along the mall down to the river. There were provisions for historic districts. There are parks and squares throughout the city. These amenities made it easy for us to say, "Look, those concepts weren't popular in their day, but look at what they've done to enhance the city." Additionally, I was really helped by a man who owned a great deal of property downtown. Bill Roberts, who was probably in his seventies or eighties, had been chairman of the Tri-Met Board [a metropolitan-wide planning and service agency] and was the chairman of the Portland Development Commission. He was much, much more conservative than I, but he and I liked each other and had great respect for one another. I recognized that he loved and cared about the city, and he felt that I did, too. Even when we disagreed, we recognized that our disagreements weren't prompted by selfish interests and arose because we saw things differently. He gave me lots of support and latitude. When he had criticisms, he gave me those criticisms privately. He had a lot of influence with downtown property owners and was very, very helpful.

Another person who owned property downtown and was very supportive of me was Bill Naito. Bill liked the idea of citizen participation. He is deserving of great recognition, not just because of his beliefs, but also because he's been active in the redevelopment of Old Town.

SINGLE ROOM OCCUPANCY HOUSING

The people involved in the central city plan were very much aware of the issue of Single Room Occupancy (SRO) housing. In fact, one of the people on the Housing Committee was Mary Burki, who had a doctorate in urban planning and worked for an agency that provided SRO housing. She also had a long history in neighborhood development. We tried hard to find and involve people who had broad experience like that. Mary argued the case for SRO on the Housing Committee. Similarly, a person who worked with a housing and social service program for homeless people served on the Social Service Committee. A number of other people on these committees recognized the need to address the problem of homelessness and to preserve the SROs. It's always easier if you can deal with problems early, rather than later on.

Interestingly enough, Bill Naito owned a number of SRO hotels. People who didn't like him called him "the slumlord with a heart" because he leased his hotels to agencies that ran them as SROs. Bill really saw a need for them and could give you a wonderful history of Old Town and how these hotels were originally built for lumbermen and sailors. Later the hotels' purpose had changed as they became housing for retired workers, mostly single men; it was as close to any home as they were ever going to have.

Since Portland had a history with this kind of housing, it was easier to convince others that we could use SROs for other groups of needy people, although we tried to get families out of that kind of housing as soon as possible and into housing in neighborhoods.

We also recognized that another big problem for homeless people is drug abuse and alcoholism. Some local agencies have tried to tie staying clean and sober to improved housing. People may start out in a shelter, but if they get clean and sober, they can move into better housing. This may provide some real motivation.

WHAT WE LEARNED FROM THE PLAN

We learned several things from the central city plan. We could probably speed up the selection process for the various committees or at least recognize that we could do more things simultaneously. I wouldn't take so long to do the preliminary planning, and at the same time I would ask for applications for the committees. If we had done that sooner, the committees could have been up and running at the kickoff. But in spite of these glitches, Portland's commitment to citizen participation continues strong. You've got to understand that once you give neighborhoods and citizens that much power, it's damn tough to take it back.

Since the initial interviews for this book, several things have happened. Among them is the much increased development on the east side of the Willamette River, especially in the area of the Lloyd Center. A new mayor, Vera Katz, and a new commissioner, Charlie Hales, have joined the city council. They are taking up the issue of relocating the east side freeway again. It's a good idea that won't die. Additional work on low-cost housing and better programs for the homeless continue. The emphasis is on permanent housing and a reduction in people on the streets or in mass shelters.

The most ambitious planning project since the central city plan has been the development of the Albina plan, which covers a number of areas in the inner northeast portion of the city. This plan has not yet been adopted, primarily because citizen input was given less attention than it deserved. Though citizens were involved, many of them felt they were being dictated to, rather than involved. Had conversations with the community been truly two-way, the plan would already be adopted with some sense of cohesiveness and consensus. In-depth involvement takes more time in the early stages but leads to a more cohesive plan with the community stakeholders arriving at a consensus that builds support and speeds the adoption process. In other words, you can put the time and money in at the front end and develop a plan that has community support or you can put the time and dollars into fighting the plan through the adoption process. In the end, they both take time and money, but true involvement produces a plan that is accepted by the community and, hence, can be more easily implemented.

My work as a volunteer, even my work as a teacher, was most helpful in preparing me for participatory planning. Ever since I was a kid—I guess I got it from my aunt—I've believed that everybody has a piece of the truth and that if you can put all those perspectives together, you're going to come up with a much better product. Unfortunately, I think that traditional planners frequently mistake education for intelligence. Sometimes planners will go out to a neighborhood and find that people don't have the "right" language. They end up not listening because they subconsciously feel that these people don't know what they're talking about. That's a mistake. People who live in a neighborhood know if there are problems, if their children are at risk because of traffic patterns, for instance. It's incumbent on planners to learn how to understand all kinds of communications; otherwise, people turn off because they feel they haven't been heard. Their being excluded has nothing to do with the validity of their ideas or their identification of the problems, but only with their inability to put their thoughts into the planners' language.

I guess what I'm saying is that cultural bias and educational hubris may be the biggest obstacle to equity planning, whether that bias is toward education, race, or other factors.

NOTES

1. The steering committee was carefully balanced both geographically and in terms of the individual's profession and interests. Most members had several overlapping areas of expertise or interests.

2. Each of Portland's four commissioners directs several departments. Strachan was assigned to planning in 1984 by the new mayor, Bud Clark.

FURTHER READING: Citizen Participation

Clavel, Pierre. *The Progressive City: Planning and Participation, 1969–1984*. New Brunswick, N.J.: Rutgers University Press, 1986.

Desario, Jack, and Stuart Langton. *Citizen Participation in Public Decision Making*. Westport, Conn.: Greenwood Press, 1987.

Filion, Pierre. "The Neighborhood Improvement Plan. Montreal and Toronto: Contrasts between a Participatory Approach to Urban Policy Making." *Urban History Review* (Canada) 17, no. 1 (1988): 16–28.

Haeberle, Steven H. "Community Projects and Citizen Participation: Neighborhood Leaders Evaluate their Accomplishments." *Social Science Quarterly* 69, no. 4 (1988): 1014–1021.

———. "Neighborhood Identity and Citizen Participation." *Administration and Society* 19, no. 2 (1987): 178–196.

———. *Planting the Grassroots: Structuring Citizen Participation*. New York: Praeger, 1989.

Henderson, Lawrence J. "Neighborhood Power in the Capitol: Advisory Neighborhood Commissions in Washington, D.C." *National Civic Review* 78, no. 3 (1989): 209–215.

Kraegel, Wilfred A. "Community Goals Projects: Citizen Participation in Urban Planning (Milwaukee Case Study)." University of Wisconsin, Milwaukee, DAI 48, no. 9: 2470-a DA88728151.

McClendon, Bruce W., and Judith A. Lewis. "Goals for Corpus Christi: Citizen Participation in Planning." *National Civic Review* 74, no. 2 (1985): 72–80.

Shearer, Derek. "Citizen Participation in Local Government: The Case of Santa Monica, California." *International Journal of Urban and Regional Research* (Great Britain) 8, no. 4 (1984): 573–586.

chapter 6

BOSTON

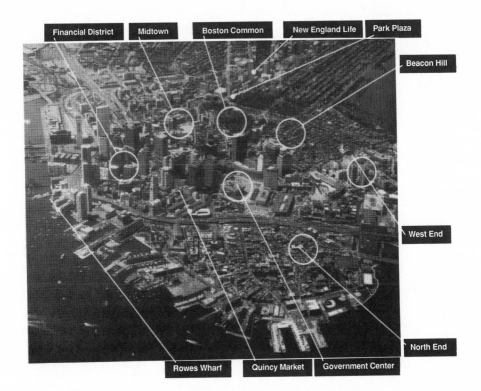

Financial District
Midtown
Boston Common
New England Life
Park Plaza
Beacon Hill
West End
North End
Rowes Wharf
Quincy Market
Government Center

How the Boston Redevelopment Authority got some respect. By permission of Aerial Photos International. By Malcolm Woronoff, Aerial Photos International, Inc.

Snapshot, 1983

Population Composition for Boston, Massachusetts, 1970–1990

Demographic	1970	1980	1990
Population	641,071	562,994	574,283
White	524,709	393,937	360,875
Black	104,707	126,229	146,945
Median family income	$9,133	$16,062	$34,377
Percentage poverty	16.2	20.2	18.7

In November 1983 Raymond Flynn was elected mayor of Boston. The Flynn administration had been given a mandate by the voters to "share the prosperity" of Boston's downtown economic boom. Peter Dreier came into the Flynn administration as director of housing for the Boston Redevelopment Authority (BRA) as well as Flynn's housing policy advisor, serving from 1984 to 1992. He is currently the E. P. Clapp Distinguished Professor of Politics at Occidental College in Los Angeles.

What the Flynn administration inherited was a city of contrasts. By 1984, Boston's economy was well along to shifting from a manufacturing base to a service-based economy, spurring the development of downtown office buildings, university and medical research centers, and high-technology industries. This economic boom created new problems and compounded some old ones. Neighborhoods near downtown or close to universities and hospitals were becoming gentrified, pricing working-class and moderate-income residents out of the market; 10,000 families were on the waiting list for public housing; lower-income neighborhoods faced redlining and disinvestment; the minority unemployment rate was twice that of the city at large; and many of the jobs held by Boston residents were in the low-paying portion of the new service-oriented economy.

Peter Dreier, a former Tufts University professor and housing activist, recognized these problems as both immediate concerns and the results of decades of uneven urban development. As BRA's housing director and Flynn's policy aide, Dreier has had significant influence in a city government that has called into question the responsibilities of the private market toward Boston's residents and has used the powers and influence of government to make sure that the benefits of prosperity are distributed more equitably.

THE POSTWAR DEVELOPMENT OF BOSTON

Throughout the postwar era, the urban development of Boston was guided by business-oriented growth coalitions in cooperation with political machines. At the end of World War II, Boston was in economic distress; in fact, only one private office building was built in Boston between 1929 and 1960. Total assessed valuation of real property fell from $1.8 billion in 1930 to $1.3 billion in 1960. Between 1950 and 1960, the city's population decreased by 13 percent (801,000 to 697,000) and the number of jobs in the city fell by 10 percent (558,000 to 500,000). Realizing that they had real estate investments at stake, the corporate community made a choice to carry out a vigorous redevelopment strategy. In the late 1940s, business leaders mobilized their political influence and helped to elect two probusiness mayors, John Hynes (1949–1959) and John Collins (1959–1968), who were responsive to the fiscal and development agendas of private interests. Hynes defeated the redoubtable James M. Curley in 1951 with the aid of the New Boston Committee, a business-based reform group.

The Hynes administration undertook Boston's first federally funded urban renewal projects in 1952, initiating the now infamous West End Project. One of the first massive slum clearance projects in the county, it displaced more than 2,600 families. He also put together the Prudential Center project, with strong support from the business community and Cardinal Cushing of the Roman Catholic Diocese.

Throughout the 1950s the business community became more politically cohesive and solidified its leadership as the Boston Coordinating Committee (nicknamed "the Vault"). The Vault's influence became a force in the Collins administration's development activities. The Vault also persuaded the state and city to create a "superagency," the Boston Redevelopment Authority (BRA), which combined the city's planning and urban renewal functions.

The BRA's urban renewal program, dubbed the "New Boston" program and led by Ed Logue, included one-fourth of the city's land area, the net result of which was sharply to reduce the number of housing units in Boston. Renewal in the South End was designed to produce "maximum upgrading" (to use Ed Logue's words) in the housing stock adjacent to the central business district (CBD), a hospital complex, and office developments in Back Bay. The Collins administration also offered tax concessions and other incentives for downtown development, which spurred the first large-scale office towers and luxury housing constructed downtown in decades. Nevertheless, the city lost both population and jobs through 1970, while it gained a significant minority population (5.3 percent in 1950, to 18.2 percent in 1970).

Collins opted not to run for mayor in 1967, and Kevin White defeated six other candidates to win the seat. During White's four terms (1968–1984), the economy, fiscal condition, and political character of Boston changed significantly.

The development activity of the Collins era continued through White's years, and the city gained an average of 800,000 square feet of office space each year from 1965 to 1974, adding another 5.2 million square feet in 1975 alone. After the recession of the mid-1970s subsided, the Boston economy began a recovery based on financial services, high-technology industies, educational and medical institutions, and tourism. This success led to increased real estate speculation in both office space and housing in the late 1970s and early 1980s. Although White had instituted a rent control program in 1968 to protect the city's large tenant population (70 percent), he bowed to real estate industry pressures and began in 1975 to dismantle rent control and, more generally, promote the gentrification of housing.

The city also faced a fiscal crisis. In 1980, Massachusetts voters passed Proposition 2½, which severely cut property taxes. This created a revenue shortage that plunged the city into severe fiscal stress. The Vault's business leader used their influence with investment banks and bond-rating firms to prevent the city's bankruptcy. The Vault gained more influence over government, and while downtown boomed, the city was forced to cut back again and again on municipal services. Mayor White had also been investigated by the U.S. Attorney for corruption and campaign irregularities, resulting in the indictment of several key aides. Realizing that the fiscal crisis, corruption investigations, and increasing contrast between downtown affluence and neighborhood decline had fatally wounded his political career, White decided not to run for a fifth term in 1983.

THE FLYNN MANDATE

The inconsistency between Boston's thriving economy and the socioeconomic conditions of the city's working class provided the Flynn administration with a mandate for a redistributionist policy agenda. The pattern of development described previously had created economic prosperity for some and had made life difficult for many others, especially in the areas of jobs and housing.

The jobs created in the growth sectors tended to be split between well-paid managerial and professional jobs on one end, and low-paying clerical, sales, and service positions on the other. By 1983, Boston residents held only 31 percent of the city's 587,000 jobs, with suburban commuters holding the majority of up-scale professional positions. Boston residents held most lower-rung jobs without real opportunities for advancement.

Boston's population began to grow again in the early 1980s, for the first time since 1950, leading to increased pressures on the housing market, which again threatened to displace many poor and working-class residents. The trend had begun in the late 1970s, and increased gentrification and real estate speculation through the 1980s had exacerbated the problem. Between 1975 and 1984, the price of a single family house had more than tripled, while rent in the city rose 48 percent between 1977 and 1981. Condominium conversions increased through the 1980s and displaced many renters. Some owners benefited from appreciating real estate values, but for working-class renters and many minorities, housing was a crucial problem.

Once in office, the Flynn administration and BRA created policies in several specific areas: linkage and inclusionary zoning, support for a growing network of community-based nonprofit developers, community reinvestment by private lenders, rent control and control of condominium conversions, and a jobs policy for Boston residents.

In this chapter, Peter Dreier talks about some of these programs, the difficult process of negotiation and implementation, and his ideas on how cities can use their limited resources and authority, not only to address immediate concerns, but also to reinvent the public debate on the relationship between development and distribution.

INTERVIEW WITH PETER DREIER

I have three careers that were on parallel tracks at first. I was a journalist, an organizer, and an academic. This job is in some ways an opportunity to do all three—plus a fourth, which is to be a government official with some power to make things happen. But you make important things happen only if there are things going on in the community that create the conditions that make it possible.

I came to Boston in 1977, to teach at Tufts. I wanted to live in Boston, in part because I have friends here, and in part because some of the people I had known when I was in Chicago had come to Boston to work at Massachusetts Fair Share, and I knew there was this really good community organizing going on.

I worked with Fair Share, helping its staff and leaders do research on different topics. Fair Share had at one point thirty to forty VISTA volunteers plus its own staff, so overall it had over a hundred staff people. It had a budget of over a million dollars. It was doing the best community organizing in the country. The fact that it didn't sustain itself over time, and didn't survive the Reagan/VISTA cuts and some other things—there are probably some lessons to be learned from that. But Fair Share was building a progressive, pragmatic movement that changed Massachusetts politics. And it was ten years ahead of the tax revolt and ahead on housing and basic economic fairness issues where you could draw people of middle and lower class, black, white, and Latino, together. Fair Share had chapters in the black community, fighting on common issues with chapters in white neighborhoods.

I saw a vacuum. Although it did some work organizing tenants, Fair Share primarily organized working-class and poor homeowners. I thought that there ought to be a tenant's component to that. During my seven years at Tufts, I took two years off and helped start the Massachusetts Tenant Organization.

Mike Ansara was Fair Share's executive director and sort of their public spokesperson, their best fund raiser. The person I dealt with besides Michael was Miles Rappaport, who I knew in Chicago, and who is now a state assemblyman in Connecticut and a leader in progressive politics there. I was friends with these people. And I think that my experience of Fair Share shaped my view of pragmatic left politics more than anything.

At the same time, for a couple of years in the early 1980s, I was on the national board of Democratic Socialists of America (DSA) when Mike Harring-ton was still alive. I became pretty close to Mike. I wrote some things with him. I tried to integrate my kind of democratic socialist politics with DSA and my organizing work. I wrote a lot for the DSA newspaper, and I was always open about being a DSA. In Boston, DSA had about 500 members. And for a while, in the early 1980s, a core group of about ten of us helped make DSA a political force in Boston. People (including candidates for office) would come to our annual dinners, our forums, our public events. We helped them create a climate that made DSA a political activist group. The people in DSA were active in unions and community organizations and in electoral politics. They helped to create a political climate where, from about 1978 to 1983, a network of people who knew one another had a common strategy, a common view of how to proceed politically. Even though we didn't march through the same strategy on everything, there was a common view of left politics.

The Ray Flynn–Mel King electoral fight in 1983 helped undermine that con-sensus. Before that, it was a sort of a friendly fight on the left, between the people who eventually went with Mel and the Rainbow Coalition and those in Fair Share, 9 to 5 (a national association of working women), some unions, and the more working-class–oriented organizers who eventually went with Flynn. I mean, the stakes were real, so it was hard to have merely intellectual conver-sations around that issue. And I think some of the reverberations of the 1983 race are still felt in Boston. Some of Mel's hard-core supporters still question the politics of the Flynn administration, although an equal number of Mel's supporters are with Flynn.

FLYNN'S EMERGENCE AS MAYOR

Through working on issues in Boston, I got to meet Ray Flynn in 1978, when he was the lone member on the nine-member city council who was interested in tenants' rights. With our help, he was always introducing bills to protect tenants from condo conversions and rent increases.

Flynn topped the ticket, winning the most votes, in the 1981 city council races. That immediately made him a potential candidate for mayor in 1983. I knew that he had mayoral ambitions, so in late 1982 I signed on to work on his campaign. I was quite impressed with him. I thought he could articulate the kinds of issues to a broad constituency that the left on its own could never do. I think that a lot of us saw Ray Flynn as a vehicle for our politics, and I think that Ray Flynn saw a lot of us (progressive organizers, activists, and academics) as a talent pool to get him elected, and to draw on our ideas on politics.

Flynn won the election in November 1983, and I went to work the day he took office. A few of the folks who went to work for Flynn in high-profile jobs, with backgrounds as organizers and activists such as Neil Sullivan (a Fair Share organizer), Nancy Snyder (director of 9 to 5), and Ray Dooley (an antiwar leader and political aide to radical state Representative Tom Gallagher), were called "the Sandinistas" in the press, and the label stuck. We were the most high-profile progressives, or the "left" in the administration. A certain amount of goodwill would sustain us among the other folks at city hall, especially our loyalty to the mayor. We tried to keep the lines of communication open—in fact, not to be viewed as a "caucus" or faction at all.

THE PROGRESSIVE AGENDA IN THE FLYNN ADMINISTRATION

I am a democratic socialist. Although in this administration there are other people with comparable views, I am probably the most outspoken progressive in this administration. And the mayor likes that. He likes to get those views. There is no single document that outlines the Flynn administration's goals. There is nothing comparable to Harold Washington's Chicago Works Together. The mayor in his inauguration speech had a vision that we helped shape and make specific as he took office. A set of thoughts guide what we are doing. A lot of them are things that the mayor articulates on a day-to-day basis, as well as in speeches, reports, and planning studies. We shape and grab hold of them. If I have an idea I want, I'll often write a speech for the mayor or an article for him and then we'll talk about it, back and forth. He has never said anything he doesn't believe. I'm not some Machiavellian who puts words in his mouth. But I am able to articulate the larger vision of what his views of the world are and then incorporate it in speeches he gives to national and local audiences and articles and testimony before Congress or the legislature or in press statements. And then that becomes the Ray Flynn stamp of approval, which gives us the ability to say, "This is what the mayor wants."

To some extent, that substitutes for a broad game plan. It also means that if you ask ten people in the administration what are the five major goals, you'll get ten different answers. That is probably a handicap to planners. On the other hand, Steve Coyle, as the chief planner of the city (Coyle was BRA director from 1984 to 1992), has articulated a kind of view, and we've written some speeches for the mayor about how we want planning in the city to be, which get broad circulation. It always incorporates planning with the participatory neighborhood focus. It always incorporates the sharing of prosperity between the downtown businesses and the working-class and poor neighborhoods. It always incorporates government as a lever, to get the private sector to do things that they wouldn't do on their own. We don't believe in "trickle down" economics. It incorporates the rezoning of the city so that the rules are clear to everybody; there are no special interests and political favorites that get special favors from developers and bankers because of their connections. The rules are clear, and they apply to everyone. So all those are things that have been said by the mayor over and over again, that have been written down in documents—planning documents, rezoning maps, reports, and the like. And those substitute for a comprehensive master plan. Mayor Flynn is pragmatic enough to know that when conditions change, you may change specific policies a bit, as is evidenced now by the fact that we're in a recession.

SPECIFIC THINGS I HAVE WORKED ON

The issues I was involved in at first were always about housing or banking. Some of them were national issues. Within a year or so, after Flynn took office, he was already becoming active on the U.S. Conference of Mayors, and I worked with him to get the USCM more involved with housing and homelessness issues at the national level. Locally, I was devoting my energy to getting linkage operating and expanding (my) work on rent control, getting the city's property disposition (abandoned property) program together. Later on, during the mayor's second term, I put together the city's antiredlining campaign to extract more money for CDCs to do affordable housing, and devised an inclusionary zoning legislation. Since I've written extensively elsewhere about the linkage program, I'll focus on the other things here.

All those topics have something in common, which is that they require a certain amount of technical work that involves drafting legal and policy documents, doing background research to help justify and explain these laws or policies. Part of my job was the technical/legal/policy side of it. But a lot of my role in trying to promote these progressive policies was as much political as technical, which meant building political support for policies that the mayor wanted adopted but didn't have unilateral power to adopt or needed to create a public climate to make these policies acceptable. Also, organizing internally in city hall to try to use the power of the bureaucracy to make things happen.

Rent Control   We knew that one of the first tests of the Flynn administration was going to be rent control. And I think that we thought that the campaign to win rent control would mobilize a lot of the activists and keep the momentum of the organizing—to unite the activists of the Flynn campaign and the King campaign—on the common agenda of fighting for rent control. In other words, we didn't have a road map of where we wanted to be in three years, but we did have a sense of how to bring people together, to organize them. The Flynn campaign and then the Flynn administration could be the vehicle for organizing them. Our vision was that you could have city hall and the community organizing together around issues of economic justice—against the big landlords and the real estate industry, against the developers around linkage, and five years later, around the banks and redlining.

Rent control had been gradually eviscerated by the White administration. Mayor White had been a rent control supporter when he first came into office in 1968. In 1970 the city passed rent control and put rent control on about 150,000 units. By 1975 Kevin White decided he was no longer for rent control. He was much more in cahoots with the real estate industry, downtown real estate, and some big landlords. In 1975 the city council enacted decontrol, permanently wiping out protections when a tenant leaves an apartment. Between 1975 and 1984, when Flynn took office, any time somebody left a unit, that unit was no longer under rent control—so eventually there was going to be a complete turnover. The turnover was about 75 to 80 percent in those eight years, so that only about 20 percent of the city's eligible rental housing stock was under rent control. Our goal was to bring it back. In the early 1980s, rents were going up very fast, and the city was beginning to feel the effects. This was a big issue. There were also a lot of condominium conversions and a lot of unfair and arbitrary evictions going on. Flynn made rent control one of the key components of his campaign in part because when he was in the city council that had been the one issue he had been the most identified with. It was one issue that attracted a lot of people like me to work for him because the city council had been sort of bought and sold by the real estate industry, and he was an exception to that.

There were a couple of problems with getting our rent control program through the city council. One problem was that there was serious opposition. The real estate industry was obviously gearing up to oppose rent control and it (through the Greater Boston Real Estate Board) elected as president a very political guy named Tom Hynes, who was a top executive in Meredith and Grew, a big real estate firm. His father had been the mayor. He knew everybody in town, and the real estate industry was gearing up; they weren't just appointing some small realtor from the suburbs. They knew this was going to be a big fight, and they knew Flynn was popular. At the same time they had an advantage, in the sense that the city council, which had been elected at the same time as Flynn, was against rent control. There were thirteen members on the city council, and we had, at best, four clear votes for rent control. So if there was going to be success in getting the rent control law passed, it was going to require changing the vote of at least three members of the city council who were opposed to it—against the power of the real estate industry and a lot of small homeowners and small landlords. Boston is a city divided into single-family homeowners, three deckers, large apartment buildings, and subsidized housing. The constituency for rent control is extremely narrow. The 25,000 units of subsidized housing are exempt from rent control (except for the eviction law) by federal law because they are subsidized. So, all the tenants in public housing and Section 8 housing developments in the city were not easily mobilized for this issue. Also, at least one-third of the city's rentals are in two and three deckers, which are exempt from rent control because they are owner occupied. So the tenants in those buildings were not mobilizable, at least on an immediate self-interest basis. The geographic distribution of the apartments that would be under rent control and stronger eviction and condominium conversion was very concentrated. These apartments basically tend to be in the Fenway, Back Bay, Allston-Brighton, and parts of Jamaica Plain—liberal neighborhoods. It was no surprise that the city councilors from these neighborhoods were with us. We thought we also had Councilman Bruce Bolling from Roxbury, although he was sort of wishy-washy on this.

We didn't anticipate how hard it would be, and we weren't ready to turn those councilors around. Part of the reason was that so many people came into the Flynn administration; we needed time to get settled, but the media were clamoring for a fight over rent control. Both the media and the progressive activists expected immediate results on this issue, before the administration was constructed internally. There was a lot for us to learn about how city government worked and how the civil service worked, and how to coordinate the departments, and how to get the political activists who worked on the campaign to work together, and we didn't have enough time. A few years later, we were much more sophisticated about how to mobilize people around such issues as banking and other issues that we won, but those first few months in office were too early to launch this major fight.

We came into office in January 1984. In April I announced the aim of augmenting the city's rent control programs, which everyone could anticipate from the campaign. The vote didn't happen until October. I think that the Flynn administration basically didn't have our political organization, the political connections in some of the neighborhoods, in place to win this initiative.

So it was going to be a difficult fight, and my first role in the Mayor's Office was to draft the bill. This itself took a few months. There was a lot of input from tenants groups and the like. There was also a recognition that we had to do more than just draft a rent control law. We had to build political support for it, and that would mean not only helping Massachusetts Tenants' Organization (MTO) to do its job but also trying to make rent control appear to be more of a universal issue than a narrow tenants' rights issue, because the MTO didn't have the political clout to change the city council, and the mayor did not control the council.

Basically, what I drafted was an extremely strong rent control law that would put all the normally rent controlled units back under rent control; it would require a permit for any landlord to convert an apartment to a condominium. It would ban the conversion of lodging houses. It included very strong eviction controls, "just cause" eviction of the entire housing stock. And it would strengthen the administration of the Rent Board.

Part of my job was to go and talk to all the city councilors and feel them out. It was pretty clear that different people in the administration should be talking to different councilors. I think it is fair to say that some of the members of the Flynn administration who, by disposition, experience, background, and their own personal histories, would have had the most affinity with the more conservative members of the city council, were also not particularly sympathetic to rent control. So we had this difficulty about how you talk to these guys.

Part of it was to organize their constituencies. The mayor has never had a "machine," he has had a personal following among people who knew him when he was a sports star and people who knew him through political work. So that is the dilemma we faced. Lew Finfer (director of MTO and an experienced organizer with Fair Share and other groups) took it upon himself, with our support, to be the lead organizer in the community. I think this campaign really frustrated him because city hall was not well organized enough to point out where the support was.

Part of the mayor's instinct was that if we were trying to get rent control through the city council, we ought to surround it with some other housing legislation, a comprehensive housing plan, of which rent control was one piece. We drafted a couple of other things, like home repairs for the elderly and arson prevention. We had these big charges, and we would go around the neighborhoods and point out why this program was important. We tried to make a case about why rent control was pro-business—because the city's employers needed a workforce that could afford housing; that, like health care, housing was a social cost that business had to bear one way or the other, either higher wages or difficulty in getting employees. We basically had this road show that we took around to neighborhood groups—that was part of my job.

In retrospect, it's clear that we were fighting a losing battle from the beginning because there was almost no way, given the demographics of the city and the weak power of the tenants' movement, the power of the real estate lobby, and the resistance of the city council, that this was ever going to pass. I was probably more optimistic than I should have been—I guess we all assumed that, with the mayor's mandate, somehow we could overcome these obstacles, but it turned out we couldn't.

I felt that the structural conditions weren't there, and yet it was being seen as a test of the mayor's political strength. So, it was a no-win situation. The bill was filed in April 1984; it didn't come to a vote until October. What we got eventually in October 1984 was a compromise measure that provided for rent adjustments of the cost of inflation (at the time it was fairly high) and strong eviction laws for the elderly and poor people. One of the problems that created, and it got worse over the next couple of years, was we kept going back to the city council every year to try to strengthen the rent control, condo conversion, and eviction laws. Every time we did that we would resubmit something similar, and every time we would get a little more. You could see the first six years of the Flynn administration as a kind of war of position, to try to get what we originally wanted but were unable to get originally. By 1987 or 1988, we had gotten about two-thirds of what we wanted. But we still didn't have full rent control, but what we did get was a patchwork system.

We now have a law that is *much* stronger than it was in 1984. There is still a big gap: when somebody leaves an apartment, the rent can go up to market level, but then it goes back under rent control; it is basically recontrol rather than decontrol. That is a big hole. When rents were still skyrocketing through most of the 1980s, that was a big loophole in the rent control law, and we couldn't get the council to fill it in. So the end of the story here is that we were fighting insurmountable odds; we ultimately fought a war of attrition or a war of position, where we got most of what we wanted but not in a way that it felt, looked, or was perceived as a big victory.

Property Disposition Committee   One of the major problems that Boston faced when Ray Flynn took office was that large swaths of vacant land were owned by the city or potentially owned by the city (meaning tax delinquent). Large numbers of publicly owned buildings had been taken by tax foreclosure by the city, and many more that weren't taken could be taken. The previous administration under Kevin White had no policy at all. When a building came through the tax foreclosure process, almost by accident, they would auction it off to the highest bidder. The city also had a number of surplus buildings because of school closures, and municipal neighborhood buildings closed down because they were no longer useful as public buildings. With Flynn in office, the city was beginning to implement its linkage policy and had the potential of having a considerable amount of discretionary housing money. So there were all these city resources. The question was how to spend them.

At the same time, there was a fledgling network of nonprofit housing groups undertaking development. Most of them were young, inexperienced, and un-sophisticated. A few of them, like Urban Edge, had been around for nine or ten years, but most were only two, three, or four years old. Most of them had had a very difficult time getting access to property in Boston. The CDCs that were in low-income neighborhoods tended not to have political clout and couldn't get access to city properties under the Kevin White administration. And ones like Fenway Community Development Corporation, which were in gentrifying neighborhoods, couldn't afford the acquisition price of private land, and since there weren't that many publicly owned properties around, had a hard time getting projects going. So they were strapped by a lack of operating resources to hire staff and to pay their overhead and to hire architects and planners to help them with projects, and more important, a lack of access to public resources for projects.

Coming into city hall, we had a view that we wanted to change city policy and encourage and nurture these nonprofit groups. But there were a couple of obstacles: most of the groups were fairly unsophisticated, and there was an incredibly hot housing market. Many speculators and real estate developers in the city saw an opportunity to make a lot of money. There were also a growing number of minority developers who wanted a piece of the pie in the minority neighborhoods. Why? Because most of the tax-delinquent properties were in minority areas, and because most of the old urban renewal land that the city had taken in the 1960s and 1970s and never had done anything with was located in communities of color.

The mayor, realizing the problem with all the abandoned property, put me in charge of something we called the Property Disposition Committee, which pulled together the heads of several city departments and tried to develop an inventory of what the city owned because the previous administration didn't know what the city owned. There was no computerized database. Our other goal was to put together a policy as to how we were going to dispose of prop-erties. Over a period of about a year, in doing the property inventory and identifying what and where the buildings were, there were some internal fights on that committee. One wing wanted basically to continue to sell properties to the highest bidder and allow the private market to do it. One problem was that the agency that owned the property (PFD) and the agency that had the CDBG money (NDEA) were separate departments. It took the mayor a while to iron out the problem. There were some stops and starts in trying to figure this out, and ultimately the mayor consolidated those two agencies into one so that we could work more smoothly.

While that was going on, there was this thing that had started under Kevin White called the Boston Housing Partnership. It wasn't going anywhere because soon after he announced it, Kevin White decided to quit. It was a show without a mission. We decided its mission was to expand the capacity of nonprofit community development corporations—to get the business community to help the CDCs. So a lot of the nonprofits in the city got their first major project, something more than five or ten units, by the aggregation of financial resources through the Boston Housing Partnership.

It seems like several things had to happen to get community development moving. Number one, Flynn had to be convinced that the CDCs could do it. There is, after all, a prejudice in the United States that the private sector is the only one that can do things. Second was an information question—getting a list of the properties. Third, you can't just go into a neighborhood and say, look, here is this piece of property, why don't we build some houses? The people in the neighborhood want to take a step back and say, wait a minute, is this Coyle or Dreier or somebody coming in here with a bill of goods? What is *our* agenda? They need some information, and they need to sit and go through a planning process. The mayor certainly had a predisposition toward CDCs and grassroots planning, but somebody had to show him that this was the way to do it, that the CDCs were in fact able to do it.

My job, in all of that, was to push the bureaucracies inside city hall to carry out the mayor's stated agenda, which was to be supportive of these nonprofit groups. The two agencies that dispose of properties have basically followed the mayor's guidelines. They have project managers that hold hands with the CDCs. Some CDCs are not up to the task, so the city's own project manager may play a stronger role—we package the subsidies, we get the state, the federal government, and the local development team to pull all the pieces together. Our architects often help design projects, although the CDCs have architects they hire to do it—it is often a kind of joint arrangement. We have done more than just dispose of property, we have done a lot of hand holding and a lot of capacity building of community groups.

The planning role here has basically been one of allocating property and funding resources and then, on a policy basis, doing things like figuring out what the deed restrictions should be, doing the legal work, getting our lawyers to fight with FHA and Fannie Mae, to fight with HUD to allow us to have long-term affordability guidelines.

Now there are probably about thirty-five to forty nonprofit groups in Boston. These include CDCs, tenant co-ops taking over HUD housing, union groups like the Bricklayers and the Hotel Workers, church groups, the Catholic archdiocese, Boston Aging Concerns (a group that does elderly SRO housing), groups that started off doing homeless shelters (like Pine Street Inn) and moved into SRO housing or transitional housing. In some cases we created organizations in order to do something we wanted to do. Somewhere between thirty-five and forty organizations, probably something like 120 projects, something like 5,000 units since late 1984. In the process a lot of groups grew and were able to go from 5 units to 50 units to more than 100 units.

But the bottom line is that there is no magic formula to solve the housing crisis in Boston (or any other city) because there is not enough money. We have done practically everything one city could do. There was a housing crisis—the mayor identified that as a key issue when he ran for office. Housing was going to be a key issue in his success or failure. We decided that the way we were going to address the housing crisis was by the nonprofit sector, and the way we did that was primarily to dispose of the resources that way.

REDLINING

I played the major role in a two-year campaign to get the city's private banks to invest more in the city's low-income and minority neighborhoods. There is nothing in my job description that says this is what I am supposed to do. Part of what a progressive equity planner should be doing is looking for opportunities to get progressive ideas onto the public agenda. There was no game plan when Flynn took office that fighting a campaign around redlining was going to be an issue. The issue emerged in part because in my role as director of housing I identified redlining as an obstacle to our goals. We designate mostly non-profits for property that the city owns; we put linkage money into projects; and then we try to get the projects off the ground. Given the climate of patchwork financing that we have to use for housing, Boston has a pretty sophisticated network of groups and a lot of support in the business community. But what we were finding was that a lot of the nonprofit groups and some of the minority developers we had picked to build subsidized housing in the black and racially mixed neighborhoods were having a hard time getting financing from the banks.

This was not a public issue at the time. I had a number of meetings with developers who were talking about this problem. They said, there seems to be a pattern here, what is going on?

It seemed to me there was some potential to make this a public issue, particularly since the banks in Boston and around the country were beginning to consolidate; they were looking for approvals from the federal government; this was a good opportunity for organizing. There was a potential for a campaign to get the banks to invest in the city's neighborhoods, not just around more favorable treatment for construction loans for CDCs, but also to provide more home mortgages, open more branches, and do other things. In retrospect, I am probably putting more coherence on what my thoughts were than I really had. I talked to Steve Coyle about it, I talked to the mayor about it. Both of them said, try to be careful that this doesn't become a racially divisive issue but a way of bringing people together. It shouldn't be an issue that pits poor whites against poor blacks, saying that poor whites are getting loans and poor blacks aren't. The facts would speak for themselves, but politically it was important to try to improve housing and community conditions in black neighborhoods without looking like it was a zero-sum game. We wanted to expand the pie rather than divide it—which meant more overall loans, more overall investment.

So I started talking to people about doing a study. I figured it would have more impact if we went outside the city and hired an "expert" who would do a study and tell us whether or not there was systematic redlining, discrimination, disparities in terms of lending. I started talking to a number of researchers and settled on hiring Chuck Finn from the University of Minnesota. Lo and behold, I went to the BRA board and I asked them for permission to hire Chuck Finn to do a study, and the board, made up of holdovers appointed by Kevin White, said no. This shocked us all; we just thought it was a formality. Anyway, I went back to them about two weeks later. In between my first request to the board to hire Chuck Finn and my second request to the board, the *Boston Globe* got hold of a copy of a draft Federal Reserve Bank of Boston study, looking at disparities in lending. It showed racial patterns, disparities in mortgage lending. The *Globe* spread it all over the front page. It created a political atmosphere where the BRA board could no longer say no, especially when Mayor Flynn demanded that they do something. The mechanism by which that report showed up in the *Globe* will remain a mystery to the public, but I think the timing was good for our purposes.

The board hired Finn. We brought him to Boston, and two weeks later he met with bankers, with CDCs, with the black developers, with housing people, policy people. Hiring Finn was a very controversial act in itself. The banks immediately started attacking his credibility, his judgement, and his research capacity.

About a year later, in January 1990, an agreement was announced at a big press conference in the mayor's office. In between, there was a year-long struggle around Finn's study. (We actually didn't release it until December, but the fact that it was coming made the impact.) We knew that the banks were doing their own internal analyses and knew what Finn was going to find. We had announced that we were going to do what the federal study didn't do, a bank-by-bank study. We were going to name names. We were going to compare banks to one another. It was very controversial and started an uproar in the city. There were a couple of reporters on the daily and weekly papers whom we cultivated very carefully. When there was a logjam getting the banks to agree on a critical part of our comprehensive plan (such as below-market mortgages), that is when we released Finn's study, to sort of push the plan over the edge. We used the timing of releasing Finn's study as leverage to get a lot of things done.

The community groups in the city were not particularly poised to do an organizing campaign around this, and it was going to be very critical for this to be successful, for there to be outside pressure, protests, demonstrations, studies, community pressure on the banks, and the kind of direct action that I think was important. I called Lew Finfer, a veteran organizer who was very helpful. I said I think this is a hot issue, I think this is something we can organize around, I think it is something we can build community support for and help strengthen the organization. I think it can be something that bridges racial neighborhoods, and I think I can get some foundation money to support and organize the campaign around this issue. Lew took the ball and ran with it. Lew contacted some of the CDCs and some of the black neighborhood organizations and other groups and put together a coalition that eventually called itself the Community Investment Coalition (CIC). There were internal tensions over race, over strategy. The Massachusetts CDC Association refused to join the CIC as a collective body. But two CDCs—the more activist progressive ones—joined the CIC.

During the next year, parallel organizing campaigns would be going on. The mayor, myself, and the city treasurer, meeting with the banks and community groups, putting together our own plan. We didn't want to beat up on the banks, we wanted to have a plan they could adopt, a community investment plan. We called for a plan that came to $1 billion. We went beyond what the data were going to show, which was that minority neighborhoods were not getting mortgages. We wanted more ATMs, more branches, more construction loans, more support of the CDCs, loans to more small business owners, more black and Hispanic people hired at the banks. There were all kinds of forums that the Federal Reserve Bank and the Massachusetts Bankers Association put on to try to demonstrate their good faith. There were all kinds of ways in which this became a major public issue. The press played a very important role, and we used the press strategically to get our issues out.

The community groups were doing their own thing, but Lew and I were on the phone several times a day during this whole campaign. The CIC had a Harvard Law School student to do its own report, and Becky Stevens, my assistant, was basically assigned not only to work with me on their city's report but also to work with the CIC on their report. So the fact that the mayor's report and the CIC report were similar (except the CIC asked for twice as much as what we were asking for) was no accident.

I had hoped that during the spring, summer, and fall of 1989 the community groups would be engaging in more direct-action organizing. Who am I to say who should get arrested, but I hoped that there would be some direct protest to keep the heat on the banks. The only group that had the troops to engage in anything like that was the Hotel Workers' union. They helped organize some actions on banks. They even threatened a lawsuit. They had a press conference and said they were going to sue the banks for racial discrimination; they eventually decided not to do that, but the threat put pressure on the banks and kept the issue in the news. So a whole series of events, public events, kept the issue on the front burner in Boston, sort of a lead issue, for the entire year of 1989, and even made it a national issue. A few articles showed up in the *New York Times* and national banking industry publications.

The more we could embarrass the Boston banking community, the more we could pressure them, the more we could have a kind of good cop–bad cop relationship with the banks. Within the city administration, Coyle and I were the bad cops. We would meet with the banks, threaten them, and tell them how we were going to sue them, embarrass them, and so on. Coyle was such an unpredictable person in the public eye that the banks were worried about him, and they knew that I was the radical behind the scenes.

Within the administration there were people who wanted to be easier on the banks, not because of our bond rating or any political clout by the banks, but because they (the city officials) had a different style than I did. What always impressed me about Mayor Flynn was that whenever there seemed to be an internal difference of opinion within the administration over how to analyze a situation, how to move forward (between those who wanted to be more confrontational with the banks and those who wanted to be more cooperative with the banks), the mayor always took the side of the more activist group.

In a nutshell, in January 1990, at a press conference in city hall, the mayor, with the CEOs of the city's major banks, black ministers, and community leaders and organizers, announced a $400 million neighborhood lending plan. For a few years, my job had been (in part) pushing the banks to do it and getting the community to agree to do it. The community coalition was very fragmented and there was, as always in these situations, a turf battle about who would claim credit for getting the banks to do this. But the bottom line is, we won a major victory that got the banks much more involved in Boston's inner city.

Inclusionary Zoning   Boston had an extremely hot housing market, and during the first two or three years of the Flynn administration, developers were knocking down our doors at BRA, which is responsible for approval of all housing development. Any private developer who wants to get a zoning relief, to get their approval, has to come before the BRA. It was pretty clear to me, very early on, that the market for private housing was going to swamp the number of subdized units we could put on line—for every one or two subsidized units we could put on public land, with public subsidies, there were going to be two or three units of market-rate housing. At the same time, condo conversions were going on, removing affordable apartments. The private market was going to overwhelm our ability to keep things in balance.

Every developer who came to BRA had to meet with a team of neighborhood planners, architects, and me. With the staff, I would look at the financing to make sure it was a viable project. The architects would often change the design, and the planners would make sure of parking requirements and the like. We'd also organize neighborhood meetings to bring each project for community review; it was not just a rubber stamp, but a real grassroots planning process. Then it had to go to the Zoning Board of Appeals for a variance because the zoning code was so out of date it hadn't been changed in twenty-five years. Everybody knew the variance depended on BRA because of the enormous powers delegated to it. It was the planning agency, the development agency, and the agency that makes recommendations (to the Zoning Board of Appeals) on zoning. It had a lot of power, and until Flynn's administration, it hadn't been exercised around affordable housing.

Around 1986, after we had gotten our act together on condo conversion, rent control, linkage, and nonprofit development, I began meeting with some private developers and telling them that the city would not approve their project unless it included some affordable housing. In essence, this meant a kind of linkage policy on residential projects, even though there was no formal linkage requirement on housing. That meant internal linkage, using profits from market-rate units to subsidize low- and moderate-rate units within the development—or pay a linkage fee so that we could do it off-site. Most housing developers, when they went through the community review process in the neighborhood, part of the Flynn administration's community review and planning process, were asked by the neighborhood groups to fix up a park or to some other public amenity, separate from and not required by the zoning code. So there already were additional negotiations over public goods, beyond what was required by the standard financial, design, and zoning requirements.

I negotiated with about eight or nine developers in early 1987 for what we called "voluntary" inclusionary housing. One of them put up a big fight, but eventually he backed off. All the others agreed to it. All but one agreed to do it on-site. One wanted to cash his way out of it, and we made him pay a penalty. We took his potential loss on the sales and doubled it. It was all seat-of-the-pants in terms of what we thought we could get away with legally. Financially we knew it could be done—we carefully scrutinized their development budgets and projections and we knew the market as well as, if not better than, the developers.

There were two problems. First, we had no legal authority. The city did have legal authority to say that under the zoning code you have to have certain designs, you have to provide certain parking. But there was no *affordability* requirement in the zoning code. But there was this incredible speculative psychology in Boston. Developers believed that housing prices would continue to go up 10, 20, 25, 30 percent within a year. In that psychological marketplace, I didn't get a lot of resistance from developers. They knew they could make a fortune and still build affordable housing as part of their mostly market-rate projects.

Another problem involved a couple of cases where developments were in neighborhoods where the local residents or community organizations didn't want affordable housing. They associated it with either poor people or people of color. Unlike city-owned property, which was primarily in areas of color, inclusionary zoning projects (market-rate housing developments) were primarily in white middle-class and upper-middle-class neighborhoods—the north end, the wealthier sections of Dorchester, the wealthier sections of Jamaica Plain, and downtown. So, having successfully done eight or nine inclusionary housing projects, and having the developers—with a little bit of arm twisting—say good things about their good deeds in public, especially to the newspapers, there was a public record that this was a good thing to do even for the development community. So I proposed to the mayor and Coyle that we legalize this through the zoning code. That was in 1987. I got some lawyers to draft the bill; I had our financial people do the financial work. I drafted a letter of support for the mayor of how important this was; he was behind it 100 percent. We got a couple of press stories about the new policy proposal.

The Greater Boston Real Estate board said that it was illegal and that they would sue the city. But I got several developers to come before the BRA's board and say they were in favor of it. By having private developers who had actually done it and said this was good, we undercut the Greater Boston Real Estate Board's argument that it wasn't financially feasible. I had two of my staff people working full-time for several weeks, getting people to come to this hearing, generating letters of support—so it was overwhelming in favor. We got Governor Dukakis's housing secretary to come to the hearings to support us. We had all the nonprofit groups. The Greater Boston Building Trades Union came and testified in favor. A lot of it was political work, as well as doing the planning and technical work. The BRA board held a public hearing in March 1987, and we were all prepared to go forward.

It then went to the zoning commission. They have to hold a public hearing and then wait a month. So it was going to be another few months before the deal could be formally in place. I thought it would be good to legalize it so that we didn't have to negotiate case by case. The law would be clear. More important, once in the law, the zoning would change the appraised value of property and would lower the acquisition prices so that developers, in buying and selling land, would have to calculate that one-tenth of their units had to be affordable, low and moderate income. They could no longer say that they didn't know this was coming, that this was "extortion," and that it would make their project financially unfeasible.

To make a long story short, the U.S. Supreme Court made the *Nolan* decision a few months later. It was a California zoning case, and the Court ruled that you couldn't use zoning for "social" purposes without compensation. We all thought that linkage and other things would go out the window. I talked to a number of real estate attorneys in the city who were liberal and sympathetic, and I talked to the city's lawyers, and they all agreed that it was not a good time to move forward because as soon as we passed the law, the Greater Boston Real Estate Board would sue—and could win. So we continued to negotiate deals on a case-by-case basis. Within a year or so, the housing market started to slip, and it seemed like the climate was no longer a good one. So we never did it officially. But it continues to be the informal policy of the city to do this. In the last year and a half, however, there have been only a few market-rate housing projects coming through the city. Almost all the housing we're doing in mid-1992 is subsidized.

FURTHER READING: Community-Based Housing

Bratt, Rachel G. *Rebuilding a Low-Income Housing Policy.* Philadelphia: Temple University Press, 1989.

Dreier, Peter. "Redlining Cities: How Banks Color Community Development." *Challenge* 34, no. 6 (1991): 15–23.

———. "Can We Save America's Cities?" *North Carolina Law Review* 71, no. 5 (1993).

Dreier, Peter, and John Atlas. "Housing and Urban Development." In *Changing America: Blueprints for the New Administration,* edited by Mark Lenean. New York: Newmarket Press, 1992.

Dreier, Peter, and Bruce Erlich. "Downtown Development and Urban Reform: The Politics of Boston's Linkage Policy." *Urban Affairs Quarterly* 26, no. 3 (1991): 354–375.

Dreier, Peter, and W. Dennis Keating. "The Limits of Localism: Progressive Housing Policies in Boston, 1984–1989." *Urban Affairs Quarterly* 26, no. 2 (1990): 191–216.

Frank, James E., and Robert M. Rhodes. *Development Exactions.* Chicago: APA Planners Press, 1987.

Goetz, Edward G. "Office–Housing Linkage in San Francisco." *Journal of the American Planning Association* 55, no. 1 (1989): 66–77.

———. "Promoting Low Income Housing through Innovations in Land Use Regulation." *Journal of Urban Affairs* 13, no. 3 (1991): 337–351.

Keating, W. Dennis. "Linking Downtown Development to Broader Community Goals: An Analysis of Linkage Policies in Three Cities." *Journal of the American Planning Association* 50 (1986): 133–141.

Tornadijo, Raimundo Herrero. "Housing Linkage: Will It Play a Role in the 1990s?" *Journal of Urban Affairs* 13, no. 1 (1991): 1–19.

chapter 7

DENVER

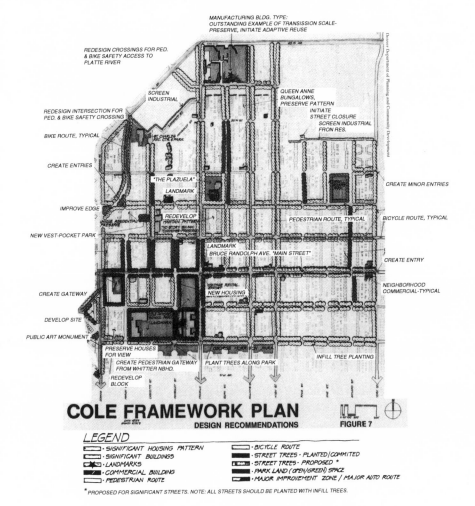

MANUFACTURING BLDG. TYPE:
OUTSTANDING EXAMPLE OF TRANSISSION SCALE-
PRESERVE, INITIATE ADAPTIVE REUSE

REDESIGN CROSSINGS FOR PED.
& BIKE SAFETY ACCESS TO
PLATTE RIVER

SCREEN
INDUSTRIAL

QUEEN ANNE
BUNGALOWS,
PRESERVE PATTERN
INITIATE
STREET CLOSURE
SCREEN INDUSTRIAL
FRON RES.

REDESIGN INTERSECTION FOR
PED. & BIKE SAFETY CROSSING

BIKE ROUTE, TYPICAL

CREATE ENTRIES

CREATE MINOR ENTRIES

"THE PLAZUELA"
LANDMARK

IMPROVE EDGE

REDEVELOP
HARIAN PATTERN
TWO STORY BLK MAX

PEDESTRIAN ROUTE, TYPICAL

BICYCLE ROUTE, TYPICAL

NEW VEST-POCKET PARK

LANDMARK
BRUCE RANDOLPH AVE. "MAIN STREET"

CREATE ENTRY

NEIGHBORHOOD
COMMERCIAL-TYPICAL

CREATE GATEWAY

NEW HOUSING

DEVELOP SITE

PUBLIC ART MONUMENT

PRESERVE HOUSES
FOR VIEW

CREATE PEDESTRIAN GATEWAY
FROM WHITTIER NBHD.

PLANT TREES ALONG PARK

INFILL TREE PLANTING

REDEVELOP
BLOCK

COLE FRAMEWORK PLAN
DESIGN RECOMMENDATIONS
FIGURE 7

LEGEND
- SIGNIFICANT HOUSING PATTERN
- SIGNIFICANT BUILDINGS
- LANDMARKS
- COMMERCIAL BUILDING
- PEDESTRIAN ROUTE
- BICYCLE ROUTE
- STREET TREES · PLANTED/COMMITED
- STREET TREES · PROPOSED *
- PARK LAND (OPEN/GREEN) SPACE
- MAJOR IMPROVEMENT ZONE / MAJOR AUTO ROUTE

* PROPOSED FOR SIGNIFICANT STREETS. NOTE: ALL STREETS SHOULD BE PLANTED WITH INFILL TREES.

Plans to revise Denver's Cole neighborhood originated with the city planning office, which then convinced the community to take the lead. Source: Cole Neighborhood Revitalization Demonstration Program, Status - 1991, Planning and Community Development Office, City and County of Denver.

SNAPSHOT, 1984

Population Composition for Denver, Colorado, 1970–1990			
Demographic	1970	1980	1990
Population	514,678	492,365	467,610
White	458,187	375,628	337,198
Black	47,011	59,095	60,046
Median family income	$9,654	$19,527	$32,038
Percentage poverty	9.4	10.3	17.1

D enver is often thought of as a sunbelt boom town, with powerful and growing markets in real estate and mineral investment and a constantly growing
population that is well trained, of higher than average income, and devoted to
a western lifestyle. Yet, traditional urban problems are not alien to the city.
Denver has major traffic and air pollution problems; at times, its air quality is
the worst in the nation; and regional growth since 1970 has taken place mostly
outside the central city.

The boom of the 1970s was spurred on by the 1973 oil embargo and the
subsequent interest in oil shale development. By 1980, ten massive projects
were planned, and between 1972 and 1983 the value of total mineral production increased from $400 million to more than $2.5 billion. During the same
period, fifty new office buildings shot up, and more than $2 billion was in-
vested in skyscraper development. The Denver metropolitan area's growth rate
from 1970 to 1978 was second to Houston's in the United States. Coping with
the side effects of unrestrained growth seemed the city's greatest problem.

But the boom was short-lived. The national recession of the early 1980s and
falling oil prices produced disinvestment rather than growth. By 1984, Denver had the highest downtown office vacancy rate in the nation: 28 percent.
Between 1986 and 1988, the Denver region lost 29,000 jobs, and for the first
time in two decades, more people moved out than moved in. The city also had
a disproportionate percentage of minorities and families with relatively low
incomes. By 1980, Hispanics made up more than 18 percent of the population
and blacks 12 percent; their educational attainment, occupational status, and
incomes were substantially lower than those of white families.

During the 1970s, Denver's political leadership emphasized growth. Under Mayor William H. McNichols, who took office in 1968, Denver encouraged downtown development via the $1 billion Skyline Project of the Denver Urban Renewal Authority. McNichols maintained a low-tax, caretaker kind of government. In the early 1980s, however, with the boom at an end, his administration was rocked by a series of minor scandals. In 1983, Mayor McNichols was replaced by thirty-six-year-old Federico Peña. Peña's election marked the first time a Hispanic mayor had been elected in a major city without a Hispanic majority.

Peña promised to open city hall to neighborhood groups, minorities, and others who had long felt shut out of city government. He also stressed the need for long-term planning. In his campaign, Peña had criticized McNichols for cutting the city planning staff and all but eliminating neighborhood planning. While asserting support for growth, the new mayor also called for planning the growth so that Denver would not become another Houston or Los Angeles. His winning coalition needed (and got) heavy support from the minority-populated districts west and north of the city. At the same time, the coalition was broad based, including thousands of liberal Denverites who had provided electoral support for Representative Patricia Schroeder and Senator Gary Hart.

As for the neighborhoods, Peña pledged that they would "have a partner rather than an adversary" in the mayor's office. To facilitate the pledge, the new mayor began a series of town meetings in each council district. He also increased the size of the neighborhood planning staff, bringing in, among others, Billie Bramhall, who had years of experience as a neighborhood advocate and neighborhood planner in Baltimore and Pittsburgh. Bramhall had worked in some of Pittsburgh's most troubled neighborhoods, helping to organize citizen representation, identifying key neighborhood projects and programs and including them in Pittsburgh's ongoing budgetary process. She believed deeply that grassroots, or "bottom–up," development would make more difference to the livability of a city over the long term than any amount of top–down development centered on downtown.

At the same time as he expanded his neighborhood initiatives, Peña made a number of new economic development proposals, mostly focused on downtown Denver. As the mayor said: "Unless the city's revenue base is substantially enhanced, further reductions in service delivery . . . will be required. . . . This is the single most compelling reason for the city to undertake a strong economic development program."

The Peña platform is one that more and more mayors seem to be adopting: focus mostly on downtown, arguing the overriding need for economic development, but also talk a strong neighborhood game and provide support as available for neighborhood planning and programs. As a result, the most imposing symbols of the Peña administration will probably relate to his economic development program. They include a new convention center, a refurbished 16th Street Mall, a downtown plan directed by the Denver Partnership (a downtown business organization), a million-square-foot new shopping mall in the Cherry Creek neighborhood close to downtown, and a new airport to replace Stapleton. But his neighborhood planning and development program merits praise as well.

This chapter is an account of how Billie Bramhall went about translating her beliefs in citizen participation and neighborhood planning and development into the day-to-day work program of her agency, the Denver Planning Department.

INTERVIEW WITH BILLIE BRAMHALL

I grew up in the South Bronx when it was a low-income but stable and rather loving community. I married a professor's son who went on to become a college professor in economics. He got his Ph.D. at the University of Pennsylvania in Philadelphia in the 1950s. I ran into a lot of people there who were city planning students and city planners. It was a very exciting time in planning. Philadelphia's renaissance was taking place; there was the urban renewal of Society Hill, a pre–Revolutionary War restoration project, and the Penn Center project, a commercial development in center city. I began to take a planning course or two.

Several things drew me to equity planning. The first was that I found myself less interested in such projects as Society Hill and Penn Center than I was in Eastwick, a primarily white but racially integrated lower-income, close-knit neighborhood destroyed by urban renewal and the building of the Philadelphia airport. I began to write term papers on things like that and on black removal, which was taking place in a number of the urban renewal areas in more central Philadelphia. I remember one of my papers had a line that struck Professor Bill Wheaton as very touching, "Where does a chicken plucker go?" I asked because there was a small businessman who was a chicken plucker, and he couldn't exactly move out to the suburbs. I thought that you could stabilize a community and still use vacant land and take advantage of development opportunities—a kind of you-can-have-your-cake-and-eat-it-too approach. I guess I've been trying to convince mayors and councilpeople of that possibility for thirty-five years now.

The second influence on me was the faculty at Penn. The university just happened to have the most wonderful and talented planners—they're old-timers now, I suppose, but at that time they were among the most progressive thinkers in planning in the country. Paul Davidoff, the "father" of advocacy planning, was there, as were housing expert Chester Rapkin, and the great urbanologist Lewis Mumford, whom I had the pleasure of hearing debate the subject of the city versus rural areas. I didn't agree with all of my teachers, but they were all stimulating, and ideas were flowing. I became friends for life with many of them.

When my husband took a teaching assignment at Johns Hopkins University, we moved to Baltimore. By that time, I was hooked on planning. I thought that it was a career in which I could use my interest in technical, statistical, and economic issues. (I had been an economics major with a political science minor at Colorado University. I now have a master's in urban and regional planning, but that degree came a little later.) My first job was with Morton Hoffman and Company. Hoffman's an old-time market analyst and private consultant. I did field work for him that included the most exciting and interesting jobs: the economic study of the Inner Harbor development, which didn't come to pass for some time, and some major downtown housing studies for Washington, D.C. I worked part-time for him for a number of years and did part-time work for the city of Baltimore while my children were young. I also taught urban studies and introduction to planning at the Johns Hopkins' night school. Those were the early years of the Department of Housing and Urban Development (HUD), so the Baltimore–Washington area was a vital place to be.

Housing integration and school integration were major issues in Baltimore. I did some analyses of Baltimore's urban renewal and found it had followed the same pattern as Philadelphia's. Baltimore did some creative things downtown—the Charles Center, for one—and it did some expansion activities for the Johns Hopkins Medical School, but the planners were really ruthless in removing black families without adequate compensation. There were no relocation benefits. I was struck with the lack of equity in the urban renewal program. I participated in a little liberal planning group called the Planners for Equal Opportunities. From all these activities I drew some conclusions that I took with me to Pittsburgh and later to Denver. One was that planners tended to be fairly liberal and were writing comprehensive plans that addressed equity issues as well as urban design, but that these plans were being put on a shelf and ignored in the cities that I was learning about by the people who were doing the work—the urban renewal authorities. This was a period of great concern about the future of downtowns, which I don't negate. I think about it as a period in urban history in which the neighborhoods themselves and the residents of neighborhoods were not even aware of what was being done to them. There was not a consciousness. It was not that residents were organizing and trying to make cities a better place and nobody was paying attention to them. They weren't even organizing. They were invisible, and the visible issue was how to keep downtowns viable. At the time, there wasn't any win–win or equity approach.

THE PITTSBURGH YEARS

This pattern held true in Pittsburgh, where in 1968 I went to the Graduate School of Public and International Affairs of the University of Pittsburgh. Graduate school was exciting at that time because two-thirds of the students came from either the civil rights movement or the Peace Corp or VISTA, and there was a large minority group. It's very hard in Denver today to find a minority person in planning school whom you can nurture and then hire. Two-thirds of my class must have been minority students (I'm guessing), but it was a very exciting student body that was asking new questions.

After graduate school, in 1970 I went to work for the Pittsburgh planning department, and I found that while downtown was growing and improving, Pittsburgh's neighborhoods were decaying. But because of the city's poverty program and the civil rights movement, we were beginning to get some stirrings within the neighborhoods, particularly the low-income minority neighborhoods. People were beginning to say, "What can the city do for us? Why have we been left out of things?"

I pushed for a neighborhood planning program that would give the neighborhoods, particularly low-income neighborhoods, an opportunity to be part of the process that allocated public resources in Pittsburgh. Luckily, the new mayor, Pete Flaherty, and his new planning director, Bob Paternoster, were supportive of this approach.

The first tool we used was the six-year capital improvement program. We initiated a public process in which we went into neighborhoods, rich and poor, and asked, "What are your top priorities for capital improvements in the next six years?" Our neighborhood planners were sent out to work with residents of the poor neighborhoods, helping them to get ready for the hearings and know what to ask for. For example, Pittsburgh had some hard-core old housing projects, built in the worst sections of town at too great a density. The city had never done anything for those housing projects. We put in playgrounds, swimming pools, basketball courts, and recreation centers. We identified the housing projects as the poorest, most disenfranchised neighborhoods in the city, and we worked with the residents to identify capital improvements that would help them. By the way, they still have the capital improvement hearings to this day; they have been institutionalized.

The second tool we had was a sympathetic building department that was willing to take a hard look at development proposals from the point of view of impacts on adjacent neighborhoods. The third thing was that, for a short period of time, we took over urban renewal, that is, took over operations from the Urban Renewal Authority (URA). Essentially, the planning department called the shots. For the first time, URA began to develop small urban renewal projects in lower-income neighborhoods that concentrated on rehabilitation instead of bulldozing. We concentrated on small-scale development that would provide employment.

NEIGHBORHOOD PLANNING IN DENVER

In 1975 my husband and I moved to Denver, Colorado. This was Dave's home state, and he wanted to teach at the University of Colorado, where he had gotten his bachelor's and master's degrees. I applied for a fairly high-level job in the planning office, just beneath that of deputy director, director of small-area planning for the city of Denver. I got the job in May 1975, at the time there was a lot of stirring in the neighborhoods. The administration recognized that it was going to have to do something in the way of neighborhood planning that was meaningful. Mayor William McNichols, like most old-time Democratic mayors, knew that when you had to do something, you had to do it, but it was better if someone else did it.

I came in and found a small neighborhood planning program. I was given permission to hire three or four new neighborhood planners. The young planners who go into neighborhood planning are really very special. They're bright and they're committed. They tend to be flexible. They tend to be technically good. I hired four people who have all gone on to bigger and better things in planning. We have a wonderful crew now, too—competent and capable people who are willing to put in untold hours and take a lot of crap from everybody because you can never do enough to solve the problems of the neighborhoods, given the limited resources of the city.

I spent about five years as head of small-area planning and as the chief planner for the city's community development agency. Then I spent three years with the Piton Foundation, which is sort of a mini Ford Foundation. I was Piton's community development program officer. Then I did three years of private consulting. My fourth job was the one I have just left. As deputy director of planning for the city of Denver, I was responsible for both neighborhood planning and community development. By receiving the double appointment I was given a powerful tool for implementing neighborhood plans, the Community Development Block Grant funding that came into the city each year from HUD. I reported to the director of planning and to Mayor Federico Peña directly. I was an appointee of Peña's.

I guess the term now for what I tried to do is *empowerment*. You're probably familiar with John McKnight? He's at the Center for Urban Affairs and Policy Research at Northwestern University. We were doing empowerment for years, but now he's written about it. It's gratifying that someone is finally recognizing the empowerment of the unempowered through city hall, as I think of it. To give you another slogan, empowerment was providing "equity of access" to public resources. I guess Paul Davidoff talked about it years ago when he spoke about raising the unempowered to the level of the middle and upper classes by giving them planners and lawyers and others to act as advocate for them.

As in Pittsburgh, I tried to give high status to neighborhood planning, to institutionalize it, to make the neighborhood plans part of the comprehensive plan. Put another way, we had the comprehensive plan specifically recognize the status of neighborhood planning. Denver's 1990 comprehensive plan contains four goals, which we call "Core Goals." Core Goal 3 is: "Protect, enhance and integrate a city of neighborhoods." That means that Denver must provide equal opportunities to all its citizens to share in its livability, whether it be ensuring adequate housing, excellent education, mobility, public health, or recreation. Denver must be a city that cares and shares with compassion and equity. We gave particular priority to ensuring educational excellence because we believed that education was the cornerstone of city spirit and at the heart of its capacity to progress. Unfortunately, the city administration has little control over the Board of Education.

When I began working for Peña, his planners had almost completed writing the comprehensive plan. But as my first task I was asked by Planning Director Bill Lamont to review the chapter in the plan on Denver's neighborhoods and make sure that it adequately reflected the direction that he and I and the mayor wanted to go. He also asked me to review the entire comprehensive plan and inject the issue of neighborhoods and equity wherever it seemed appropriate.

In the comprehensive plan we divided the neighborhoods into three types: stable neighborhoods, developing neighborhoods, and "opportunity neighborhoods," which is a euphemism for low-income, deteriorating ones. Denver concentrates its neighborhood planning in the opportunity neighborhoods, although we also draw plans in developing neighborhoods where a major new development is going to have an impact on the residential areas. Most of our stable neighborhoods don't have land for new development. Of the twenty or so neighborhood plans that have been completed since I was in charge the second time around (which are the plans that I feel are most reflective of how I would like neighborhood planning to take place and what I want it to be), only one or two are not focused on low-income, deteriorating neighborhoods. That's important to note because the middle-class neighborhoods in Denver are extremely well organized and powerful. In every neighborhood in which we have worked, if the residents haven't started out that way, they have ended up being very well organized and powerful.

THE NEIGHBORHOOD VISION

Instead of becoming a typical mini-comprehensive plan, the neighborhood plans became the vision of the neighborhoods. We started out by going into a neighborhood and getting everybody together. We never did neighborhood organizing per se because there was always somebody in the neighborhood to do that once the residents realized that could really have an impact. But we would organize meetings and try to bring to the meetings representatives of all racial groups and geographic areas, as well as renters, homeowners, businesspeople, developers, and neighborhood institutions such as churches and schools. Sometimes, in order to get people to come in large numbers, we'd have to say: "Come and hear what the city's planning to do to your neighborhood." Boy, then they'd come out!

Then when they got there, we'd say that we weren't really planning to do anything except talk about a neighborhood plan. The response was, "Oh, great."

The first thing we'd ask them to work on was a vision. "What would you like your neighborhood to be in five years? It's not going to be Cherry Hills, which is Denver's upper-income suburb, but given what you're starting with, what's your vision? What do you want?" We would spend quite a bit of time envisioning. We would bring pads and magic markers. A number of people from the planning department and even from other city agencies would come out and help us, so we weren't alone out there. The mayor told them to assist us, so we always had a traffic engineer and a parks and recreation person at the meetings, or somebody from storm sewers, if the problem was drainage.

We would start with envisioning and then we would ask, "What do you like about the neighborhood and what are its problems?" By the end of the first meeting, we would have accomplished four things. We would have the residents' vision for the future and a sense of the neighborhood's strengths and weaknesses. The third thing we would do would be to describe the process of working on a neighborhood plan in order to get their commitment to the planning effort. Finally, we established a hard-working representative neighborhood steering committee.

They'd see that the same neighborhood planner who was going to help them prepare the plan would be assigned to work on implementing it for the next five years. Each neighborhood planner—we had about six—worked on one or two neighborhood plans simultaneously, as well as on the implementation of three or four others. That was their job load, but they got a lot of help from the zoning administrator, the traffic engineer, and staff of other city agencies.

We encountered very little opposition. Denver has two councilpeople elected at large and eleven elected by districts. Even the district people liked our approach. They understood that they were not going to get everything they wanted, but they respected the process and participated in it. They got a lot of the credit. Once we got all the neighborhood's recommendations, then each year the plan's steering committee established its five priority goals. They'd say this is what we want to get in the capital improvement budget more than anything else; this is what we want from city services, and so on.

In the normal course of working on a neighborhood plan, the neighborhood planner would organize three or four major meetings during the first year to report back to the entire neighborhood on what the steering committee was doing and to get further insights. The planning process ended with a document that focused on those issues that were of greatest concern to the neighborhood. For example, if there were no problems with zoning, then we didn't deal with zoning.

We never had to deal with the kinds of triage issues that Pittsburgh and Baltimore dealt with. We never got to the point of actually saying that some of our neighborhoods are so bad there isn't much point in investing capital improvement money in them.

The neighborhood plans were then approved by the planning board and adopted by the city council as amendments to Denver's comprehensive plan with public hearings, fanfare, and celebrations.

THE COLE NEIGHBORHOOD

The oil bust hit Denver, so in 1988 HUD foreclosures began. Before we knew it, we had 2,200 vacant HUD units within the city. We had never before had a vacant-housing problem. These were single-family, owner-occupied houses that were foreclosed when people lost their jobs and couldn't pay their mortgages. For example, we woke up one morning and realized that several hundred houses in Denver's Cole neighborhood were vacant and boarded up. The foreclosures happened over a six-month period. Even though we had a neighborhood planner out there, her attention was focused on the business strip at the time. When we realized the dimensions of the problem, we immediately began looking for funds. We asked the mayor and the city councilperson: "Do you want to save this neighborhood? Because if you do, it's going to take extraordinary means. You can't fight this with just community development money and capital improvement money and neighborhood planning."

Cole was an unorganized neighborhood. In fact, it was a neighborhood that had had some bad experiences with neighborhood organizing. The residents were predominantly black with a fair number of Hispanics and a few Anglos. The neighborhood abutted an industrial area that was close to downtown but not close enough to experience a boom. It had historic houses, but they were small; they had been built for working people, so they didn't have the pizazz that some other Victorian neighborhoods had. Cole had everything going against it, including a lot of disillusioned, poor residents.

We tried various approaches and finally chose to recommend that, over the course of three years, the city invest $1 million from the capital improvement budget in Cole. At the same time, we maintained our efforts in Cole on other capital improvements and on community development, which was already pretty high. In other words, we said let's really put some time and resources from every department in the city into saving this neighborhood, into reclaiming and stabilizing it. The goal was to bring private investment back. The million dollars would be used for housing and streetscaping programs, not for typical capital improvements such as parks and recreation, streets and sewers.

Are we just reinventing urban renewal? we asked ourselves. And we said, "Yes, in a way, but in a new way." We felt three things were essential to Cole's successful renewal in addition to financial resources. Money alone wouldn't do it. First, we recognized that we had to organize the residents and organize them in large numbers. Eventually the neighborhood had to take control of the program. To be sustainable the program had to go from being city driven. Here we were telling this neighborhood: "Your neighborhood is dying. We want to help you save it, but you have to take control." The neighborhood had to get organized so that it would become a neighborhood-driven program.

Two, the program had to be comprehensive; it couldn't just be bricks and mortar and the things that our staff feels most comfortable with, such as parks, streets, housing. We had to provide social services, job training, and public safety because gangs, graffiti, and everything that could go wrong was present in that neighborhood.

The third thing we recognized was that we did not have enough money to do the job ourselves. We had to bring in the foundations and corporate and lending communities. We asked them to make Cole one of their prime activities for a three-year period. We sold that agenda to them. Developing that partnership was what I worked on primarily for the past two and a half years. It was a very important program to me because our hope was that we might duplicate this partnership in some other neighborhoods.

It was an exciting, taxing, up-and-down project. But it's happening. While there's been virtually no new construction, substantial rehabilitation of the vacant houses is taking place. For example, we devised a homeownership program called Home Start. The residents wanted to keep Cole a single-family, owner-occupied neighborhood, so we found ways of helping their friends and relatives to relocate there. When we began, people weren't exactly lining up to move into the neighborhood; even the poor had better opportunities to buy a house than in this neighborhood.

The first thing we did was to organize the residents. They can now mobilize 200 people at the drop of a hat. But in the beginning it was just twelve of us screaming at one another in the basement of an alcohol abuse center. The few neighborhood people we could get to come out kept saying that they didn't trust the city. It was a nightmare, but our neighborhood planner, a white woman named Susan Foley, simply would not give up.

Susan and I got together twelve to twenty people—the neighborhood leaders with whom we had worked in the past, plus representatives of all the institutions in the neighborhood, such as the principals of the parochial and public schools and the church leaders. A few neighborhood organizations, such as a merchants' association, had survived the bad times and were also able to get involved. Then we asked this small group to develop a mission. I want to highlight the ending of their mission statement because it describes how we proceeded. It states: "Therefore, be it resolved that we the undersigned residents, businesspersons and service providers of Cole neighborhood join together as the Cole Coalition for the common purpose of creating a Cole neighborhood people's organization by the Fall of 1990 and establishing a partnership between the public sector, the investment community, service providers, the private non-profit foundation community, and the people of the Cole neighborhood." We twenty sat for six months and fought over the wording of this declaration.

After the mission statement was written, the city agreed to give the Cole Community Coalition $1 million a year (it turned out to be a little less than that). Then Central Bank of Denver said, "We'll give a $100,000 grant per year to this neighborhood for three years to match the city's million dollars." We gave the coalition a great deal of freedom to decide how the city's money was to be spent. It went primarily for housing, which was the priority the coalition set.

They also started a major tree-planting program and an alley program. They established an office with a staff of three people. Foundations are giving them money. It's moving.

BIG VERSUS SMALL PROJECTS

Mayor Peña's most visible legacy to the city is going to be the big projects: the biggest new international airport in the country, the convention center. During his administration, the upscale, million-square-foot Cherry Creek mall was built. The Central Platte Valley is going to be redeveloped, including a new ballpark for Denver's major league team. Yet he truly believed in the neighborhoods and in tending to the needs of lower- and moderate-income people. He mobilized city agencies to give quality services and a high level of capital improvements to the neighborhoods. He held city technicians accountable for these things. For example, during his administration we rewrote the zoning ordinances governing the location of industry to give greater protection to the neighborhoods.

The housing authority, with support from his administration, has put forth a scattered-site public housing plan that is now being implemented, although, perhaps surprisingly, the housing is not located predominantly in the so-called opportunity neighborhoods because we determined that they are generally overimpacted. In planning for the scattered-site public housing two or three years ago, our public housing authority did not act as sensitively and carefully as it should have. The plan broke in the press before there had been discussions about it in the city council. The planning department was called in to help facilitate the disagreement that arose between the city council and the neighborhoods. Bill Lamont and I and our housing planner helped organize a citizens' housing task force to which each councilperson appointed two representatives. The housing authority also appointed representatives from each of its housing developments. We got this group of twenty-eight people together and accompanied them through a complex process that produced an intergovernmental agreement between the planning office, the housing authority, and the city council. It was agreed that scattered-site low-income housing would go into *all* Denver's neighborhoods. The opposition to dispersed public housing came primarily from moderate- to lower-middle-income white people. With a Hispanic mayor and many minorities on the city council, those groups felt extremely alienated. I think our process was helpful in healing some wounds, which are important to heal.

Unfortunately, when Mayor Peña took office, relationships with the business community were not close. There was little connection between the two, and it hurt the vision and dreams he had for the city. Because of the oil bust, neither he nor the city council nor the planning department was able to put the kind of pressure on the business community to extract what has been extracted from business communities in other cities. We couldn't do linkages between new developments and disinvested neighborhoods because nothing was being built. That's why Peña got the airport and the convention center going. At least these large developments created some construction jobs and would, we hoped, lead to some long-term economic stability.

RETROSPECTIVE THOUGHTS

Despite our advocacy on behalf of Denver's neighborhoods, we never lost touch with the fact that we were technical planners working for city government, that we were professionals. I am absolutely convinced that with the right value system on the part of the city administration and the right kind of staff, any planning department in the country can have a high level of citizen participation, can do neighborhood planning, can do equity planning—without getting into tremendous, unsolvable adversarial situations. It is possible to make equity planning a win–win situation for developers, neighborhoods, and city governments.

The reasons more planning departments aren't involved in equity planning is that many planners are afraid of it. Publicly negotiating plans is a frightening experience to contemplate. People on all sides can become angry. Planners are not sure how to keep professional standards and respect budgeting limitations. Denver has done it successfully, however, as have many other cities. In fact, we've gotten excellent publicity for our programs. That's an accomplishment in itself because it isn't often regarded as news when a bunch of people get together to plan a neighborhood or plant a thousand trees. It's news if a group of people are spitting at each other over the construction of a road, with the developers saying, "We've got to have a 40-mph speed limit on this road and it's got to go through this neighborhood," and the neighborhood people saying, "Over our dead bodies." That's news.

I've been in this field for twenty-five years. I keep saying that if I ever lose my idealism, if I ever get totally cynical, I'm just going to leave the field. But, believe it or not, when we start a new neighborhood plan and a hundred people come out and they start envisioning their neighborhood, I still get excited.

FURTHER READING: Neighborhood Planning and Capital Budgeting

Clay, Phillip L., and Robert H. Hollister, eds. *Neighborhood Policy and Planning*. Lexington, Mass.: D.C. Heath, 1983.

Fasenfest, David, and Penelope Ciancanelli. "Public Costs, Private Benefits: The Pitfalls of Capital Budgeting for Reindustrialization." *Journal of Urban Affairs* 10, no. 3 (1988): 291–307.

Jones, Bernie. *Neighborhood Planning*. Chicago: APA Planners Press, 1990.

Mier, Robert, Kari Moe, and Irene Sherr. "Strategic Planning and the Pursuit of Reform, Economic Development, and Equity." *Journal of the American Planning Association* 52, no. 3 (1986): 299–309.

Morgan, David R., and William J. Pammer, Jr. "Coping with Fiscal Stress: Predicting the Use of Financial Management Practices among U.S. Cities." *Urban Affairs Quarterly* 24, no. 1 (1988): 69–86.

Nunn, Sam. "Budgeting for Public Capital: Reinterpreting Traditional Views of Urban Infrastructure Provision." *Journal of Urban Affairs* 12, no. 4 (1991): 327–344.

Pagano, Michael A. "Fiscal Disruptions and City Responses: Stability, Equilibrium, and City Capital Budgeting." *Urban Affairs Quarterly* 24, no. 1 (1989): 118–137.

Rohe, William M., and Lauren B. Gates. *Planning With Neighborhoods*. Chapel Hill: University of North Carolina Press, 1985.

Toulmin, Llewellyn. "Equity as a Decision Rule in Determining the Distribution of Urban Public Services." *Urban Affairs Quarterly* 23, no. 3 (1988): 389–413.

HARTFORD

SCALE IN FEET
0'   1000'   2000'

City neighborhoods with neighborhood organization boundaries, Hartford, Connecticut. From the Hartford Planning Department.

Snapshot, 1992

Population Composition for Hartford, Connecticut, 1970–1990			
Demographic	1970	1980	1990
Population	158,017	136,392	139,739
White	111,862	71,169	55,869
Black	44,091	46,131	54,338
Median family income	$9,108	$14,032	$24,774
Percentage poverty	12.6	22.5	27.5

Hartford, Connecticut, was founded in 1635 on the banks of the Connecticut River. Hartford was one of the first incorporated municipalities on the east coast. Both the Connecticut River and later the development of the railroad (originally built to link the emerging coridor between New York and Boston) helped Hartford establish regional prominence as a vital industrial and manufacturing hub in the 1880s. The first industries to emerge provided a wide array of goods including firearms, typewriters, bicycles, and, for a short while, automobiles. Insurance was also an important early industry.

Hartford is generally considered the only truly urban area in central Connecticut, although it is a very small city of only eighteen square miles. Located halfway between New York and Boston, this arrangement affords Hartford excellent locational advantages. The city enjoys the regional amenities of the urbanized Boston–Washington corridor, while not experiencing the extreme congestion, pollution, and sprawl of many of its northern and southern neighbors. This relationship has also allowed Hartford to maintain some of the most affordable housing on the east coast.

Manufacturing in Hartford has followed the same downward spiral as it has in most older American cities. But the situation is exacerbated in New England because of the regional disadvantages of high labor and energy costs. In the 1980s, for example, the average price of energy to the final user in New England was 40 percent higher than in the rest of the continental United States. Hartford has also been hard hit by the effects of suburbanization. This is largely due to the fact that Connecticut is a "home rule" state, and each of the

169 towns is independently run. There is little incentive for regional cooperation. Since New England cities do not have the option of annexation, the cities
themselves must investigate other avenues to expand a constantly dwindling
tax base.

A recent city document sums up Hartford's status in its greater metropolitan
region:

- Hartford is the major employment center of the metropolitan region,
  although this role is declining;
- Job growth is occurring faster in the suburbs than in the city;
- White collar office jobs (mostly in finance, insurance and real estate) are
  those most likely to be retained in the city;
- Hartford's function as a retail center has greatly diminished;
- A wide disparity in income (one of the widest in the U.S.) exists between the city and suburbs, and Hartford is home for the metropolitan
  region's poor.[1]

PEOPLE AND NEIGHBORHOODS

Throughout its history, Hartford has served as a port of entry for waves of
immigrants coming to this country. These have included not only the early
European immigrants who arrived by way of Ellis Island but also many minorities who migrated to the city, lured by a bustling economy.

The city flourished during its developmental years between 1890 and 1910.
During this period, Hartford saw its population expand from 53,000 to 99,000.
By and large, residents were employed in the city's established manufacturing
and retail sectors. Hartford continued to maintain a modest rate of growth until
the mid-1950s when the population reached its all-time peak of 177,000. The
past forty years have witnessed a gradual population decline, down to a 1990
level of 139,739. Racial and economic shifts have also been significant with
a recent study concluding that "nearly 70 percent of Hartford residents are
minority while only 8.3 percent of suburban residents are minorities."[2] The
large influx of minorities resulted mainly from workers in the tobacco fields of
the fertile Connecticut Valley.

Hartford has a mix of neighborhoods that have substantial political muscle,
define the city, and give it its character. The downtown neighborhood is the
core of the city, and a mix of traditional office, commercial, and retail uses
predominate. The city's primary industrial zones fall in the North Meadows and South Meadows districts. Secondary industrial zones are located in

the Parkville and Charter Oak–Zion neighborhoods. The remaining fourteen neighborhoods are primarily residential.

Neighborhoods located closest to the central business district have mixed land uses, with interspersed medium-density residential, office, and "strip-retail" development along the major arterials. These include the South Green, Sheldon-Charter, Oak, Asylum Hill, Clay Arsenal, and Frog Hollow neighborhoods.

The outer neighborhoods were the last to be settled and constitute some of the most desirable real estate in the city. These low-density, single- and two-family residential areas include the South End, South West, Charter Oak–Zion, Parkville, West End, and Blue Hills neighborhoods.

PROJECTS AND POLITICS

By the 1960s, Hartford had become polarized in its economics and demography. On one hand, the city was the state capital and contained the headquarters of six of the nation's largest insurance companies. On the other hand, the resident population was fast becoming an enclave of minority poor.

These changes produced reforms in the old, isolated power structure that had been led by the banking and insurance industries. The newer model of the 1950s was driven by relatively liberal business interests using the chamber of commerce and its talented executive director, Arthur Lumsden, as the vehicle for participation. Lumsden played an intermediary role between the corporations, increasingly active community organizations, and city government. According to Jack Dolard, an architect involved in several civic projects at the time:

> It seemed to me like there was the city over here, and over there, across a moat, there was a castle where the companies were. Every once in a while we in the city would need something, and it would be like shouting across the moat. The drawbridge would then come down, and Lumsden would come out. We would talk, and he would go back, and then after a while he would come back out with something.[3]

This coalition adopted three forms of public–private cooperation during the 1950s and 1960s. The first strategy was the use of urban renewal, which produced the city's first major urban renewal project—Constitution Plaza. Constitution Plaza was a classic downtown renewal project of the 1960s: a vast expanse of concrete and office towers that would ultimately house most of the commercial and insurance industries in Hartford's downtown while displacing hundreds of families and small businesses in the process. As a later city document noted:

> During the first five years of Hartford's Urban Renewal Program commitments were made to clear 190 acres of land in and immediately adjacent to the Downtown. . . . More than 1,200 households and 750 businesses were forced to relocate at a time when urban renewal programs did not provide adequate relocation assistance and had no means to build new housing for lower income citizens other than public housing.[4]

One reaction to urban renewal was community action that moved beyond physical planning and housing to education, community organizing, and social programs with a minority community that was increasingly restive. In 1962, at Lumsden's insistence, the city established the Community Renewal Team (CRT), with black representation from North Hartford. Gradually, the CRT approach became more prominent, and the organization of minority neighborhoods became a higher priority. Nevertheless, Hartford was to suffer a series of riots and acts of arson and violent confrontations in the summers from 1967 to 1970. Confrontations between minorities and police further transformed Hartford's approach to urban policy. Remedial programs became more urgent, as did neighborhood organizations, led in the 1960s by the South Arsenal Neighborhood Development Corporation (SAND). SAND and other neighborhood development corporations (NDCs) got support from city governments and the corporate community, which offered money and expertise. SAND and other NDCs also initiated elections on the neighborhood level, thus offering greater control to autonomous neighborhood coalitions as well as stimulating similar political efforts at a grassroots level. Long-neglected housing issues were pushed to the fore. The Sheldon Oak Co-op, Chapelle Gardens Co-op, and Martin Luther King housing developments sprang from this effort. Also, a sizable investment in the city's public education facilities was introduced in 1968 with a $44 million bond issue approved by city residents for the erection of two additional high schools, as well as two new middle schools.

But the major effort of the 1960s (and Lumsden's most ambitious effort at social engineering) was the Greater Hartford Process, a program to build new towns in Hartford's North End and in the suburbs. It was an attempt at a truly regional approach that projected a population of 20,000 to the new suburban community with profits from the venture earmarked to subsidize revitalization efforts in the city's North End. The approach was imaginative, but ultimately the Greater Hartford Process built neither the suburban nor the North End new towns. It fell victim to rising interest rates and shifts in the political climate of the Nixon administration.

During the 1970s, Hartford saw the continued growth and power of the neighborhood movement, which for a time was harnessed by City Councilman Nick Carbone and Assistant City Manager John Alschuler. Carbone, in particular, played a powerful role as advocate for Hartford's "have-nots" until his defeat for reelection in 1979.

Hartford followed the ebb and flow of the prevailing national economic trends of the 1970s, which, with the advent of the 1980s, saw a reversal of long-standing federal funding for urban areas under the Reagan administration. The Reagan era "new federalism" decreased the federal government's role in funding assistance for cities and emphasized greater local funding and control. The net effect of all this activity on Hartford was further decline. The city was forced to turn to other revenue sources, its private sector, state funding sources, and an already strapped tax base for the revenues needed to continue even the most basic services needed by an increasingly poor and isolated population.

Howard Stanback became city manager in 1992. He recognized that, historically, Hartford has never been especially strong in development planning, exemplified by a "here are our programs, here are our funds, you come and get it" approach to social equity programs. Stanback's strategic planning includes working on smoothing city–suburban disparities, enterprise zones for minority enterprises, strengthening linkage issues, and increasing the role of empowerment programs. The following interview is a frank discussion with him concerning his role as city manager, the challenges his office faces, and his ideas for implementing the strategies he sees as central for the development of the city in particular and the region in general.

INTERVIEW WITH HOWARD STANBACK

Prior to coming to the city manager's post in Hartford, I was doing air-port development consulting in Chicago for three years. I got into that as a result of having been commissioner of aviation under Eugene Sawyer when he was acting mayor. Before that, I had two roles in Harold Washington's administration, the last as deputy to the mayor for infrastructure. Rob Mier was director of development, I had infrastructure, and in that I had public works, streets and sanitation, water, sewer and aviation departments. The responsibilities largely involved budget planning, personnel, contracts, finance, and a general reorganization that we were trying to institute at that time. Earlier still, I was deputy director for employment and training, which is what I went to Chicago initially to do.

Before that, much of my adult life, at least fifteen years of it, was in academia. My first teaching job was at Atlanta University. Then I was at the University of Connecticut in the School of Social Work. I was associate dean. I received a doctorate in economics from the University of Massachusetts at Amherst. My specialties were in labor, history, and development. I got my master's degree from Case Western in Cleveland, in social administration. John Turner was the dean then, back in 1969. Just before going to Chicago, I taught at the New School for Social Research in the Graduate Faculty, Economics Department.

I was brought up in the North Carolina middle class. My father, at the age of seventy-five, still owns and operates a photography studio. It is a very small operation. At one time it was the largest black photography firm in the country. That was before the desegregation of the public schools. I was an undergraduate at Wake Forest and went to Salem. My roommate and I were the first two blacks to graduate from there in 1969.

I had been close to Hartford people before. When I did my doctoral work at Amherst, I lived there and taught at the School of Social Work, and my activism got me involved in a lot of political activity. The current mayor, Carrie Saxon Perry, became a close friend in the process. I did a lot of her issues work in her campaign for state legislature in 1980. Of two of the current city council-people, both women, one was a colleague of mine—actually I supervised her at the School of Social Work—and the other was a former student. There were a couple of other council members that I knew who were new to the council and had run on a progressive slate and won. They approached me, and with some twisting and pulling and gnashing of teeth I agreed to come back to the public sector. It's a challenge to try to turn a poor city around. I had turned down a few opportunities to do that because there was still a lot of pain and a lot of distress associated with the affairs of Harold Washington and the energy associated with that. I remarried three years ago. I have a fourteen-month-old daughter, and the idea of coming back and doing this was not necessarily the highest priority of mine. But because of who the people were and the opportunity I thought it presented, I would give it a shot, at least for a while, to see what I could help put in place.

STRATEGY FOR HARTFORD

To start in the most broad way, Hartford city government has never been in the forefront of development planning. It has always said, "Here are our programs, here are our funds, you all come and get it," and there were no efforts to apply social justice criteria, equity criteria. Goals were largely defined by the federal government in terms of what funds they made available. There was little definition from the state. There wasn't very much leadership in terms of setting forth either a vision or a comprehensive program in the city. That always came from the corporate sector, largely from the insurance companies.

This failure to think about priorities was one reason why for years there has been this strong inequality. Hartford is a poor city; it has one of the greatest income disparities between the suburbs and the city in the country. During the 1980s, some of that was ameliorated because there was such a tremendous real estate boom here, and the city was getting fat. That is, the fat were getting fatter and the leanest were getting little. But the government became even more fragmented, even more disassociated from any leadership role. Simultaneously with that, the insurance company leaders began to turn over the companies to more technocratic leadership, and that created a real vacuum for economic development vision. The city just moved from corporate leadership to no leadership. So a part of the problem is to get the city administration into a culture and a way of thinking so that they can in fact be leaders and set the tone for development programs.

That's not an easy task because we've got a series of departments that, while they are good technically, lack vision. One of the things I have done is to bring Rob Mier in to do some strategic planning work with the departments and look at things on a case-by-case basis: look at projects, look at programs, look at the vision and the way of thinking and how we can be creative about it. Making deals happen, but making them happen in a way that they have a critical social justice component.

There are one or two examples of how this is working. One is a black female engineer who owns a fiber optic company in the enterprise zone in Hartford. She came to the city looking for some operating capital, to the tune of about $300,000. Well, the only thing we have in the pot is the Community Development Block Grant funds. But $300,000 is too much to go to one company. We don't have that big an allocation. That is 10 percent of our total allocation. The furthest our staff could take it was to the banks. The woman was committed to doing local hiring, training, and so forth. That was the easy part of the deal. The hard part was finding the money. Rob sat down with the staff. I sat down with them, and we looked at the deals and said, "Hey, this is a venture capital deal." Our people really didn't understand venture capital. They said, well, the banks looked at it. Well, the banks are not venture capital. We have a local major citywide development corporation, and it is not venture capital. So we began to get them hooked up with some of the more socially conscious venture capital firms around New England. They began to look at how this woman can raise her funds. Part of this is really an exercise in vision, in creative thinking.

Another example is a firm that has been around here for years that does metal fabrication. The firm is heavily tied to the defense industry. The owners know that that is not going to last. They are looking for nondefense markets. Our staff members threw up their hands. They said we don't know what we can do to help you. We got them now talking to technology resources' global marketing group out of one of the business schools. They are looking into getting some state funds to retrain their staff because they are going to have to do some retooling. They made a commitment with us to make 50 percent of all new employees Hartford residents. We are looking for new facilities for them. Part of this was just a process that the staff had to engage in to help them recognize that a lot of the resources they needed were not inside city government and not necessarily in state government, but were in some of the universities and in the neighborhoods.

The University of Hartford ran this technologies resources' group for small businesses. All the businesses they were helping were in the Boston area. They weren't helping any businesses in the Hartford area. Some of us were just trying to find the resources and link them up.

Another area is corporate relations. I've been going around to all the major corporations and trying to establish a line of communication because it has not been there. Finding out what the companies' interests are, what our interests are. Trying to define some common interest, both in terms of neighborhood investment and large projects that the city may need, including job access.

Taxes   We have a relatively unique situation in Hartford in a sense that because this is the state capital, 40 percent of our land, our real property, is nontaxable. This winds up being a situation where 76 percent of our property taxes, which is all of our tax revenues except what we get from the state, falls on the major corporations. This does not exist in any other city in the state. It is actually the reverse. We have a very small residential property tax base, and to the extent that it is rental property, it is taxed at a rate that is roughly $2.50–$2.80 a square foot, whereas towns right over the line are charging only $.90 a square foot, so we are very uncompetitive.

I have been arguing—not arguing because they have agreed—with some of the chiefs of our corporations that one of our mutual interests is having a tax reform measure that generates either a commuter tax or increases the reimbursement on state property. We do get a 26 percent reimbursement on state property, but that needs to double, at least. So we can cooperatively engage in some revenue reform that can benefit not only the major corporations but also the average homeowner, the average taxpayer, the average resident in the city. This is probably an issue where we have as common an interest as I can imagine.

If we could levy a 1 percent earnings tax on suburban residents who work in Hartford, we could raise about $50 million a year. That might let us cut our property taxes and make investment in the city attractive. There are other areas of mutual interest. The insurance companies have a major capital stock investment, and they understand that in order to protect that they need to be more aggressive in investing in the neighborhoods and in the conditions of the people who live there. They are coming around to that, and we are engaging in dialogues on a number of issues to see how that can be done more creatively. So it is mostly a question of encouragement and negotiation.

There are also some linkage issues. We have a couple of major redevelopment areas where we have recruited businesses, and they are looking at linkage deals: some distribution companies, car dealerships, mail-order houses, a couple of back-office operations. There are linkage deals in all of them that have to do with local employment, and most of the employers have created a home mortgage assistance pool in their hiring agreements for employees to

purchase homes in Hartford. A couple of other linkage items have been negotiated, but the primary ones have been mortgage assistance, first-source hiring,
training, and, depending on the nature of the company, some neighborhood
investment activities.

City Investment in Neighborhoods We have just begun a targeted investment
strategy for neighborhoods in the city—something we worked on with Rob in
Chicago. We identified small, almost subneighborhoods, typically from nine
to fifteen blocks, where we work with the neighborhood people to identify
blighted housing units for redevelopment. We are trying to target the drug
houses, the chop shops, and other problem locations. We have expanded our
powers of acquisition and eminent domain and our power to attach landlords'
assets beyond that particular piece of property so that we can either attach or
seize. We have some rehab money and are using local community organizations
to do the rehabilitation. We are working on how to get the houses occupied in
a way that people feel accountable for the neighborhood. We encourage owner
residency. We have a mix of Section 8 and non–Section 8 rentals. We have combined that with community policing of satellite centers that we are going to be
putting in. We are creating one-stop social service shopping. We don't call it
that, but that is what it amounts to. The state has funded that. An example is
that we are merging the intake and case management from our job training and
social services departments and housing assistance so that people who come in
from those neighborhoods will not only get social services but can get access
to job training, housing in the neighborhood, day care, and other services they
need on the development side. We are tying those same individuals to these
hiring projects and giving them priority with some community redevelopment
areas, as well as small business assistance programs in those neighborhoods.

Our capital improvements are focused on neighborhoods. We do the capital
programs for the Board of Education, which gets the bulk of it right now because we're in a school revitalization period. Most of our capital spending for
the next five years is slated for neighborhood improvements, whether it's street
or sidewalks, public facilities in the neighborhoods, libraries, or property acquisition to turn over for development activity. Most of our general obligation
bonds are associated with that. We do have some revenue bonding capacity
through our redevelopment agency that we really have not used. We haven't had
to use it historically because we are able to get a lot of these projects paid for
through state bonds. But we do have some capacity, both GO and state bonds to
do additional projects that we are defining this year so that we get into the next

capital budget and next capital improvement program with some additional neighborhood focus reflected. A lot of the current capital budget was done before I got here, but it does have enough of a neighborhood orientation to it to be able to tap into it from some of these other projects.

REGIONAL ISSUES

I'm fairly cynical about our ability to achieve any short-term success in linking the suburbs to the problems in Hartford's inner city, although it must be tried. I'm cynical mainly because everybody was going on about it when I got here in 1974, was going on about it when I left in 1981, and is still going on about it. To the extent that we have to wait on regional solutions, I think we are making a mistake in terms of public housing and even in terms of our education, although there is a major court case that comes up in November about regionalization of education.

Ideally, I'd like to tear down some of the worst public housing in the city, such as Stowe Village, and rebuild 1,000 or so units in the suburbs so that low-income people could have a choice in location. Suburbs like Avon, Simsbury, and West Hartford should make more of a contribution to the city—should do their part. I know these ideas are not popular, but they are the right thing to do. But if a black professional like me is not willing to put them on the table, who will?[5]

We aren't pressing for a regional busing approach right away. Regional housing and access are really the first issues and then two-way busing would probably follow. It would cost us right now to bring our school systems up to capacity, and even up to code; it would cost us over $300 million. That's a major capital burden for a city of this size. While we are going ahead and pursuing it, it does dip into our other capital requirements fairly heavily. We need to do some regional education projects that, as long as they are two-way, everybody, at least from a city standpoint, should be satisfied. That is, we would bus some public school children out to the suburbs, and they would bus some public school children into the city.

Vouchers are an option. We would be terribly opposed to that under certain conditions. I think we might be willing to try the voucher system as opposed to the regionalization system. We do have a good magnet school system in the city; it is just not big enough. To the extent that we can use that as a way of starting to attract people to spend vouchers, some of our magnet schools are the best in the region. So I am not urging any one of those, whether it's a regional system or whether it's a magnet system or a voucher system or whether it is just a cross-district busing process. I am not particular, I just know that on schools and on affordable housing we need some regional solutions.

In the meantime, we have to create as positive an environment as possible in the city for low- and middle-income residents so that Hartford is affordable. Otherwise, with many of these programs, if we start getting access to jobs in the suburbs, which we do have to some degree, but if we get the transportation to them, our people are going to get the jobs and are going to leave. They are going to buy cheaper housing in the suburbs. Actually, decent housing right now is cheaper in the suburbs than it is in the city because of the tax break associated with it.

Of course, transportation issues are connected with this. We are fighting to influence the regional bus system. They allocate a certain amount of resources to services that provide city residents with access to key employment areas outside the city, but they must do more. It is going to take some legislative initiative.

Frankly, we really don't have a plan right now. The state runs the public busing system. There is a regional district transportation district through which the state operates public transportation. I have been meeting with state leaders to deal with this reverse commute issue in terms of access. The only thing that is on the table right now is a proposed rail line that is at least eight or nine years old, if it happens at all. It certainly would be nice to have, if we land it correctly. There are some pitfalls. Right now, we need buses leaving the city and going to jobs elsewhere because that's where most of the job growth is going. Now we want to create job growth in the city as well. Right now, the people, frankly, just need work, period, and public transportation has to help them get and keep it.

POLITICS

Ninety-five percent of the initiatives we are trying are supported by the city council. The only reason that it is not 100 percent is because we have a major split on the council, and 5 percent is caught up in politics. This fundamental approach, this philosophy, is that it gets approved. When I need council action to make approvals, I generally get it. Sometimes it will get put on hold until somebody else can take control of it or take ownership of it. I understand that, and I let it happen to the extent that it doesn't interfere, but by and large it goes off all right.

The establishment is an issue. I think that, given the strain in relations over the past several years between city government and the general establishment, there is a lot of instability in this office. I'm the sixth city manager in eleven years. There is an election here every two years. There is a lot of instability at the top, and while I think leaders are receptive to my ideas and I can get them to participate, I think the level of energy and enthusiasm they give is largely on a wait-and-see basis to see if I can actually put certain services and programs on the street and not get bogged down in the bureaucracy. A lot of them are waiting to see if I can deliver or not.

Taxes   I've met with the senior vice presidents of most of the corporations. They have all nodded, they have all agreed, and they are now arranging for more discussions. In the next two or three weeks I am going to be making a presentation to the CEOs of ITT Hartford, Aetna, and Travelers. Three options are under discussion. One is a major reform in the state's payment in lieu of tax assistance, which would at least double our reimbursement rate. The second would be a commuter tax, and the third would be a payroll tax. I would say that if they had to rank the three, the reform idea would be number one. The key issue for me is not which of the three is chosen but that they take some ownership of this because basically we have had the ownership. We don't have the votes, we don't have the clout. The state legislature in Connecticut is not dominated by the largest cities. It clearly is dominated by suburban communities, and they are not going to vote to allow Hartford to enact a commuter tax or a payroll tax unless Aetna, which owns property in these other towns, and Travelers and ITT Hartford really use their clout to get it done. I am trying to get Aetna, Hartford, Travelers, Connecticut Mutual, and United Technologies to step out there and take this on as a corporate mission on their own, because their finances are at stake as well.

Neighborhood Groups and City Hall   In Chicago, Rob Mier had a long and distinguished history with neighborhood groups. He helped set up many of them, gave them technical assistance. Yet when he was in city hall, the relationship was sometimes a rocky, difficult one. I was a part of some of that. In fact, I was Rob's cannon fodder at times.

But Hartford is pretty good. I had a good relationship with most of the neighborhood groups when I was here earlier. I was in an activist role. I led the fight for civilian review boards of questionable police actions. This council finally passed it, and I'm implementing it. I worked with a number of community organizations for funding and programs. I actually did tutoring in summer youth programs for a couple of community groups. Most of the people in these groups know me. They knew me from eleven years ago. So far, it has been good. I think I have gotten out to meet with most groups, even some of them who compete with one another. I have been on tours of various neighborhoods. They have taken me on tours to show me what's happening. In some neighborhoods I have been on two or three tours, depending on the number of groups they have.

What I've done in this targeted investment program is just said that we are willing to work with you. We want your leadership. We are willing to put resources here, but what you have to do is to start working together. Groups actually are doing it. Groups that were historically pitted against one another are now sitting at the table talking about setting development priorities in their neighborhoods and defining target areas. It is not without problems, but they are sitting at the table together. Historically, there were groups that were largely property owners versus renters; now those groups are sitting at the table, at least in four areas we are dealing with. Responses have been good. We have gotten commitments from universities and hospitals for money. Not just in-kind services, but money and staff to help work with the organizations to coordinate this activity. We have gotten some foundation commitments from both local foundations and from the Ford Foundation to help fund community groups to do the planning. We've gotten commitments from the Local Initiatives Support Corporation to expand their program here. The governor's office has agreed at our urging to create an urban community economic development bank, for which they are going to use about $100 million of state bond funds to leverage another $500 million in bank funds to guarantee the loans. The private sector has agreed to put up some of the money: Fleet Bank and Bank of Boston.

Larger projects may be key to attracting or expanding local businesses who would want to hire locally. We are hoping that with that pool it will mean probably as much as $100 million in capital funds for Hartford. It will mean that some of this will be spread around the state, but we gave them the model, they loved it, and it is going to be going through the state legislature. In the meantime, we are sort of pulling state money from where we can find it. There is some excitement generated at the neighborhood level and at the state level.

I think the corporations are a little cautious right now, but they like the idea, they like the concept. I think they're interested because it could be the key to freeing up some of their own dollars in investment activities for the neighborhoods. There has been a long history of alienation here, a lack of engagement between the corporate community and city hall, and it didn't have a lot to do with ideology. Let's put it this way: I don't think there has been a lot of engagement between the city and the corporate community on the development issues. There are always projects, but not much has dealt with the overall economic development picture. As a matter of fact, I would say virtually nothing that deals with overall economic development policy or tax reform.

A PROGRESSIVE AGENDA

The critical issue for somebody like me is how to bring a fairly progressive agenda to the table. Usually we have some other options available to us, and this situation can burn you out pretty fast and you get cynical about it. So one issue is longevity.

That is particularly true for minority public administrators. You either wind up becoming jaded by the bureaucracy or you get enticed into the private sector or into teaching. I think one of the high risks in this is that you get worn out by the frustrations of the bureaucracy. I don't get jaded by politics because I love it. But you could get frustrated by the bureaucracy and the difficulty of moving things. That is one of the risks that could happen to people who like to implement progressive ideas. Still, the opportunity to introduce a progressive agenda to local government is worth all the risks.

NOTES

1. *Economics & Development,* Comprehensive Plan of Development, City of Hartford, Commission on the City Plan, 1984, p. 21.

2. *1990 Census Data Release,* City of Hartford, Department of Planning, November 16, 1991, p. 2.

3. Pierre Clavel, *The Progressive City: Planning and Participation, 1969–1984* (New Brunswick, N.J.: Rutgers University Press, 1986), p. 21.

4. *Hartford: State of the City,* Hartford Planning Commission, July 1983, p. 7.

5. It should be noted that Stanback's office was heavily involved in a Negotiated Investment Strategy arising from Connecticut's 1988 law encouraging regional fair housing compacts (Connecticut Public Act 88-334 55 1:1988). The NIS has led to agreements to provide up to 10,000 units of affordable housing in two regions: Bridgeport and Hartford. See Michael Wheeler, "Regional Consensus on Affordable Housing: Yes, In My Backyard?" *Journal of Planning, Education, & Research* 12, no. 2 (Winter 1993): 139–149.

FURTHER READING: Regional Issues

Baldassare, Mark. "Citizen Support for Regional Government in the New Suburbia." *Urban Affairs Quarterly* 24, no. 3 (1989): 460–469.

Bloch, Robin, and John Friedmann. "American Exceptionalism in Regional Planning, 1933–2000." *International Journal of Urban and Regional Research* (Great Britain) 14, no. 4 (1991): 576–601.

Bollens, Scott. "Constituencies for Limitation and Regionalism: Approaches to Growth Management." *Urban Affairs Quarterly* 26, no. 1 (1990): 470–482.

Bowman, Ann M. "Competition for Economic Development among Southeastern Cities." *Urban Affairs Quarterly* 23, no. 4 (1988): 511–527.

Burnell, Barbara S., and James D. Burnell. "Community Interaction and Suburban Zoning Policies." *Urban Affairs Quarterly* 24, no. 3 (1989): 470–482.

Kantor, Paul. "A Case for a National Urban Policy: The Government of Economic Dependency." *Urban Affairs Quarterly* 26, no. 3 (1991): 394–415.

Rubin, Irene. "Regional Political Economy: Looking Forward from the Past." *Urban Affairs Quarterly* 23, no. 2 (1987): 309–317.

Turner, Robert S. "New Rules for the Growth Game: The Use of Rational State Standards in Land Use Policy." *Journal of Urban Affairs* 12, no. 1 (1991): 35–47.

Wheeler, Michael. "Regional Consensus on Affordable Housing: Yes, in My Backyard?" *Journal of Planning, Education, & Research* 12, no. 2 (1993): 139–149.

Wrightson, Margaret. "Interlocal Cooperation and Urban Problems: Lessons for the New Federalism." *Urban Affairs Quarterly* 22, no. 2 (1989): 261–275.

chapter 9

SANTA MONICA

"The bottom line is that Santa Monica will not become another Westwood or Century City"—Derek Shearer, planning commission chairman. From *Planning*, January 1985. Original map drawn by Cleveland State University.

SNAPSHOT, 1978

Population Composition for Santa Monica, California, 1970–1990

Demographic	1970	1980	1990
Population	88,289	88,314	86,905
White	81,935	75,696	71,961
Black	4,218	3,594	3,920
Median family income	$10,793	$22,263	$51,085
Percentage poverty	12.0	9.9	9.4

Before World War II, Santa Monica was a sleepy seaside city near Los Angeles, a place with small bungalows and apartments, known for its beaches and pier. During World War II, the availability of work at Douglas Aircraft and other war-related industries drew new residents to the city. Most of them became renters, filling the mobile homes that had been installed on back lots and the small apartments that began to spring up. Many elderly persons sought out Santa Monica as a retirement site, most of them as renters. With its lovely beaches, soft air, and sunshine, the city had much to recommend it. By 1960, the population was growing, and 69 percent of the housing units in the city were rental units. At that time, the median family income of Santa Monica's residents was slightly lower than the $7,646 median in the Los Angeles metropolitan area, while monthly rents and housing values were slightly higher.

Completion of the Santa Monica Freeway in 1966 changed all this. Major investment capital began to seek out Santa Monica, and pressure for new development began to grow. Land prices and rents rose steadily and steeply, while larger housing units were converted to multiple smaller units. Pressure also began to build on the city's middle-income homeowners and especially its renters. From 1960 to 1980, median rents shot up from $83 a month to $269, while the proportion of renters in the city increased from 69 to 78 percent. This set the stage for sharp changes in local politics.

Until the early 1970s, Santa Monica was run by a coalition of local bankers, businessmen, landlords, and homeowners. A city manager ran the day-to-day business of government, but a conservative alliance dominated the city council, and the emphasis was on growth. The first public issue precipitating the imminent shift in local politics was a proposal by the city manager to demolish the famous Santa Monica pier. The pier was to be replaced by a high-rise development built in the bay on a new island constructed of landfill. A coalition made up of local liberals and environmentalists challenged and defeated the proposal.

A second factor leading to the change in local politics was the political involvement of a group of liberal activists, many of whom had recently moved to Santa Monica's Ocean Park neighborhood. Derek Shearer and his wife, Ruth Goldway, were among these activists. Shearer was a journalist who had just completed his Ph.D. He had taken urban planning courses and been impressed with the work of Jane Jacobs and Paul Goodman, but had not taken his degree in planning. During the 1960s, he had been involved in antiwar protests and had played a role in California state politics. Goldway also had strong political interests, having organized a consumer boycott and run unsuccessfully in 1977 for a seat in the California Assembly.

The main issue precipitating the political shift in Santa Monica was rent control. In a community where 78 percent of all households were renters, all under pressure by inflationary rent increases, rent control was an obvious political issue. It emerged for the first time in the form of an initiative petition for a rent control ordinance on the June 1978 ballot. The early work on the issue was done by retired labor union officials, but the activists in Ocean Park established themselves as part of the alliance. The rent control initiative of 1978 was defeated after being heavily outspent by property interests. Nevertheless, it provided the impetus for a wider coalition and victory less than a year later.

The broad coalition formed around the rent control issue was called Santa Monicans for Renters' Rights (SMRR). It began with a core of forty to one hundred workers and aimed at influencing city government by campaigning on the rent control issue. Shearer and Goldway were important members of the coalition.

SMRR won a series of electoral victories beginning in April 1979. In that election, the rent control initiative was approved by voters, and Goldway and two other rent control supporters were elected to the city council. Rents were rolled back to April 1978 levels in all buildings of four or more units, and annual rent increases were limited to landlord-documented cost increases. An elected five-person rent control board, which was shortly dominated by SMRR members, supervised the process. Once enacted, the rent control law stimulated its own broad political constituency so that by the end of 1979, SMRR had won three of the city council's seven seats and all five rent control board seats. In April 1981, SMRR won other council seats and swept into control of Santa Monica's city council with a five to two majority, a majority that lasted for the next four years. Ruth Goldway served as mayor and leader of the majority coalition, and Shearer was appointed to the city planning commission.

SMRR's initial success was based on rent control, but the organization attempted to tie that issue to larger, equity-oriented concerns. Derek Shearer was key to this broadening effort. He was a pragmatic progressive who was also policy oriented. His vision of the "ideal city"—small-scale, participatory, fair and equitable—came to be an important force in the years ahead.

SMRR's first initiative was to set up a number of citizen task forces to study various issues before Santa Monica city government. One sought to broaden citizen participation in general government affairs, another sought to involve citizens in rethinking fundamental concepts underlying land development and the public's interest in regulating it. SMRR also had to develop initiatives dealing with crime control, housing for low- and moderate-income people, racial and gender matters, and other ideas percolating through the organizations and activists that made up the base of their coalition.

What follows is Derek Shearer's account of how an activist, progressive coalition devoted to the ideals of equity and citizen participation thought about making these ideals operational through governance.

INTERVIEW WITH DEREK SHEARER

I was brought up in what in retrospect is a model for how I came to think about cities. I grew up in Culver City, which is surrounded by Los Angeles on all sides. Culver City is a city of neighborhoods built around a neighborhood park and a neighborhood school. It wasn't designed by anyone famous; it was designed as a real estate development by a man named Harry Culver, who wanted to build a middle-class community. I grew up on a street of single-family homes built after World War II. I could walk to a public park. I could walk to a classic 1950s candy store. I could walk to the drugstore. I could walk to the corner market. And I could walk to my grammar school. Each one of Culver City's neighborhoods had a grammar school attached to it, which funneled into a central high school. And all the city parks were linked by a municipal sports league. I always had the sense that I lived in a certain neighborhood, but because of the sports league, I had friends who lived in other neighborhoods.

Culver City, which had a population of 35,000, was relatively homogeneous in terms of income. There were some slightly better and some slightly worse neighborhoods than mine, but the extremes of high and low were not that great. Socially and culturally, we all related to greater Los Angeles; we went to the movies all over Los Angeles, we rooted for its sports teams and enjoyed a big-city lifestyle. But we still felt that we belonged to a neighborhood community, and I had all the benefits of growing up there.

It made sense to me that every neighborhood have a park, a school, and neighborhood-oriented shops. Our city also had one of the first shopping centers in southern California, where we could go for larger items. I could ride my bike there; I did a lot of bike riding. We also used mass transit a lot before its decline in Los Angeles. I used to take the bus with my friends down Venice Boulevard and transfer onto a trolley car, one of the last trolley lines left in Los Angeles, the last remnant of the massive electric urban railway system the city once had. I would ride the trolley cars to the L.A. Coliseum for the UCLA football games. I would also ride the bus to the beach. Again, you had the sense that you could live in a particular neighborhood but still avail yourself of all these metropolitan amenities. Culver City wasn't your typical eastern suburb, isolated from the central city, at all.

I also did some traveling because my father was a journalist, which meant that I got to go to Europe, where I saw pedestrian-oriented mass transit systems. I enjoyed riding on the French and British subways and trains and walking in European cities and observing city life. That was a formative experience. Later, when I was at Yale, I observed the urban renewal of New Haven, which is a now-classic case of how *not* to do urban renewal. At the time I was at Yale, in the mid-1960s, New Haven was the recipient of the most federal money for urban renewal per capita of any city in the country.

We saw the effects of massive urban renewal in our daily life at Yale because a black ghetto abutted the college. The ghetto had been bisected by a freeway exit, and the black community was very bitter about that. Individuals took it out on us students, so we had to worry about our safety, which I didn't like. I remember quite clearly some lectures by Vincent Scully, the great architectural historian, in which he compared the building of the freeways through urban neighborhoods to the coming of Genghis Khan and the barbarians. This was barbaric megaplanning that destroyed neighborhoods. Activists at Yale were involved in urban planning struggles in New Haven—some of them friends of mine—and they wrote community-oriented critiques of urban renewal at a very young age.

At Yale, I majored in international relations, and I studied Russia and China, and I studied politics. I took one course in city planning from Christopher Tunnard, one of the great humanist planners. I read his books, and he, too, was a critic of urban renewal in New Haven. We read Paul and Percival Goodman's book, *Communitas,* which had some influence on me. We read Jane Jacobs's *Life and Death of American Cities,* and Herbert Gans's *The Urban Villagers.* They were important to me because of their observations on neighborhood life and the importance of human scale. I remember quite clearly Gans's story of the fight against urban renewal in the Italian section of Boston. I went and looked at it myself, walked around, ate cannoli and drank cappuccino, and saw the neighborhood, which helped me understand more clearly what he had written. I visited Greenwich Village, about which Jacobs had written. These books reinforced my own feelings, values, and bias toward being concerned with people, with how things actually work in daily life. One of the things I felt about some of the "famous architects" we studied in Vincent Scully's course was—and Scully was critical of them on this point himself—that they were building monuments to their own egos or to that of their corporate sponsors. They were more concerned with building art or making a public statement than with how the building operated for the people who worked or lived in it. I didn't have good feelings about any of the "famous" American architects.

So I had this background, but I didn't go on to get a formal degree in city planning. I was much more concerned when I got out of college with the antiwar movement, journalism, and international affairs. After I had been involved in the antiwar movement, doing some research on the economics of the military–industrial complex, I served for a few years as an editor of a weekly newspaper called the *Boston Phoenix*. There I also got involved in urban planning and urban political issues, such as how the city was run and some of the struggles around urban renewal in Boston. By that time I was familiar with the work of Chester Hartman and the group called Urban Planning Aids because I was teaching a course in political economy. Some of my students worked as interns at Urban Planning Aids, so while I had students who were getting involved in urban planning issues in Cambridge, I was not doing that myself.

When the Vietnam war ended and the antiwar movement dissipated, I decided to move back to California. I settled in Santa Monica because I wanted to live in a city of a manageable size. Santa Monica has about 90,000 residents, and I knew that it had distinct neighborhoods. I didn't want to live just anywhere in greater Los Angeles. I felt Los Angeles was so big that it would be hard to get a handle on it. My wife and I moved into the Ocean Park section of Santa Monica. The reason we picked Ocean Park is because it is a very distinct neighborhood of California bungalow-style houses that had attracted a number of 1960s activists. You also had renters and homeowners, blacks and Latinos, so it was one of the few somewhat integrated neighborhoods in Los Angeles. At the time, Ocean Park was a relatively cheap place to live because it had been redlined by the banks.

POLITICAL BEGINNINGS IN SANTA MONICA

Although my wife and I were both still more involved in state and national politics than local politics at the time, we became part of a community effort to save the Santa Monica pier. The pier, which is one of the last of the great wooden piers on the West Coast, was going to be demolished by the city council as part of an urban renewal scheme. They wanted to knock it down and build an artificial island out in Santa Monica Bay and put high-rise condos there. That immediately struck me as the kind of ugly, awful, mega-urban renewal that had been going on in the eastern cities in which I had lived or had read about.

After we helped save the pier, we got involved in a couple of state campaigns. I served as policy advisor to Tom Hayden in his unsuccessful race for the U.S. Senate. My wife and I both worked in Governor Jerry Brown's first administration on state issues. Then my wife, Ruth Goldway, decided to run for the state assembly from a district that included Santa Monica as well as west Los Angeles. I was her campaign manager. Ruth narrowly lost by 1 percent of the vote to Mel Levine, who later became our U.S. congressman, but in the process we met more and more local people.

Because Ruth had become so well known in Santa Monica through the state assembly race, a group of local activists asked her to run for city council. These were the people who had worked on the "Save the Pier" initiative, as well as on a failed initiative to change city council elections from an at-large to a district basis. People thought that only if we had district elections would Ocean Park and some of the other more progressive neighborhoods ever be represented in the council, which was dominated by conservatives, Republican bankers, and real estate types—a typical growth coalition city council.

The issue that was clearly on everyone's mind was renters, who constituted about 75 percent of the population in Santa Monica. Once the Santa Monica Freeway was completed in the mid-1960s, making it easier to live in Santa Monica and commute to other parts of Los Angeles, there had been a tremendous boom in the building of apartments in Santa Monica. The real estate interests that dominated the city council rezoned the southern part of the city to make it easier to build apartments, with the result that there were more and more tenants—mostly elderly people who had retired and who were well-educated but not terribly affluent, and a significant minority of blacks and Latinos. These people tended to vote Democratic, as renters usually do. In fact, although the city had voted for Barry Goldwater in 1964, it went for George McGovern in 1972. But there was not a great turnout in local elections, and the few liberal Democrats who had run for the city council didn't do terribly well.

When Ruth ran for the council, we decided to form a coalition of all the progressive groups we could find. We decided that the most pressing issue was housing, particularly controlling rising rents and protecting renters from eviction. The sponsors of Proposition 13 had promised tenants that if they voted for it, landlords would get a tax break and then they would pass along their savings and the rents. Of course, that turned out not to be the case. Proposition 13 passed. Santa Monica voted for it, as did most of the state, but rents continued to go up. Evictions continued, condominium conversions continued, and there was a real sense among middle- and working-class tenants that they were the losers in this game and that nobody was speaking for them. Our political coalition was called "Santa Monicans for Renters' Rights." Our platform included support for rent control initiatives, participatory democracy, and human-scale development.

We passed the rent control initiative, which had a provision for an elected rent control board, the first one in the country. Our coalition won all five seats on the rent control board. I had worked with Ralph Nader early on in my career. Nader came out and endorsed Ruth and our rent control efforts. Ruth and one other coalition candidate were elected to the city council, where they were in the minority. Ruth immediately began raising city planning issues, in addition to issues of housing and enforcement of the rent control law.

We ran not only on development issues; we recognized that crime was an issue. We felt that local liberals had not taken crime seriously enough, especially in terms of how it affected the quality of urban life. They were analyzing crime as a problem that related to failure to have full employment, but that kind of mega-analysis didn't speak to the genuine fears of people. We campaigned on a community-based crime strategy, which now, interestingly enough, has become the new paradigm of community-based policing, but we were one of the first communities to advocate it and put it into practice. Our program was called Neighborhood Watch. It entailed having the police department come out and give people a security check on their house or apartment. The police would advise them on their locks and how to clean up their shrubbery so that they would be safer. They put ID numbers on homeowners' goods in case they were stolen. The city also increased foot patrols and bicycle patrols. We now have police on horses within our parks. We also have a community service program in which officers help with neighborhood dispute resolution and neighborhood problems. In short, we did not come in with a hostile attitude toward the police or toward the police chief.

Our coalition was in the minority for about a year and a half, during which time we raised several issues involving urban development. One of the issues concerned an ice skating rink downtown that had been a very important, community-oriented facility; even though it was privately owned, lots of people went there. Some developers wanted to knock it down to build a high-rise office building. Ruth successfully fought them on that issue, and we started to raise the level of consciousness about massive high-rise development. We also fought a downtown redevelopment scheme involving a fully enclosed, suburban-style mall. We wanted the developers to open it up to the city. Again, there was a standard notion of what should be developed and the way development should proceed, which we fought. We lost that battle.

When the next city council elections came up, our coalition ran a complete slate of candidates and the coalition put together a complete program. I was instrumental in outlining a number of concerns besides rent control, such as articulating what kind of development we thought appropriate. We weren't no-growth. We wanted to be very clear about that. We thought that no-growth was an elitist position that elite suburbs and elite neighborhoods in other cities had taken. We argued for "balanced" growth. The notion was that you could have a city plan that pushed growth in more human-scale, neighborhood, and community-oriented directions. We won the election, and Ruth became the mayor. I was subsequently appointed to the planning commission, which meant that the coalition had to go beyond trying to affect single projects and implement a new plan for the entire city of Santa Monica.

EARLY INITIATIVES

We already had a vision for the city that reflected the weather and traditions of Californians instead of a style that could be anywhere in the United States. We called it a "city where people come first." Now we had to put into place some new processes. We were dedicated to much greater participatory planning. Previous administrations had not even notified tenants when development projects affecting them came up. They would notify only the owners of the buildings. We immediately changed the notification rules. We also decided to subsidize the local public radio station, KCRW, which is the largest National Public Radio affiliate in California and one of the largest in the country. Our support enabled KCRW to broadcast the city council meetings live. If you couldn't attend the meetings, you could at least hear them. We wanted to get neighborhood people involved as much as possible in the planning process.

There were two reasons for that. It was the right thing to do, and it was a strategic decision. If the council and the planning commission alone issued these new plans and rules, we were going to be politically vulnerable to attacks that we were these awful government planners. But if it was a bottom–up process that we were facilitiating, then politically it would be much harder for our opponents to say, "Well, that's Derek, the planning czar," or, "That's Ruth's plan." If developers had to sit down with the neighborhood people who lived next to their planned developments and negotiate with them, then we weren't dictating an outcome so much as a process. When we said, "Look, we won't even look at your project until you go through that neighborhood process," then we were actually *building* support for the project and making it much likely politically that it would actually get done.

Another part of our policy was that each neighborhood ought to have a democratically constituted neighborhood organization to represent its interests. We funded neighborhood groups in the poor parts of town so that they could hire organizers and issue newsletters. We also made money available for technical assistance to support neighborhood organizing and development. The other thing that we decided on was some big projects, because we wanted to show some results. For example, Ruth almost immediately started a downtown farmers' market. It was based on her experiences as assistant director of the State Department of Consumer Affairs under Jerry Brown, where she tried to set up ways for farmers to market food directly to consumers in the city.

The Santa Monica farmers' market did a couple of things that we liked. It provided healthy food at a lower price, and it helped to animate the city. As I said, the new downtown mall tended to push people into parking structures and into a building in which all the shops were those you see in any mall around the country. We wanted to get people out of their cars, out of buildings, so that they could interact in ways that we thought were more human. Having a downtown farmers' market was one way to do it. It turned out to be a tremendous success. It's still going today. Interestingly, the chamber of commerce initially called the farmers' market "socialism in action." I asked, "How can a farmer selling directly to consumers be construed as socialist by any stretch of the imagination?" They said it was because the city organized it, because it took place on city streets. This seemed shortsighted to me.

We also became engaged almost immediately in a large development project. One of the largest development firms in the world wanted to build its national headquarters and an office building in Santa Monica. Using the state planning law, we entered into a development agreement that would allow us to expedite the project if the developer agreed to certain things. We wanted traffic management, which meant that the firm would encourage employees to use mass transit or ride-share. Second, we required that they put in a day-care center. We were one of the first cities, maybe *the* first city, in the country to raise the issue of including day care in development projects. Now this has become a very popular thing for private firms to do. Actually, it benefits them because their employees benefit, but at the time we proposed the concept, there was resistance. We also required the developer to buy a hundred units of off-site, affordable housing that would be turned over to our city housing agency.

They argued, of course, that they shouldn't have to do that. The way the state development laws work is that you have to show that the development fees or impact fees that you're imposing are related to costs that the project might be bringing into the city. We successfully argued that large-scale developments could raise the cost of housing in the city and, therefore, that a large project could legitimately be asked to help offset the problem by either building housing or paying into a housing fund or whatever. This project was important not only because there were tangible benefits but because it let us work out some of the principles we wanted to apply to the entire city.

A NEW CITY PLAN

But we didn't want to go along forever on a project-by-project, negotiation-by-negotiation basis. We felt that we might be vulnerable to legal charges of playing favorites with developers. We needed to put together an entire city plan, which California law requires every municipality to have. Ours had not been updated since the 1950s. It was wildly out of date in terms of the current development pressures on the city. For example, it allowed for much greater density than anybody realized. We knew we wanted to rezone the city, and we also wanted to address as a whole package all the different planning, housing, and transportation issues that we had been addressing piecemeal in individual projects.

State law requires public hearings on the updating of city plans. We conducted ours in an innovative and creative way. First, we hired a professional firm to do the best economic, traffic, and environmental analysis one could do. We attempted to be scientific because we wanted to protect ourselves. In case of a legal challenge we wanted to show that we had a rational basis for what we were proposing. Then we moved the public hearings out of city hall and into the neighborhoods. We held charettes—intensive, focused planning sessions—at which people could blue-sky what they might like to see. They could also play planning games and come up with ideal solutions and then figure out how to allocate scarce resources.

Early on in this process, we hired a new city manager, a man named John Alshuler, who had been a deputy city manager in Hartford, Connecticut. Like most of us, he was in his early thirties. John and I had met through a national organization called the State and Local Conference on Alternative State and Local Public Policy. I had been one of the founders of this in the early 1970s, recognizing that people who had been activists in the antiwar movement, the women's movement, and the civil rights movement were getting older and settling down in neighborhoods and communities. While they weren't yet being elected to Congress or the Senate, many of them were either being elected to the city council or the state legislature. The organization was a way to share experiences about innovative programs and policies that actually worked.

In the mid-1970s, I was appointed by President Jimmy Carter to the first board of the National Consumer Cooperative Bank, which Ralph Nader had been lobbying to create as a means of lending money to cooperative enterprises. Because of such national experiences as these, I was asked to be a guest teacher at the UCLA Graduate School of Urban Planning.

In Santa Monica we ended up hiring as junior planners many of my UCLA students. We deliberately tried to hire people who were smart and technically competent, and who shared our social values and visions. Many of those students worked out very well. One has just become deputy city manager of Beverly Hills, while others are working for national housing organizations or have become planners in other cities. To the extent that we could, without wholesale firing, we tried to create a new bureaucracy. We brought in a new planning director and a new assistant to the city manager. The other thing we did was to create new commissions. We created an arts commission and a women's commission, which focused on issues from a woman's perspective. And we appointed new people to existing boards and commissions. For example, we appointed community-oriented architects to the architectural review board.

MAKING THE RULES

The most important thing about the new city plan we developed was that it allowed us to rezone the city. We wrote height limitations and specific tradeoffs into the plan. For example, we said that we would not allow buildings higher than four stories, except under certain circumstances. To get the extra stories, we specified the kinds of things a developer had to do in terms of providing on-site housing or day-care centers.

By making the rules explicit, we eliminated fights over these issues on a case-by-case basis. The one thing we had learned from dealing with developers is that developers will live with the rules if you make them clear, and if you make it clear that you are going to enforce them. The worst situation is when you say, "Here's what we like, but what do you have to offer?" Then everything's open to political bargaining, and we didn't want that. The other thing we did that was very important was to formulate an economic development strategy for the whole city. Then we made the zoning fit the strategy.

We were for growth because we wanted to do other things—we were upping the level of social services, of art programs; providing financial help to the schools, even though the city wasn't required to do so; operating senior meals programs; trying to build more affordable housing. Under Proposition 13, we couldn't raise property taxes; one of our few sources of revenues came from sales taxes. We needed a strategy that allowed for more commercial activity. We decided to figure out our assets—we have a great location, we're on the ocean, tourists should want to come here, potentially even conventions—and then we asked how can we take those assets and make use of them in such a way that it won't reduce the quality of life for the people who live here but will increase our revenues? Hotels seemed to be one way. They provide a bed tax, and since most people don't drive to them in off-peak hours, their environmental effects are relatively benign.

Given our great beach location, Santa Monica had very few good hotels, so we included in the plan a zone for large, luxury hotels near the ocean, but not right next to residential areas. At the same time, we also redesigned and remodeled the oceanfront to make it an urban park. We redesigned what was supposed to be a four-lane highway near the water, cutting it down to one lane each way, and we used that extra land to create tree-shaded areas, a bike path, places for people to have picnics. Wanting to revive our historic pier, we created a separate nonprofit corporation, so that it wouldn't be subject to city council politics or being micromanaged by the planning commission. I've always believed that we need public entrepreneurs, people who can use business and entrepreneurial skills to develop projects in the public interest. The Pier Restoration Corporation, of which my wife is still chair, took on the job of renovating the pier, including everything from repainting the historic horses on the carousel to trying to land new shops and restaurants to building new play areas for children.

We also set up a Third Street Mall Development Corporation to revive our old main street, which the city had closed to vehicle traffic in the 1950s. When the new suburban-style mall opened downtown, it killed off what was left of the old mall. We decided to revive the old mall, but to do it strategically. We wouldn't look for chain stores; we'd look for one-of-a-kind stores that filled a particular market niche. We wanted the old mall to become a festival marketplace, similar to the pedestrian-oriented streets I had seen in Boston, Baltimore, Vancouver, and Toronto. I think our most important decision was to make the old mall an entertainment district. We said to movie theaters that if they wanted to locate in Santa Monica, they would have to locate at the Third Street Mall. There's good parking there, we'll give you all the help we can, but you're not going to get a permit to go to the northern part of the city near the residential areas.

The old mall has been a tremendous success, and it's brought all kinds of life and activities into downtown. Once you get a critical mass, then market forces take over and people come in on their own and set up new restaurants and new shops. But we did the physical planning, the strategic planning, and fit the zoning into the strategic plan. We also tried—and this was the hardest task—to include clauses regarding the training and hiring of minority youth. Under current American law, you can't really dictate resident-only hiring. You can only encourage firms to advertise jobs in your area. Nonetheless, we tried to do some employment tie-ins and we had some success. We got a few hotels to recruit at our local high schools and local community colleges to hire minority youth as management trainees.

My sense is that most general plans are nothing more than zoning maps that protect single-family homeowners and validate market trends and development. What we tried to do was to lay out the direction in which we wanted the market to go and to make plain our vision of what Santa Monica ought to be. As far as I can tell, our plan is fairly unique in that we were trying to build in equity. We wanted to make *every* neighborhood in the city a decent, friendly, and safe place for people to live, regardless of their income levels or their race. We tried to encourage neighborhood-oriented shopping centers, traffic management plans, and housing affordability programs so the life style I knew in Culver City, where everybody had a decent neighborhood, parks, school, and shops, was possible for everybody in Santa Monica. Given the city's history, we couldn't make everything perfectly equitable. What we tried to do was articulate our vision in concrete terms in the plan and then use various city programs to implement that vision and encourage a participatory planning process so that concerned citizens in each neighborhood would fill in the gaps in the plan.

INSTITUTIONALIZING THE VISION

In California, a city plan has the force of law. A general plan is like the constitution of the city and the state requires a complicated process to change it. Once we went through this very arduous, two-year process of rezoning and strategic planning, with the concomitant expenditures of money, it would be very hard for someone to come in and do that all over again, which they would be required by law to do. Fortunately, our coalition has governed for ten years straight, even though Ruth and I no longer hold high elective and administrative posts. One of the reasons for the coalition's longevity is that we've made various modifications to try to institutionalize more citizen involvement. For example, in fighting for tenants' rights we recognized that we didn't want to be seen as being against homeownership. We made a modification in the rent control law that stipulated that if a certain percentage of the tenants would sign on, we would allow condominium conversions, which we had initially banned outright.

There has also been a political and philosophical shift in the city so that the people who used to run things are not even players any more. Our coalition's values became the dominate values.

The people who were totally against renters' rights and rent control or who were for high-rise office buildings—the people who were what I would call Reaganites—they're no longer strongly represented, they've largely withdrawn. Instead, our opposition comes from people who are our age, who claim that they share, and in some cases they do, most of our values. They just disagree with our means. But they've accepted renters' rights, rent control, human-scale development—an exciting, animated city. Also, what many businesspeople have found is that good planning is good for business. We have been a tremendous asset for anybody who owns property in this city. Property values in Santa Monica have been steadily rising.

Santa Monica is now a very desirable place to live. One of the reasons people want to live here is because they feel it's such a great, alive, exciting community. We've been written up in *Vanity Fair* and *Travel and Leisure* as the hip, neat place where all the good restaurants in Los Angeles are located, where all the artists' studios are, where the interesting shops are, where you can still walk, where you can ride your bike, where you can know your neighbor and still have a sophisticated life. Some of the praise is a little trendy and silly, but what's interesting is that the things that the writers are raving about largely happened because of our planning and citizen involvement. Without that, the old urban renewal model—where people live in the suburbs, drive to their high-rise offices during the day, and go home at night, leaving the city dead or to the poor—would have proceeded. If we had left the developers to proceed unilaterally, they would have made Santa Monica look like high-rise Miami Beach. They weren't concerned because that was not their job. Their job was to make as much money off land as they could. Some developers from Asia bought a piece of land because they wanted to build a twenty-story skyscraper. I told them their plans ran counter to our zoning. The developer said he had never heard of zoning. "We don't have that in Taiwan," he said, "we do whatever we want."

I think that what we did is unique in one sense. We were lucky in that, unlike Cleveland or Detroit, we had a lot of assets and desirable land that people wanted to use; we were part of a relatively diverse and growing regional economy. I don't think that you can do everything we did in industrial cities that have tremendous economic problems, although I do think our principles of planning and development are adaptable to any city that wants to manage growth. Some of the tradeoffs we developed, such as day-care centers and housing tie-ins, have become policy in San Francisco, Boston, and around the country. It wasn't that we did anything particularly new. We tried to do what was being done by progressive planners around the country in a comprehensive way, in a strategic way.

This is not to say that Santa Monica is a utopia. We had political opposition. We had lawsuits filed against us. We were physically attacked. But I will say that we carried out a good 70 percent of what we wanted to do. And it's on-going. We set up the mechanisms and the structure so that Ruth and I and a few other founding fathers and mothers didn't have to be there forever, which is nice. Our decision to use the various commissions as a kind of training ground was deliberate. We would appoint somebody to a lesser commission and then they worked their way up until they sat on the planning commission or on the city council or on the rent board. This gave us a farm system for developing citizen talent. We actively recruited people from the minority community. Now there is a Latino on the city council. We were trying to maintain a continual flow of talent into the structure we built so that the process didn't become dependent on particular individuals.

ON PLANNING EDUCATION

I think students should study planning as a part of politics and economics. They need to understand that you can't simply study architecture or physical planning; you have to understand governmental structures, the political process, why citizens participate or don't, how political campaigns are waged. You have to have an appreciation for the history and inner workings of a particular city.

When we set up a community housing corporation to build some affordable new housing, we conducted a political analysis. Why did people not like public housing? One of the reasons was that it looked like housing for the poor. Our affordable housing looked almost like upscale condos. We won awards from Reagan's HUD for being among the best community housing projects in the country. We brought in some smart, efficient builders and we used local architects. We had competitions to come up with designs. People can go and look at the project. There is also a slide show on it. I feel that planning school ought to be more involved in looking and learning from real experiences in cities around the country. I call it learning from ourselves.

There's a lot of talk about "planning theory," which I don't find very useful. I think the most useful things are case studies. For example, in Cleveland, you can read the books on populist mayor Dennis Kucinich. Why was that opportunity not fulfilled? What's our analysis of the politics in Cleveland? What did get done in terms of local neighborhood development that we can learn from? You study these kinds of questions so that when you become a city planner, you will be able to analyze the opportunities at hand. You know you'll have an opportunity in this neighborhood or on that project because you know what's been done elsewhere, you know your choices.

Getting out and walking around and seeing how cities operate and function is also very important. A lot of it is common sense. If you go into a building, it's obvious if it's not functioning well, or there's no place to sit comfortably in a park or a square. I feel that planning school ought to be more involved in looking and learning from ourselves. Although I'm a believer in learning from experience, a planner must also have values. My bias is toward the values of neighborhood, community, and human scale. If you have those values and you're hardheaded about picking your opportunities, then you can have real equity planning, real planning for people.

FURTHER READING: Progressive Planning and Participatory Democracy

Boggs, Carl. "The New Populism and the Limits of Structural Reform." *Theory and Society* 12 (1983): 365–373.

Capek, Stella, and John Gilderbloom. *Community vs. Commodity: Tenants and the American City.* Albany: SUNY Press, 1992.

Coit, Katherine. "Local Action Not Citizen Participation." In *Marxism and the Metropolis,* edited by William K. Tabb and Larry Sawers, 297–311. New York: Oxford University Press, 1978.

Feagin, Joe R. *The Urban Real Estate Game.* Englewood Cliffs, N.J.: Prentice Hall, 1983.

Heskin, Alan David. *Tenants and the American Dream.* New York: Praeger, 1983.

Levine, Ned, Eugene J. Grigsby III, and Alan Heskin. "Who Benefits from Rent Control?: Effects on Tenants in Santa Monica, California." *Journal of the American Planning Association* 56, no. 2 (1990): 140–152.

Moberg, David. "From Rent Control to Municipal Power." *In These Times,* January 1983, 11–13.

Schiesl, Martin J. *The Politics of Efficiency: Municipal Administration and Reform in America: 1880–1920.* Berkeley: University of California Press, 1983.

Shearer, Derek. "How the Progressives Won in Santa Monica." *Social Policy,* Winter 1982, 7–14.

———. "Planning and the New Urban Populism: The Case of Santa Monica." *Journal of Planning Education and Research* 2 (1982): 20–26.

———. "Left in Santa Monica Loses a Battle, But Not the War." *In These Times,* April 3, 1983.

———. "City Profile—Santa Monica." *Cities,* November 1983, 107–112.

———. "In Search of Equal Partnerships: Prospects for Progressive Urban Policy in the 1990s." In *Unequal Partnerships,* edited by Gregory D. Squires. New Brunswick, N.J.: Rutgers University Press, 1989.

chapter 10

SAN DIEGO

San Diego, 1992. Photo used by permission of the San Diego City Print Shop.

SNAPSHOT, 1991

Population Composition for San Diego, California, 1970–1990

Demographic	1970	1980	1990
Population	696,769	875,538	1,110,549
White	619,498	674,268	745,406
Black	52,961	77,508	104,261
Median family income	$10,166	$20,133	$39,318
Percentage poverty	9.3	9.2	13.4

From the mid-1980s to the end of the decade, San Diego, California, underwent a period of unusually high growth. Population rose by about 235,000 during the 1980s. The number of annual housing starts authorized by the city went from 4,000 in 1982 to 19,200 in 1986. This rapid growth took place at a time when federal government support for assisted housing was being cut by more than 75 percent. Construction of new public housing was brought to a virtual standstill, and federal subsidies to private developers building affordable housing were sharply reduced.

While this rapid growth was taking place, the city and region were plagued by problems of inadequate infrastructure and public facilities. Antigrowth and growth control sentiments, some of which reflected concern for the environment, grew vigorously, and two growth-management initiatives were placed on the ballot in 1988. This set the stage for political conflict between growth control and progrowth forces that, under the leadership of developers, banks, and businesspeople, had long dominated San Diego's politics.

The net result of rapid growth in population and market housing and no growth in affordable housing was that, by 1988, San Diego was one of the least affordable cities in the nation for renters and home buyers alike. The median-priced home was $175,000, almost twice the national median. Rents were also disproportionately high. By contrast, growth in local employment was heavily concentrated in low-paying service and retail industries, which represented 44 percent of San Diego's employment in 1988.

By the end of the 1980s, the rate of local homeownership slid below 50 percent, and only 18 percent of the population could afford the median-priced home. A total of 26,000 households lived in substandard dwellings, and 19,000 households could not meet their rent payments without doubling up and living in overcrowded conditions. By the end of the decade, an estimated 5,000 people in downtown San Diego were homeless.

Despite these conditions, the city had virtually no nonprofit housing development corporations and no active housing advocacy organizations. The San Diego Housing Commission (SDHC), founded in 1979, had not proved effective in generating either the supply or support for affordable housing. SDHC had come into existence at the beginning of the Reagan era and had been weakened by law suits, a grand jury investigation, and the eventual departure of its first director under charges of corruption. In 1988, however, the SDHC hired an energetic new director. A new chair, who was a former resident of public housing, was also appointed to head the commission. Both were highly motivated individuals who were determined to move the commission forward toward "making a significant dent in the affordable housing problem."

Kenneth Grimes was a member of the SDHC staff who, along with other staff members, introduced the new director to the concept of a Housing Trust Fund (HTF) as a means of attacking the housing crisis in the city. They later convinced the director and the rest of the SDHC to establish a task force to study the possibilities of an HTF further and to make recommendations.

Ken Grimes was a senior planning analyst in the SDHC, where he still works at this writing. Originally from England, he was a planner who had a background in community and labor organizing. At this time, he was working on his thesis on redistributive planning in the graduate program at San Diego State University. Grimes was interested in the strategic relationships between urban planning and lower-income groups. As the lead planner working on HTF, Grimes realized that technical work—needs assessment, analysis, and careful plan preparation—would be necessary but perhaps not sufficient to ensure the plan's adoption and implementation. The adoption of the plan, after all, would be intensely political in a political arena noted for laissez-faire. It was also redistributive, demanding that at least some of the funding would come from the powerful development community and that some of the benefits would flow to the poor.

Grimes and his colleagues thought about the issue long and hard. They feared a reaction from the powerful real estate and construction industries if they sought to fund the HTF solely through development linkage fees. They also feared the fund might be diverted from the goal of affordable housing.

They decided to develop a three-pronged strategy to gain the adoption of HTF. The strategy would be based on (1) building a coalition to provide the widest possible base for community support; (2) carefully framing the issue for public discussion in a way that would deemphasize the redistributive aspects of the HTF and emphasize aspects appealing to business; and (3) building a structure of funding sources and beneficiaries that would lead to consensus and acceptable compromise.

The result of their efforts was the successful adoption of an HTF that was one of the largest in the country. It is a redistributive program in the form of a large pool of money derived, for the most part, from development linkage fees and designed to provide housing for those most in need. It will be primarily used by nonprofit developers, and its resources will be largely controlled by community groups committed to affordable housing.

The interview that follows suggests ways in which equity planners, devising creative strategies, can develop and implement redistributive plans under often difficult conditions.

INTERVIEW WITH KENNETH GRIMES

I come from England. For generations, on both sides of my family, the men worked in the shipyards in Southampton and were involved in union activities, which leads to a much greater awareness of class and one's position in society and the expectations that accompany being at a certain level. My family was also a strong supporter of the Labour party. I would say that my background made me acutely aware of social differences and economic inequality and gave me a predisposition to equity planning.

I've been at the San Diego Housing Commission (SDHC) about four years now. I started working there part-time when I was working on a master's in planning at San Diego State University. Before that, I worked for about ten years in the labor movement. I worked for a number of international unions and was involved in contract administration, labor–management relations, and contract negotiations. Most of my work with the labor movement involved organizing new members. Before that, I worked briefly as a social worker. Now I'm a senior planning analyst at SDHC. I work in a small department that's basically a research and development unit called Policy and Program Development. The department consists of four people and is overseen by the deputy director, second-in-charge of the agency. Before any major steps are made, we normally have a meeting with the executive director.

Of all the projects I've initiated at SDHC, the Housing Trust Fund (HTF) is the most significant. HTFs are set up by government legislation as ongoing sources of revenues directed at the provision of housing—mostly low and moderate. The revenues are set aside in a special fund earmarked and allocated for housing. They can't be mixed in with other city revenues. While HTFs can't replace declining federal money for low- and moderate-income housing, they can help make up crucial shortfalls. Whether HTFs are progressive depends on a number of issues: who the beneficiaries are, who controls the decision making, the duration of affordability controls, and, where the money comes from to fund the HTF.

Our HTF is fairly progressive. It's an ongoing source of revenues earmarked for low-income housing that's derived from a linkage fee, that is, a fee of about two dollars a square foot on office development and a little bit less for retail, hotel, research and development, and warehouse developments. A small amount of money is also derived from the city's hotel-room tax. Control of decision making is vested by and large in the nonprofit community groups that helped make it happen. At the time of its adoption, the fund was projected to earn $13 million a year, but with the recession that figure has been more than cut in half. Of course, the outlook for commercial development in San Diego is good. In future years, I'm sure we'll be back up to $13 million a year. The city's only 70 percent built, so there'll be a lot more commercial development.

INTRODUCING THE CONCEPT

At the outset, nobody believed either an HTF or linkage arrangement could be done in San Diego. I don't think many people took the idea seriously at first. I don't think that anyone in the city felt that the housing commission had the wherewithal to propose something like this and aggressively see it through to implementation. Quite frankly, the commission does come up with all kinds of ideas and proposals, and it can be very frustrating because many of them are shelved and never heard from again. Some of them are not as bold as the HTF proposal, but nevertheless good plans and ideas that come out of the commission are often not implemented. When the idea really began to take root, and support started to gain momentum, it was like the commission coming out of the barn with both guns blazing. People were shocked and didn't know quite how to respond.

Not that we unveiled the idea at any one moment. It was a question of fog lifting rather than a curtain being thrown back. Success depended on a lot of things. Some just seemed to come together; some we helped make happen. An HTF made a lot of sense for San Diego, given the housing affordability crisis. The city was among the least affordable places in the country for everybody but very-high-income families. The housing commission had documented that, as had lots of other agencies, but nothing much was happening. Then, in 1989, two new players came on the scene, Evan E. Becker, the new director of the housing commission, and Councilman Wes Pratt, the new chair. Both were energetic and motivated to do something about the housing crisis. The question was, what?

Very early on, we met with Wes Pratt and introduced him to the HTF concept as an effective thing to do. He bought the idea, and later we convinced the rest of the SDHC commissioners to adopt the idea and set up a HTF task force to study the issue and make recommendations.

A number of questions arose: Who would serve on the Task Force? Would the Task Force actually recommend establishing an HTF? How would it be funded, structured and controlled? Who would present and support the proposals? But the immediate question was: How was it going to be possible to get the support of the city council? We knew that although lower-income groups have considerable stake in an HTF, they were not organized locally. So the SDHC planners identified the community-based groups and other nonprofit organizations interested in low-income issues and tried to pull them together into one organization that would create the political pressure necessary to adopt an HTF. In an attempt to make the HTF coalition as broad as possible, labor unions, religious groups, and environmental activists were all considered as potential supporters and contacts.

We developed a long list of everybody we could think of in the city who had any influence whatsoever, public or otherwise, and we contacted those people and tried to set up meetings with them. We said that the director of the housing commission and/or Councilman Wes Pratt, who was the chair of the commissioners, would like to talk to them about the housing crisis in the city and about some ideas that the housing commission was developing for attacking that crisis.

At the same time I was meeting with various potential grassroots supporters around the city. Altogether, we probably met with a hundred or more business and civic leaders and grassroots activists. Some people simply turned us down; they were too busy or were not interested. But many others were flattered that a council member or the director was interested in their opinions. These meetings created a ripple effect, and I think we actually built a good deal of support among some of the more liberal elements in the business community. Pratt is a skilled politician, and he's a coalition builder. And Becker, the executive director of the commission, is a sincere and genuine man whose integrity is obvious to all who work with him. Another important outgrowth of these meetings was that we began to learn more about what type of opposition was out there. In these private meetings we gathered a lot of intelligence about the way these people were thinking, about the way they were likely to react. That, in turn, helped us formulate a proposal that in some form or another addressed some of those concerns.

One of the first things we heard about was an initiative that was being undertaken by the Building Industry Association of San Diego. Their idea was to establish a nonprofit organization in San Diego rather like the Bridge Corporation in San Francisco. The idea was to create the impression that we didn't need a Housing Trust Fund and a mandatory linkage fee in San Diego because the construction industry was going to contribute to solving these problems voluntarily. They weren't overtly opposing the trust fund as such, they just argued that it was not necessary and pointed out that it was not their obligation to solve the housing crisis.

This was, in fact, one of the industry's strongest points in opposition to the HTF. It was a line of thinking that went: "Yes, we've got a housing crisis and yes, we need to do something about it, but, it's not our fault. We're the construction industry, we build houses, we didn't create these problems. It's not fair to put the burden on our shoulders and make us foot the bill to solve these social problems." Our response was to agree. "Yes, we need more resources than you have," we said. "We need resources from the community at large. It's a communitywide problem and it demands a communitywide response." But all along we intended to make sure the development community would be involved in the funding in a very important way.

Eventually it became clear that more organized community pressure would be needed to ensure council support. We made a decision to pull about thirty groups together in a single meeting. Interestingly enough, although a number of these organizations had an interest in housing, and one or two of the nonprofit organizations had actually developed a limited amount of housing in the past, most of the organizations had no idea that the others existed. When we brought them all together in a meeting, many people became aware of each other for the first time. They looked around in the room and said, "Well, it's not just me—there are thirty groups represented here, and I don't know half these people. Who are you?" It was empowering. The thrust of the meeting was informational, to let them know what the housing commission was proposing and to emphasize that the SDHC couldn't make the HTF happen by itself. If it was going to happen, it would be because people like them demanded it for their constituents. We did everything we could to alert them to the fact that if they supported the proposal, they needed to organize and create the political pressure to ensure the support of the city council.

I was very much afraid that this initial meeting might just peter out without moving the idea of an HTF forward. Sometimes that happens; people leave a meeting feeling good, but without taking any responsibility for further action. To head off that possibility, I asked Nico Calavita, a friend who teaches at San Diego State University, to join the meeting and help move things along. Sure enough, when the meeting looked like it might end without a call for further action, Nico proposed that another meeting should be held, independently of the SDHC, to pursue the idea of organizing some kind of coalition. Another meeting was held, and the coalition was born.

The HTF coalition was led by Jean Ertle, from the San Diego Catholic Diocese, and Linda Martin, an activist in the environmental community. It included church groups, labor unions, service organizations, environmentalists, fledgling nonprofit housing corporations, and professional social workers. The coalition eventually organized large numbers of people to lobby city council members, write letters to the editor, speak to potential support groups, and vigorously promote the HTF at a conference on affordable housing cosponsored by the coalition, the housing commission, and some industry groups. The coalition also participated in a forum, organized by the commission and the Sierra Club, on "Affordable Housing and the Environment," which explored reasons why environmentalists should support affordable housing. They did a lot of things to build support. During the whole process, the coalition worked closely with me and other housing commission staff. Too often, city staff members see community activists as "crazies," and activists look at city staff as part of the problem. This makes it difficult or impossible to work together—even when they share substantial agreement. The HTF's success reflected our success in building a strong relationship between the city staff and community supporters.

Another important element in the campaign to establish the HTF in San Diego was the decision, which I helped shape, to define the need for affordable housing in broad terms. The problem could not simply be defined as the city being in need of more low-income housing units. That was true, but most decision makers are far removed from the lives of low-income families and are not highly motivated to alleviate hardships endured by the poor. We framed the problem in moral terms, but we also strongly emphasized the impact of escalating housing costs on the ability of employers to recruit professional and technical staff from outside the region. As a result, we argued, high housing costs were acting as a major disincentive to companies considering locating or expanding operations in San Diego. This was a clear threat to regional prosperity, and it struck a familiar chord in the business community.

We also stressed that the housing crisis was a problem for the middle class. Young professionals are often unable to buy houses in San Diego, and many young people are simply living in their parents' homes, unable to afford to move out and live on their own. To solicit the support of more middle-class constituencies, and to make the proposal more rounded and attractive, we said that 10 percent of fund revenues should be set aside for first-time home buyers. Obviously these people are not among those in the greatest need, but we made a strategic decision in an attempt to enlist broad support. The HTF coalition opposed this provision at first because home buyers' difficulties were not a priority for them, but they came around to our way of thinking in the end.

There was some risk for SDHC in calling these groups together, lobbying and getting deeply involved with them. Council might have seen it as political mobilization (which it was) and could have punished us. But it had to be done, we thought, and it turned out to be no problem.

I worked very closely with the leadership of the coalition. I attended some of their meetings as a silent observer, yet one who was available to give them advice, to pass on information. We developed a very constructive relationship. The HTF coalition grew to more than fifty groups and organizations, including the National Association of Social Workers, churches, some local unions such as service employees unions, community groups, minority groups, and non-profit organizations who either had developed housing in the past or wanted to develop housing in the future.

At the time, the nonprofit housing development sector in San Diego was underdeveloped; until then, there barely was a nonprofit housing development sector. After the HTF coalition was formed, the few community development corporations that existed and one or two other community organizations that had ideas about doing housing began to see the trust fund as a source of money that was going to be there primarily for their purpose. The groups, who were among the most active in the HTF coalition, later organized a nonprofit housing development federation, so the HTF coalition still exists today, although in a slightly different form. I continue to work with these people, and we're trying to develop a subcommittee that would act as a watchdog for the trust fund. The subcommittee would attend the trustees' meetings of the fund, which is administered by a city council–appointed board of trustees. It's important that community representatives attend these meetings to speak up and make sure important issues are on the agenda, and so on. We've also continued to work together on other housing policy issues in the city. The federation is at present pursuing an inclusionary zoning policy being proposed by the SDHC.

THE APPROVAL PROCESS

Before we brought our proposal to the city council, we had to go to the housing commissioners. The San Diego Housing Commission is governed by the seven-member Board of Housing Commissioners. At the time of the evolution of the HTF, there were four members from the San Diego City Council and three citizen members, two of whom were public housing residents. Now there are four citizens and three council members. The chair of the housing commissioners currently is the mayor of the city.

We had to go through a series of steps in the approval process. First, we went to the housing commissioners with the proposal to recommend establishing an HTF. This required the housing commissioners to make two decisions. One was to accept the concept of the trust fund, the other was to direct the staff to continue developing the idea. The first is a dangerous step. In one or two other places in the country that have adopted the HTF in concept, they have argued for the next three, four, five, six years about the sources of revenues. But, anyway, the San Diego commissioners approved the idea of the HTF in concept and directed the staff to bring back a proposal. Staff immediately began meeting with council people. It soon became evident that there was not a council majority in support of HTF.

The relationship between the housing commission staff and the city council historically has been uneven. The agency went through a difficult period about five years ago when it was allegedly involved in some corruption and the former director resigned in disgrace. Relations improved after that for a time. Right now, they're at a low ebb because the new director of the housing commission, who has been here for three years, has stepped on the mayor's toes on a couple of occasions—one involved the HTF. In any event, the mayor initially opposed the trust fund. She wasn't a housing commissioner at the time the fund was conceived, and I think she felt she wasn't kept as sufficiently well informed as she should have been. Although her initial opposition was not a barrier to going ahead with the project, and she finally voted for the HTF, she did hold up the appointment of housing commission trustees and succeeded in her insistence that all HTF trustees' decisions must be approved by the city council, thus undermining its autonomy.

Because of the latent opposition of the mayor and other councilpersons to the HTF, we decided not to bring an HTF proposal back to the housing commissioners. Instead, we recommended that they appoint a task force, a broad-based, working committee, not just a group of "yes" men and women, to struggle and negotiate over the issues that needed to be decided in order to get the city council's approval. A lot of fighting took place on that task force, but as a result there was not a lot of controversy in any of the public hearings. The three times that we went before the city council for the approval of task force recommendations, there was no real public opposition; the real struggles had already taken place and had been largely resolved within the task force. Even when the HTF ordinance was finally passed by the council, only three speakers were against and eighty in favor.

There are a couple of ways to test whether an HTF is equitable: where the money comes from, and what it's used for. In our case, the housing commission task force identified five possible sources of funds: a linkage fee on new commercial development, a new hotel tax, a business gross receipts tax, a utility users' tax, and a park maintenance fee. And the task force recommended that 70 percent of the fund be set aside for very-low-income households.

The task force recommendation was considerably enhanced by the report of a consultant, David Rosen, whom we hired to do the economic "nexus" study that is legally required before implementing a linkage fee. Rosen did an exhaustive study of a variety of revenue sources from which the task forces selected the six listed above. We also had access to a wealth of information about the experiences of cities with existing HTFs, prepared by Mary Brooks from the Center for Community Change. Mary provided us with a great deal of informal assistance and encouragement.

A good deal of this research was included in the *Final Report of the Task Force,* which was written by staff in a nontechnical, accessible manner so that it would be readily understood by decision makers. Arguments and facts strengthening the case for an HTF were presented as convincingly as possible, stripped down, and simplified to make it easier for supporters to use. The task force report was distributed much more widely than the staff report, which was necessarily more "objective" and less partisan.

All this in-depth research proved invaluable in the public hearings before the city council and had the effect of making the proposal seem all the more authoritative and well thought out. Commission staff invariably had good answers to difficult questions posed by council members opposed to the trust fund.

When the proposal was approved by the city council, they adopted a city-wide linkage fee on new commercial development and dedicated a percentage of the existing hotel-room tax to the HTF. They cut our proposed $54 million fund to $13 million, but that still made it one of the largest HTFs in the sunbelt. They approved the task force recommendation that at least 70 percent of the fund would support affordable rental housing for very-low-income families and that these units would remain affordable for fifty-five years. The HTF would be administered by an eleven-member board of trustees, and although the board would include neighborhood, business, and labor representation, there would be a neighborhood/labor majority. All in all, this was a very satisfactory package.

The media were helpful in this process. The housing commission had a public information officer, and one of her strengths was building relationships with the newspapers' editorial boards. I, in turn, developed fact sheets and other materials they could use. One of the things I've learned about the media is that if you do the job for them, they'll pretty much reproduce your story. If you give them a good story and you write good stuff, the media will reproduce a lot of it. In general, we did get some good coverage from the three papers in San Diego and the *Los Angeles Times,* which has a fairly wide distribution in San Diego. All gave us fairly good coverage most of the time, although the *San Diego Union* eventually opposed the HTF on its editorial page, despite doing good stories on the proposal as it progressed. We have a system of impact fees and development fees in San Diego, and the editorial board thought this was another fee that was going to burden the development industry and impede growth somewhat. To be honest, it's hard to disagree with this argument. We simply believed the need for affordable housing superseded the need for unrestrained growth.

The *San Diego Tribune* didn't oppose us, and they gave us moderate support. But the *Los Angeles Times* in its San Diego edition gave us strong support. Our public information officer was successful in getting op-eds published that I drafted for the housing commission director and chairman, and the chairman of the HTF task force, who was a fairly liberal developer. An op-ed under his byline appeared in the *San Diego Daily Transcript,* which is the daily business paper in San Diego. We believe these op-eds were very influential in building support for the HTF and in overwhelming the opposition.

SERENDIPITOUS DEVELOPMENTS

We were also helped by the widespread recognition that affordable housing is a very serious problem in San Diego. I think it was this understanding that enabled us to be most effective in quickly catching the public's attention. We proposed the HTF at a time when housing prices were going through the roof. Report after report in the media, from the National Association of Realtors, and from other sources called San Diego one of the least affordable cities in the nation for renters and home buyers in terms of the cost of housing relative to income. Housing is more expensive in Honolulu, for example, but wages there are a good deal higher. San Diego has very high housing costs coupled with relatively low salaries compared to cities of similar size.

Affordable housing really was a crippling problem, not simply because expensive housing hurts poor people—we felt that focusing on the needs of the poor was a losing strategy from the beginning—but because it was going to cripple the city economically. Without a low- to middle-income labor pool, growth and development would be hampered. That's what we argued. I felt that it would be counterproductive to argue for a big pool of money to house lower-income people because these people were seen by many as undeserving. Opponents would say, "Why should we do this? They should get a job." The ethos of our time is that you pull yourself up by your own bootstraps, and we had to adapt our strategy accordingly.

At the same time that the issue of housing heated up, the political environment in the city shifted to our advantage. As I mentioned earlier, the city council in San Diego was not favorably disposed to the trust fund idea when the proposal was initially introduced. I think we counted five votes in opposition and four in favor. But at the time the fund was initially proposed, many years of effort to establish district elections in San Diego finally bore fruit. The abolition of citywide elections and the introduction of district elections occurred at almost the same time that the HTF task force made its final recommendation to the housing commissioners. In the new district elections, two new council members were elected to the city council, and they both unseated conservative city council people who had been opposed to the trust fund. Members of the HTF coalition were heavily involved in their election campaigns and helped turn them into HTF supporters. That was an important—maybe the key—piece of work on their part.

The election of those two council members was necessary to the establishment of an HTF in San Diego, but it wasn't the end of the story. It created the conditions under which the trust fund could happen, but it didn't guarantee its adoption, by any means. The HTF coalition did a lot of very hard lobbying from the time the HTF task force made its recommendation until the HTF was approved by the city council six months later.

This story of HTF in San Diego illustrates how important it is for planners to keep bringing up sound planning programs and policies that may be seen as overly ambitious or that have been shot down in the past. A planner must be aware of new conditions, new issues and concerns, and new players and must work with them in order to tailor old ideas to new conditions.

RETROSPECTIVE THOUGHTS

One of the things that always bothered me in retrospect about my adolescence was that my elders often dismissed some of the things I said because they were "idealistic." That's an awful criticism to make of anybody. I think it's important to be idealistic. It's important to hold on to your ideals and to struggle for them, that's what makes life interesting and fulfilling. We're never going to fulfill all our ideals, but we can fulfill some of them. It's important to keep ideals out there as goals to struggle for.

I think many people in fields like planning (and social work and labor relations for that matter) become disenchanted and embittered because they're not able to achieve all their goals. Their aspirations are squeezed out of them. I think it's important not to let that happen. You must make achieving your ideals an integral part of what it is you are trying to do. In my experience at the SDHC, it has been possible to make important things happen. If you are willing to take some risks and if you incorporate equity issues into the work your agency or department is chartered to do, you will find a constituency of support willing to work with you.

When I first developed the Housing Trust Fund idea and began to form a strategy, our director had not been with us long. He was motivated to make some significant policy changes, and was open to new ideas. I took his support at face value and decided there were things that needed to be done to advance the trust fund idea. A lot of times, mayors, directors, and supervisors in general will allow you to run with ambitious proposals and schemes on the understanding that if something goes wrong, you carry the can. I think a good planner understands that and uses it as an opportunity to advance good ideas, even if it means taking some risks. I never thought that my job was at stake at SDHC, and I wasn't worried about negative feedback from the development industry or the press because, at each step of the way, we had the support of our housing commissioners, four of whom were city council members. So I was just an insignificant planner implementing the wishes of the housing commissioners and the city council.

If you want to perpetuate the status quo, you don't have to take such risks. But if you want to bring about social change or important policy changes in a city or state, then you have to take some risks. Change involves, by definition, a step into the unknown, and there are always people who are going to be opposed to stepping into the unknown. As far as housing in concerned, you're in an especially critical, volatile area. There's no way around it. Real estate is a powerful industry. There are big bucks to be made and big bucks to be lost, and planning decisions have a big impact on that.

FURTHER READING: Housing Trust Funds

Brooks, Mary. *A Guide to Developing a Housing Trust Fund.* Washington, D.C.: Center for Community Change, 1989.

———. *A Survey of Housing Trust Funds.* Washington, D.C.: Center for Community Change, 1989.

Calavita, Nico, and Kenneth Grimes. "The Establishment of the San Diego HTF: Lessons for Theory and Practice." *Journal of Planning Education and Research* 11 (1992): 179–184.

Calavita, Nico, Kenneth Grimes, and Susan Reynolds. "Zigzagging toward Long-Term Affordability in the Sunbelt: The San Diego Housing Trust Fund." In *The Affordable City: Toward a Third Sector Housing Policy,* edited by John Davis. Philadelphia: Temple University Press, 1994.

Connerly, Charles. *A Guide to Housing Trust Funds*. Washington, D.C.: Neighborhood Reinvestment Corporation, 1989.

Housing Trust Fund Coalition. "Income, Housing, and the Local Economy: How the Housing Trust Fund Can Avert a Local Recession." An informal paper prepared by members of the HTF coalition, San Diego, 1989.

Rosen, David. *Housing Trust Funds*. Washington, D.C.: American Planning Association, 1990.

Schwartz, David C., Richard C. Ferlauto, and Daniel N. Hoffman. *A New Housing Policy for America*. Philadelphia: Temple University Press, 1988.

chapter 11

LESSONS LEARNED

W e believe that there are dozens, perhaps even hundreds, of urban plan- ners whose work might have appeared in this book but did not. Every interview we conducted provided more leads, most of which we were unable to follow up. If we had the time, we are confident we would be able to fill a number of books with interesting interviews with equity planners. Each one of them would have illuminated different insights into the problems of their cities and how social equity planning might have made a difference and improved things.

But at some point we had to stop, assemble what we had, and get it out into the world. Although each of the accounts in this book is revealing, together they make up a series of insights and lessons. In this final chapter, we attempt, first, to generalize beyond these accounts, making broad statements that might be useful to other planners, encouraging their own efforts at social equity plan- ning and redistributive justice. Ideally, if the reader is a practicing planner, he or she will say, "Well, this isn't Chicago (or Portland or San Diego), and I'm not so-and-so, but our situations are similar, so why don't I try what worked for them?" Second, we want to reflect on the question raised in Chapter 1: Does the experience of equity planners move cities beyond the "palliative" state to one that allows them more serious problem-solving capabilities?

First, the generalizations. This is a hazardous task; we don't want to claim too much, but we don't want to overlook important themes either. We realize that no planners will ever be in exactly the same situation as our respondents, but their stories suggest issues and possibilities, traps and opportunities to look out for and take seriously.

Perhaps we should begin with a few qualifications.

- We know that individual respondents chose what they wished to reveal about themselves, and they were unlikely to reveal themselves as fools or naifs. Also, our subjects' accounts may be at variance with other versions of the same events. To the extent possible, we have checked out our subjects' version of a story with other accounts of the same issue. Mostly, alternate sources confirmed the views presented.
- Our sample was small, and we cannot be certain what a representative sample would consist of. We do know that virtually all our interviews ended with the recommendation by the subject that we ought to go to another city and talk to so-and-so, who is "doing very interesting social equity work." On that basis alone, we are confident that much more equity planning is taking place than is being reported. We also tended to focus on large cities and not on equity planning opportunities in small cities or rural areas, although we are confident opportunities to do equity planning exist at every planning level.
- Our sample was not broadly representative. We had to depend on our own networks, and these were mostly white males, like the editors. Much more effort is needed to reveal more extensively the equity planning work being done by women and minority urban planning professionals.
- People, even urban planning professionals, do change their minds about events and about their roles in events. Time changes people's views as well. If our subjects had been interviewed two years earlier or five years later, time and circumstances might have shaded their views. Roles change, too. Individuals who have gone from being practitioners to academics (e.g., Mier, Dreier, Bertsch) are probably more likely to be outspoken, while those remaining in city hall or in nonprofit agencies (where they do not award tenure) are more likely to be circumspect and guarded in their remarks.

Having gotten these few qualifications out of the way, what can we learn from these stories?

DIFFERENCES

Social equity planners can be of either sex and of any race. They can be of urban or rural origin. While most of our subjects were brought up in urban areas, some—Strachan, Moe, Stanback, Bertsch—hailed from farms or small cities.

Equity planners' approaches were varied. For some, the work was difficult; for others, things came more easily. Most had clear ideas from the beginning about what they wanted to accomplish and why; a few had no particular intention to do equity planning but were drawn into it because it seemed like the ethical or logical thing to do. Most would do it again, a few might not. Success has led most to write about their work to provide a record and encourage imitators in other cities. In that regard, Bertsch, Dreier, Grimes, Mier, Moe, and Shearer have written a great deal; others have made fewer attempts to broadcast their work.

Some of our subjects knew economic deprivation in their youths. Cohen reports growing up in Boston public housing projects and Arturo Vazquez grew up next to the steel mills in Chicago's south side. But others reported living a middle-class life in stable, middle-class neighborhoods. For example, Derek Shearer evokes a nostalgic reminiscence of the nurturing, small-scale, but accessible neighborhoods of his youth.

Some equity planners did their work in progressive cities, such as Boston under Ray Flynn, Chicago under Harold Washington, and Santa Monica under Ruth Goldway and the SMRR coalition. In Portland, Margaret Strachan was a key part of the elected government—the commissioner in charge of city planning—an enviable position for innovative policy development. Stanback enjoyed the authority of city manager in Hartford. In these instances, the equity planners were responding to the mayor's wishes or, at least, were enjoying a reciprocal relationship between planning and politics. In other cases, however, for example Ken Grimes in San Diego, the equity planner was creating policy and building support in a very uncertain and not necessarily supportive political context.

SIMILARITIES

Most respondents reported that the origins of their interest in equity, justice, and fairness went back to their childhood and that these early teachings were elaborated by training and experience. Rick Cohen moved from his youth in public housing to a job in a homeless shelter; Ken Grimes spoke of his family's close involvement with and support for the British Labour movement; Vazquez's parents were also strong labor supporters in Chicago; Bertsch talked of his parish priest, who sharpened his concern for people; and Kari Moe spoke of her family and teachers as providing role models. Many of our respondents had backgrounds in which politics was an important component. When they were interviewed, most of them fell into the age range of 40–55. They were old enough to have lived through the turbulent 1960s, and many reported that the events of that decade helped shape their ideas. Rob Mier, who served as an advisor to the navy of South Vietnam, found that his head was turned around by his Vietnam experience; Shearer spoke of his participation in the antiwar movement, as did Arturo Vazquez. Vazquez also recounted his reconnection with his Mexican roots in the march from Delano to Sacramento with Cesar Chavez. Clearly, most of our respondents learned their social activism during the 1960s; but three decades later, they're still at it. They may now have settled into middle-class comforts, but their interest in change and social ferment remains.

Most of our respondents showed a character that can only be described as remarkably persistent and energized for what they were doing. In an era where people speak of fading energy, a reluctance to face the same battle again and again, and burnout, our stories suggest just the opposite. For example, Billie Bramhall took her observations and idealism from Philadelphia, Baltimore, and Pittsburgh to Denver over a period of more than two decades; Janice Cogger, briefly discussed in the Preface, who worked so hard on equity-oriented transit issues in Cleveland in the 1970s, was still working on the neighborhood beat in 1993; Kari Moe, in 1993 chief of staff for U.S. Senator Paul Wellstone, still speaks passionately of the need for planners personally to engage the issues of racism and poverty and try to figure out how to put coalitions together to overcome them. In their work, our respondents were captured by more than just ordinary interest. They were not simply attached to their work but hooked, driven, possessed by an unusually high level of excitement, an excitement that most of us do not ordinarily experience in our work. Most of the equity planners we talked to seemed to be convinced that the struggle for a more open, egalitarian society offered them not only the hope of a better life for others but a measure of fulfillment—even pleasure—for themselves.

Simple courage was also a factor. Aside from the danger of alienating a key politician, which Cohen, who was periodically fired and rehired by his mayor, describes so well, physical danger was sometimes a problem. Bertsch says that after a heated public hearing on his fair share housing plan, he did not know if there would be anything left of his car after he turned the key on; Moe took the "rage of kids intended for their absent or abusive parents."

Most of our respondents hedged or disregarded the informal rules of planning bureaucracies. Under these rules, agencies may consult with interested groups, but not take a hand in organizing them; may inform groups of significant developments, but not persuade them to energize their membership to take action; may routinely advise the press of activities, but never carry their case to the media.

In almost every instance, the equity planners disregarded these rules. They worked often and intimately with grassroots organizations and public bureaucracies and dealt with the media as an important portion of the planners' attempt to educate and build political support. They seem to believe that creativity in administration is superior to routine. The business of leadership, they imply, is not the guarding of privilege or the administration of existing machinery through organization charts and channels, but the anticipation of social needs, the invention of new forms, and the opening up of government.

People involved in equity planning discuss the process as more than simply planning or problem solving. Instead of merely horse-trading with other participants, they seem to be caught up in a process of learning and discovery that alters their own goals, expectations, and even language. They also saw themselves as instructing or teaching others about the importance of government and the responsibilities of citizenship. Hanna Pitkin describes this set of altered relationships well. "In the process, we learn to think about the standards themselves, about our stake in the existence of standards, of justice, of our community, so that afterwards, we are changed. Economic man becomes a citizen." [1] Perhaps this uniform persistence is based on a persuasive sense of optimism—the conviction that one person can make a difference.

STRATEGIES AND MAJOR THEMES

Building Coalitions   Most respondents rejected the notion that they might have accomplished what they did on their own. They felt that leadership was important but that coalition building among other members of the bureaucracy and lower-income interest groups was central to success. In this, they rejected one of the informal rules of government bureaucracy, which is to keep down the level of interest-group activity—that is to say, demands on government. Ken Grimes painstakingly built a coalition among church groups, labor, social workers, and advocates for the poor, all of whom shared the objective of affordable housing, but didn't even know of one another's existence. Grimes's act of bringing together this disparate coalition of advocates and focusing them on the San Diego Housing Trust Fund may have been his most important contribution. Virtually all the other respondents talked about their extensive coalition-building efforts.

Mier describes the use of the capital improvement program to build coalitions in white working-class neighborhoods in northwest and southwest Chicago that had initially opposed Harold Washington: the neighborhood organizations in these communities, banded together in a coalition called SONSOC (Save Our Neighborhoods Save Our City), eventually began to find a common ground with the black and Latino organizations.

Billie Bramhall's plans for the Cole neighborhood in Denver and Rick Cohen's and Peter Dreier's efforts to link downtown and waterfront development to affordable housing goals could hardly be brought to successful conclusions without the building of broad, supportive coalitions. And Margaret Strachan's city plans were entirely based on extensive citizen participation and were all coalition driven.

For many, coalition building was a way to institutionalize their social change policies so that they would remain in place when administrations changed. Virtually every one of the equity planners stressed the need for broadened citizen involvement in government and the need to form and work with neighborhood organizations that would then presumably back the policies they had helped formulate. Bramhall thought this was the *only* way to rebuild disinvested neighborhoods.

Cohen, who successfully sought coalitions with federal and state agencies as well as local groups, pointed to a danger: empowering neighborhood organizations did not always result in progressive policies. He pointed to one group that his agency had helped empower that had organized the poor right out of their Jersey City neighborhood. And Mier observed that "community empowerment is at once liberating and a very conservative and racist force," emphasizing that the first community organization in Chicago pushed for racial exclusion.

The techniques of coalition building varied from case to case. In an earlier book, *Making Equity Planning Work,* author Norman Krumholz described the cautious building of coalitions with Cleveland's neighborhood groups. Compare that with Margaret Strachan's ebullience in Portland to build a coalition of support for the Central City Plan: "We did some programming on cable T.V. . . . We did programs in classrooms with fifth and sixth graders (to involve their parents). . . . We set up a geodesic dome with interactive computer programs all talking about the plan." The result was the participation, Strachan says, of "over 100,000 people."

To be sure, neighborhood participation was well established in Portland. By contrast, Ken Grimes might have had a difficult time convincing the mayor that he was not organizing and energizing a potential political enemy. As a result, much of his organizing had to be low key.

Defining Planning Responsibilities Broadly   Perhaps alone among city hall employees, urban planners have much freedom to define activist roles for their agencies because planning practice is not uniform by law or tradition. To an extent, urban planning may be seen as an area of broad administrative discretion. Beyond the narrow powers and responsibilities mandated to planners by their city charters, the scope and content of the urban planning function to a large extent waits to be defined by the planners themselves. If planners choose to be limited by the descriptions of planning powers in their enabling charters, they will probably not engage in social equity planning. The same is true if they listen closely to the broad and general observations of most of their political leaders. Exceptions exist, of course, but politicians such as Harold Washington and Ray Flynn, who consistently articulated equity objectives, tend to be rare. Politicians must seek consensus in their search for the broadest possible support; in the process, they deliberately blur objectives. But planners must have clear goals and objectives in order to make rational plans and measure accomplishments.

The equity planners in this book defined their roles more broadly than anyone had any right to expect. Dale Bertsch took the HUD directive to include a housing component in his work program as meaning he should do a regional fair share housing program. Grimes's work on the San Diego Housing Trust Fund put an innocuous agency at center stage. Howard Stanback raised issues of regional equity that were bitterly resisted by Hartford's suburbs. No one told Kari Moe or Billie Bramhall to include considerations of race, poverty, and equity in their work and emphasize them in their policies; they justified doing so, and they did it.

Strategies for Success   Planners and others plot strategies in order to develop paths of minimum resistance toward their goals. Planning agencies have the freedom (within limits) to choose among alternative roles; the choice will depend on their objectives, their personal taste for risk, or estimates of the effect of each strategy on the general image of the planning agency or on the city's administration.

Many equity planners spoke of the strategy of making their chief executives look good. Cohen showed Mayor Cucci how to transform into policies and programs the vague ideas on fairness and justice that the mayor had verbalized during the election campaign that swept him into office. Mier, Vazquez, and Moe put Harold Washington's ambitious social ideas into plans, negotiations, and meat on rhetorical bones. In helping poor neighborhoods get a fair share of capital improvement funds and helping them plan for the future they wanted, Billie Bramhall also helped Federico Peña build his constituency and win elections. Her work in Denver's poor neighborhoods may have made Peña not only a winner in local elections, but famous enough on the national scene to be appointed U.S. transportation secretary in 1993. Dreier and his mayor, Ray Flynn, had reciprocal objectives: "A lot of us thought of Ray Flynn as a vehicle for our politics. But Ray Flynn saw a lot of us (progressives, activists, academics) as a talent pool to help him get elected." None of these equity planners were reluctant to get into the rough and tumble of politics.

Quite the contrary. Cohen publicly contradicted Mayor Cucci, who wanted to make linkage payments voluntary, "like passing the plate at church," by insisting that they be "voluntary mandatory," implying that if you didn't pay, you wouldn't get your permits; Mier successfully sought the commissioner of economic development post in Chicago because he feared the transition team was going off in the wrong direction; Bertsch deliberately worked to change his citizen board to one made up of elected officials.

Cultivating a direct relationship with the media was an important part of the agenda among most equity planners. Unlike most city agencies, which believe that controversies at city hall should be kept from the media, equity planners took special efforts to inform the media and gain their support. The backbone of Dale Bertsch's support was the solid backing he received from Jim Fain of the *Dayton Daily News,* who editorialized against any politician who spoke out against the fair share plan. Cohen shared his documentation, thinking, and analyses with the newspapers, and Dreier cultivated a couple of reporters very carefully. Virtually all the others made special efforts to deserve the support of the press. They did so by being open and accessible to reporters, by explaining their objectives and the reasons they were pursuing them, and by presenting themselves as honest, competent public servants.

A sensitivity to political realities was central to their dealings with the media and other groups. Planning in graduate school is learned as a largely technical activity. Students in courses on planning methods and implementation typically use survey research, forecasting, computer modeling, and other "scientific" methods to discover "facts" and shape their plans accordingly. But, in practice, these equity planners often used their speech and writing only partially as a scientific argument, but mostly as a political argument to convince others to accept their preferred alternatives. For equity planners, these alternatives often did not reinforce the prevailing view of an issue but presented another important but neglected perspective. The planners, then, had to be extremely sensitive to how the media, the mayor or city council, or the public at large would construe their utterances.[2]

Direct contact with the press was only one of the many ways the planners managed to organize public attention. Some—Bertsch, Strachan, Bramhall, and the group from Chicago—drafted and published formal plans. They and many of the others also provided timely technical work and often wrote speeches for their mayor. A few—Cohen, Dreier, Grimes, and Mier—wrote letters to the editor of their daily paper and op-ed pieces for the editorial page. Others appeared on commercial radio and television to discuss various issues. Strachan sought broad support everywhere, including displaying kids' drawings in a "huge geodesic dome." Clearly, there are many ways to organize public attention, and the planners explored a wide range.[3]

Persistence Essential Early on, Ken Grimes conceived the need for a Housing Trust Fund in San Diego, but there was little support for it on the city council. But politicians and politics change. When they did, the Housing Trust Fund idea was taken to the new council, where it was enthusiastically accepted by the new political majority. It seems to be important for planners periodically to resurrect good ideas that have been rejected in the past and put them back on the public agenda. No one else in local government is as well positioned as urban planners to do this. In any event, equity planners are often trying to change long-established policies, procedures, and understandings. This is bound to be more difficult than simply following the status quo, and persistence may be an essential ingredient in success.

The Business Terminology of Equity Planning The equity planners in this book were conscious of the fact that business is a big player in our cities and in our society. To the extent possible, they tried to enlist the support of business behind their efforts. Their objective was to convert business executives, often predatory birds of passage, into responsible, long-term stewards of the public interest. Some did this by adopting terminology that business people found familiar and comforting. Dreier argued that rent control in Boston was pro-business in that employers would either have to pay higher wages (in a noncontrolled market) or have difficulty getting employees. Grimes made much the same argument regarding the rocketing cost of housing in support of San Diego's housing trust fund and succeeded in enlisting substantial business support. Stanback sought state tax reforms with business support, arguing that Hartford and Hartford's businesses would both be better off with tax reform.

The equity planners consciously avoided taboos in terminology—centralized planning, social engineering—that would have killed their proposals before they could reach the discussion stage.

Others used analyses of cost effectiveness that were recognizable in business practice. For example, they asked whether it was more cost effective for the city to maintain impacted racial reservations for the poor with all the costs this implied or to try a comprehensive approach that would be more cost effective in the long run. When Rob Mier speaks of the need for educational reform in Chicago, he wants to enlist the support of business, which is concerned that it must spend $90 billion a year on retraining, or manufacturers who must replace the instructions on their machines with pictures because their entry-level employees can't read.

Equity planners found many ways to transcend the advocacy pluralism mode and make appeals to the more general public interest. Mier, Vazquez, Moe, and the Chicago planners appealed to the American tradition of fairness with their Chicago Works Together (CWT) plan. Margaret Strachan and her planning committees spoke of the legitimacy of broad-scale citizen involvement. Billie Bramhall and the Denver planners wrote of the logic and efficiency of true comprehensiveness.

Publishing a Comprehensive Plan   Publishing a comprehensive plan was seen by some as important for several reasons: stating goals clearly, helping build support among others of a like mind, and justifying budget expenditures. Mier found several advantages to doing CWT. First was the feeling that if you "codify what you're all about and what you want to do, then the more likely you are to have people understand it and buy into it and operate as if that is the game plan. Second, CWT was a great team-building exercise . . . it created a reason for the commissioners to get together regularly and helped some of these staff people to get in contact. Third, it was an occasion to broaden the external constituency base."

Shearer moved the Santa Monica planning commission into a comprehensive planning process some time *after* the Santa Monicans for Renters' Rights (SMRR) majority did a series of development agreements, partly to generate support on a broad rather than ad hoc basis.

Margaret Strachan in Portland used the Central City Plan as a focus for intense citizen involvement. Bramhall's planning department in Denver also found publication of downtown and citywide comprehensive plans to be useful, both in terms of organizing thinking and harnessing external support and of organizing neighborhood-related capital expenditures.

Other equity planners specifically did *not* engage in overall comprehensive planning exercises. Dreier never made a formal plan in Boston; his planning staff had an agenda, which was internally understood, but one that was developed informally. Cohen operated similarly in Jersey City. Bertsch did the fair share housing plan in the Miami Valley but did not undertake a more comprehensive planning effort. None had an animus against comprehensive planning; they simply went along without a formal plan.

While it is an important theme in the planning and public administration literature, Mier thought about the issue of long-term planning versus ad hoc decision making this way:

> Basically I don't think that ad hoc versus agenda is the right question. The question is how does an agenda and operating ad hoc go hand in hand. On a day-to-day management basis, there was a continual tension between the agenda and the peculiarities of the situation we were in. There was constant interplay. For example, the development plan had some fairly clear principles in mind, one of which was "jobs are the bottom line." In any particular development, we had to figure out what that meant. In figuring it out, our whole understanding of jobs was reshaped. I think the tension between structure and day-to-day actions was alive and palpable.

Using Dramaturgy to Manage Attention   Ken Grimes's strategic orchestration of the start-up efforts leading to San Diego's Housing Trust Fund included stage directions to move the process forward. Fearing that an initial meeting with Housing Trust Fund advocates would simply peter out, Grimes asked a friend in the group to call for further action. It was a shrewd step and helped move the process along. Bertsch, to ensure the passage of his regional fair share housing plan, bused supporters to public hearings, seated them down front, and made sure they were vocal. He also deliberately added sections to the plan that his commissioners, by prearrangement, could and did remove without affecting the plan's integrity.

Mier was always being accused of putting his own framework on Chicago events. Against some standards, this was true. But, basically, we can think of many of the equity planners as having selected and emphasized information in a different way: it is always a matter of debate what interpretation to put on events; and if the local press or business coalition was to put one interpretation on them, then it was up to the equity planners to call attention to a different frame. The equity planners simply emphasized issues of inequality and human needs, rather than size of investment and rate of return. They understood that private interests and public interests may come into harsh conflict. If unlimited private indulgence means there are not enough resources for education, health needs, or decent housing, than a planner, concerned about his city's future, attempts to limit private indulgence. The planner's selection of different information to emphasize may be castigated as being "divisive," but it is easily justified.

Dreier tried hard to manage an antiredlining campaign, making sure community groups knew when information was coming out, cultivating friends in the local press and trying to get his own framework on the issue into their hands.

The many equity planners who wrote speeches and papers for their mayors thought it helped strengthen bonds of trust. It helped the planners say to others, "This is what the mayor wants." It was also a way of building the status of the planning agency and the influence of the planners. There is no question that when the word gets out in city hall that some planners are writing speeches for the mayor, the planning agency's stock will rise.

Talking about Race   Like the rest of the urban planning profession, the equity planners in this book did not talk easily about race. Although they would agree that racial discrimination—black, white, Latino—is a central issue of our time, we had the impression that the language of race interaction was not up to the problems cities faced in the 1990s. Failing to articulate apt metaphors, equity planners fell back on other issues. Class was the dominant one; or people power, or neighborhood power, or occasionally environmental goals.

Mier was a partial exception. His experience with Harold Washington unleashed his abilities at race-conscious integrative metaphor making. He said:

> I think the dynamics of race in this country is the most powerful force confronting, shaping who can and should do planning. It is the central issue facing planners, and it's got to be confronted in every aspect of the daily work, daily life, of planning. Planners have to focus attention on it. I think a lot of planning is attention shaping. Plans shape people's attention. So planners have consciously to admit that they are confronting race.

Others, doing work in the interest of minority neighborhoods, nevertheless spoke in generally nonracial language. The Chicago planners, Cohen, and Stanback spoke of the need to have their staffs represent racially the community they served; others did not. Billie Bramhall, working in the Cole neighborhood, a black neighborhood in Denver, spoke mostly in terms of working for low-income people. Bertsch and Grimes, to gain support, deliberately emphasized housing affordability for "people just like you." The Cleveland planners briefly discussed in the Preface adopted the transit-dependent population of Cleveland as a client without discussing the fact that in Cleveland, the transit dependent were mostly black.

It is a dilemma: equity planners tend to be mostly white males and females. They often represent the interests of people of color. As these interviews make clear, they manage to produce tangible benefits for minorities. The interviews also make clear that equity planners have adopted two approaches to issues of racial empowerment: (1) economic populism, which appeals to all low-income people around their common economic interests; and (2) rainbow politics, which recognizes differences and, to a degree, makes a case for community control. The dilemma is whether white equity planners can work effectively for black or Hispanic community control without contributing to the fractioning of solidarity in communities of color. The stories in this book make clear they can, but the issue requires much more research.

A Sense of Loneliness   Equity planners talk to one another and to organizations of their constituencies, such as neighborhood and housing groups, but not nearly as much as they would like. Shearer described his role in creating in the 1970s the Conference on Alternative State and Local Policies, which served as a forum for some of the people we interviewed, but it was not clear what other national or regional forums existed. Planners Network was useful to some equity planners, but not others. What seems universal among these planners was the feeling that they were alone. Cohen said, "My staff members would sometimes say that they felt as if they were on a spaceship with nobody else out there." Kari Moe spoke of the difficulty of "fighting a war with someone else's army" and "swimming upstream."

It was better being an equity planner in cities with "progressive" mayors and council majorities, though the accounts here blur the distinction. Clavel, writing about such cases, noted that planners and governing coalitions faced a new set of problems, not that life got easier.[4] Thus, Derek Shearer, as part of Santa Monica's planning effort, concerned himself with institutionalizing innovations. It is about what the equity planner leaves behind. Shearer's comment about using the various commissions set up in Santa Monica as training grounds for persons who eventually become city council members and take other important posts is apt. Mier describes the advancement of many of his colleagues after the death of Harold Washington.

But in some more tenuous situations—Cohen in Jersey City under Cucci— we heard talk of getting gains on the margin and being happy in the end. Institutionalization was not a possibility, did not happen. In fact, in those situations, the history of what happens tends to be obliterated. The equity planner is in effect lost to memory, particularly as far as the mainstream press and opinion are concerned.

BROADENING THE OPTIONS FOR CITIES

We hope the narratives presented here make the case that there is, in the accumulated work of the equity planners, a fund of useful experience that is now available to American cities. Too often, though, all this is ignored in a nation that pursues other objectives; the work of equity planners is underutilized, their successful initiatives forgotten so that later generations cannot build on the best of their efforts.

It would be better if the *profession* of city planning could incorporate more of the practice represented by the equity planners. Earlier, we found precursors and hopeful signs, but also a majority mode of operation that, like the society generally, tended to deny the efficacy of equity work, participated in futile giveaways to growth-oriented projects that failed to produce jobs and seemed not to emphasize the populations equity planners served.

Nevertheless, we think it is possible for the profession of city planning, the professional schools, and the larger community of city politics and interests to take steps to put the work of equity planners more squarely at the center of professional and city policy work. These steps include the following:

1. At the most general level, we need to dispense with the market fetishism that has marked both academic life and politics in the past two decades. The market, and the singleminded pursuit of gain that is an indispensable part of an efficient market, has to be placed where it belongs: as an instrument of policy, rather than an end. Let the business schools, businesspeople, and their specialized interest groups focus on market thinking. We need them. But, for public policy, the problem is to figure out where the market is an appropriate instrument and where other instruments—voting, bargaining, or planning— are more appropriate. This is an old idea in planning and economic theory, and we need to reestablish it.[5]

2. Professional planning schools, in collaboration with practitioners, need to develop the practical and methodological side of equity planning. As long as curriculums and professional journals feature mainstream methodology, while bringing in equity planners for inspirational lectures, the interests of the growth coalition will be safe. It is time for the center of the profession and its

academics to do serious studies and codification of the ways equity planners actually get things done.

3. Not only planners but city politicians, planning board members, and a range of city administrators need to create a national organization devoted to the interchange of information and practice of the sort that equity planners represent. The Conference on Alternative State and Local Policies, which ran national meetings of equity-oriented administrators and elected officials during the 1970s, and which published a distinguished set of conference readers and specialized publications, is one model for this. A start would be the reissuance of many of these publications, but a formal and durable organization is needed.

4. Professional schools, university archives, or both could pour more effort into the tracking of equity planners' experiences. This should cover interviews, stories, and histories such as we have collected here, as well as documents, deep analyses of methods and practices, new legislation, and administrative procedures.

5. Equity planners themselves could do more to promulgate their work. One effective medium is the letter to the editor or op-ed column of local newspapers. Another is to use the regularly scheduled meetings of the planning board to publicize positions. Still another way is the virtue of making oneself and one's opinions visible. While many equity planners have already operated effectively in this manner, many have not, despite having compelling stories to tell.

6. Professional schools could put more emphasis on interaction with practice, particularly through mounting outreach efforts and courses that place students in direct contact with the work of the equity planners. This is a logical function for professional schools but one that is underrealized, perhaps because of administrative pressure to become "scholarly." We think the best professional schools are those that balance scholarship with practice, more or less evenly. And we think that balance should occur within individual careers, not simply by hiring a token practitioner or two or a few token theorists. We advocate opportunities to broaden academic careers, as has happened in a few, but only a few, cases. We believe it would be extraordinarily useful for academics to take positions in city government for a time, not only to get a leg up on the complex problems of implementation but to begin measuring their success, not in numbers of papers produced, but in actual improvements in the lives of needy city residents.

7. Foundations should support the flow of personnel from practice to academic life, and vice versa, at both professional and scholarly levels. MIT's Urban Scholars program, which provided community organizers with an opportunity for academic retreat in Cambridge, needs to be replicated in several places. Out of the Cambridge program, a number went on for higher degrees, and in most other cases the community organization function was strengthened and burnout was reduced.

8. Equity planners, mainstream planners, the professional schools, and city government and administration need to move forward in connecting race, gender, and ethnicity to core liberal institutions: tracking the ethnic and gender composition of schools and agencies is one key component that can move ahead immediately so that data are available to hold the responsible administrators accountable for fair representation. Rob Mier's observations on race, quoted earlier, are correct: equity planners must take every opportunity to push race to the forefront of discussion. If this is true for the profession, it is also true for the professional schools, where the profession, by and large, recruits its members and reproduces its practice.

9. We need to reintegrate notions of "fairness"—often put on the back burner—with those of organizational effectiveness in agencies and schools.

10. The planning profession and schools can take the lead in creating and publicizing indicators of distribution: wealth, income, municipal services, health outcomes, and other information that provide a baseline accounting of the state of "equity" in our cities and nation. The idea of a "public balance sheet," authored by David Smith and publicized by the Conference on Alternative State and Local Policies a decade ago, is one example of what we are talking about.

Beyond Pluralism   The biggest problem with these suggestions and for equity planning practice is the perception that they represent simply an expanded pluralism. Since a part of what equity planners do is to make contact between city hall and an increasingly diverse set of publics, it is easy to fall back on the proposition that each of these publics has a claim on public resources and recognition, without the responsibility to integrate each claim into an overall city policy that a majority can support.

The problem initially raised by advocacy planners in the period after Paul Davidoff's 1965 article was whether they represented a real advance for the "have-not" clienteles. Advocacy planners included middle-class white professionals and students who, at least some of the time, found themselves imposing alien values, professional "solutions," and entanglements with city hall bureaucracies on indigenous populations. These challenges put advocate planners in difficult positions. Some withdrew, others "deprofessionalized," making the choice to work with communities as organizers at the cost of giving up some of their more elaborate design interests. Some of the retrospective evaluation suggested that "planning" was in itself the problem: what was needed was not plans, but indigenous organizers. If there was a role for outsiders, it was as organizers, not planners.

What this produced, insofar as the larger metropolitan polity was concerned, was a kind of pluralism that insists that no outsider can know the real interests of inner-city neighborhoods and people. What is possible is perhaps a federation of interests with some balancing, but no overarching vision. This at least was the lowest denominator of the message.

The question is, did the equity planners add much to this? We think the experience of the "equity planners" suggests a very different point of view. We admit it is ambiguous. One part of it is that the situations our cities are in are so extreme and varied compared to the relatively mild crises out of which the city planning profession developed that often no overarching view is possible; the only thing to do is fight for the needs of the locality, regardless of what arguments are put together by the "growth coalition" or other elite power.

Even if this were all that characterized the worldview of equity planners, their work would be important. For it provides us with an alternative view of U.S. city development. This view, reflected in many citizen groups and some professional and academic literature, transcends growth coalition perspectives with a different vision of cities and American culture. The growth coalition perspective, still dominant in many places and among many elites, because it promises jobs and profits and accords with many traditional values, suggests in many respects a stable program. It proposes to tap sources of capital for investment; it mobilizes a coherent business leadership; it presents graphic pictures of new buildings in centralized downtown locations; and it repeats the JFK aphorism that a rising tide lifts all boats, thereby suggesting not simply a class interest but a formula for the public interest. Against this, protest was initially a mere ritual. Without a program for replacing this engine, this structure of power, the opposition only revealed its own weakness and added a corollary proposition: growth, while good in the long run, was bound to ruffle some working-class feathers. Up to a point, there was nothing new in protest.

As neighborhood protest developed in the 1970s, an opposition viewpoint went one step further. In this newer viewpoint, both the elite power structure and culture and the oppositional movements at the grassroots are changing and unstable. Business elites are not supporting upward redistribution and rejecting corporate liberal approaches out of long-term strategy and class preservation but are doing it out of desperation and their own crisis.[6] Capital is not operating as a rational market, but is "hypermobile."[7] Political systems are not pluralist systems that self-correct, but are in a state of unstable decay.[8] From this view, equity planners are innovators in the profession, carriers of a new culture, valuable witnesses to what is going on, with insights not available to those still operating within the traditional mind-set.

There is another meaning embedded in the equity planners' experience. We do not think that simple grassroots advocacy is the ultimate answer for the profession or for the communities. Even equity planners' roles as reported in this book make them more like transitional figures, somewhere between the first two interpretations between a growth coalition program and simple grassroots reaction. Equity planners all work in city hall; they all have some connection with groups that are marginal to the central political process. In their approaches to this experience they vary in viewpoint: some are modernists with a conscience; others identify mainly with the periphery, sitting on the outside looking in, despite their (sometimes temporary) position as officials in government.

Nor do we believe that city planning can become "postmodern" in the sense of abandoning its search for a fixed position from which to survey and prescribe for communities. The profession would lose its meaning if it did so. As the Goodmans argued in *Communitas,* the basic reason for city planning is a concern for the city's heavy investments—bridges, roads, and buildings that will last a long time and affect livelihoods and life.[9] David Harvey made a trenchant critique of the postmodern view:

> But postmodernism . . . takes matters too far . . . nothing remains of any basis for reasoned action. . . . Worst of all, while it opens up a radical prospect of acknowledging the authenticity of other voices, postmodernist thinking immediately shuts off those other voices from access to more universal sources of power by ghettoizing them within an opaque otherness, the specificity of this or that language game. It thereby disempowers those voices [of women, ethnic minorities, colonized people, the unemployed, youth, etc.] in a world of lop-sided power relations.[10]

Instead, we prefer that grassroots advocacy simply be recognized as one of the ways in which communities and their planners innovate; at the same time, others remain squarely in mainstream practice. The Chicago Works Together plan, after all, while an attempt to re-create Chicago's civic values to give a voice to the neighborhoods, was a claim on the older national tradition and a general model against which the claims of other groups, themselves diverse in their interests, might be measured. A tension between the creation of central values and plans, and what the equity planners show us are the legitimate creations of smaller communities, is what we would seek.

As with much else, the way the planning profession—and the culture generally—deals with these issues is likely to be played out on the issue of race. One viewpoint is that of the growth coalition, which at times seems able to deliver rewards across race and class boundaries. This promise of equal rewards will most often be made in a difficult economy, but it will not be delivered. Instead, there will be symbolic rewards along with the pretensions of race-blind (and class-blind) policies, while deeper structural forces continue situations of unequal opportunity and unequal welfare. Equity planning will play a role in ameliorating these situations, as we have argued, without fundamentally changing them.

An alternative view tends to come, not from elites, but from the grassroots. Absent a fairly massive effort at cooptation and repression of the sort that has recently failed in South Africa, there will also be increased efforts at cultural self-development. This will include not simply African Americans and Latinos, the most prominent voices in past decades, but other groups and subdivisions of these groups. Equity planners will work hard in these efforts, even with minimal government funding.

The planning profession, we hope, will continue to bridge both growth and postmodern viewpoints. They will help strengthen the first, partly because some of them will act as equity planners even in places where no serious alternative to the growth coalition exists. We hope that something more promising will develop in these places. And the planners will also help develop the second approach. Down the road, perhaps the two approaches, despite their tensions, will develop into identifiably new approaches to city development. In the meantime, equity planners will have made their important contributions.

NOTES

1. Hanna Fenichel Pitkin, "Justice: On Relating Private and Public," *Political Theory* 9 (1981): 327–347.

2. Some of the recent research dealing with urban planning as an attention-shaping, rhetorical argument may be found in: Howell Baum, *Planners and Public Expectations*

(Cambridge, Mass.: Schenkman, 1983); John Forester, *Planning in the Face of Power* (Berkeley: University of California Press, 1989); Charles Hoch, "Doing Good and Being Right," *Journal of the American Planning Association* 50, no. 3 (1984): 335–345; Seymore Mandelbaum, "Telling Stories," *Journal of Planning Education and Research* 10, no. 3 (1990): 209–214; and James A. Throgmorton, "Planning as Rhetorical Activity," *Journal of the American Planning Association* 59, no. 3 (1993): 334–346.

3. The multiple possibilities for organizing and managing attention are discussed in great detail in Forester, *Planning in the Face of Power*.

4. Pierre Clavel, *The Progressive City* (New Brunswick, N.J.: Rutgers University Press, 1986).

5. Robert Alan Dahl and Charles Edward Lindblom, *Politics, Economics, and Welfare* (New York: Harper, 1953). This is perhaps the best-known statement on this, which became the postwar liberal consensus, after a fierce debate thought to pose too stark a contrast between "planning" and the "market."

6. Samuel Bowles, "The Post-Keynesian Capital–Labor Stalemate," *Socialist Review* 65 (September–October 1982): 45–72.

7. Bennett Harrison and Barry Bluestone, *The Deindustrialization of America* (New York: Basic Books, 1982).

8. Ira Katznelson, "The Crisis of the Capitalist City: Urban Politics and Social Control," in *Theoretical Perspectives on Urban Politics*, ed. Willis Hawley (Englewood Cliffs, N.J.: Prentice Hall, 1976), pp. 214–229.

9. Paul and Percival Goodman, *Communitas: Ways of Livelihood and Means of Life* (New York: Vintage, 1960).

10. David Harvey, *The Condition of Post Modernity* (Oxford: Basil Blackwell, 1989), pp. 116–117.

INDEX

THE AUTHORS AND PLANNERS

Dale F. Bertsch is a professor in the Department of City and Regional Planning and the School of Public Policy and Management at The Ohio State University. He was the first director of the Miami Valley (Dayton, Ohio) Regional Planning Commission.

Billie Bramhall is a planning consultant in Denver who also speaks and writes extensively on community development and neighborhood planning. During the 1980s, she was Denver's deputy director of planning and community development. She has a master's degree from the University of Pittsburgh's Graduate School of Public and International Affairs.

Pierre Clavel is a professor of City and Regional Planning at the College of Architecture, Art, and City and Regional Planning at Cornell University. He is the author of *Opposition Planning in Wales and Applachia, The Progressive City,* and has recently co-edited (with Wim Wiewel) *Harold Washington and the Neighborhoods.*

Rick Cohen is a housing and development consultant in New York City. During the 1980s he was director of Jersey City's Department of Housing and Economic Development. He also served as a vice-president for the Enterprise Foundation in Columbia, Maryland.

Peter Dreier is the E. P. Clapp Distinguished Professor of Politics at Occidental College in Los Angeles. He was director of housing for the Boston Redevelopment Authority (1984–1992), and Mayor Flynn's housing policy advisor. His articles on housing, urban politics, and community organizing have appeared in many journals. He has a Ph.D. in urban studies from the University of Chicago.

Kenneth Grimes is a senior planning analyst at the San Diego Housing Commission, San Diego, California, and the co-author (with Nico Calavita) of "The Establishment of the San Diego Housing Trust Fund: Lessons for Theory and Practice." He has a master's degree in city planning at San Diego State University.

Norman Krumholz is a professor of urban planning at Cleveland State University's College of Urban Affairs. He served as planning director for the city of Cleveland (1969–1979) and is a past president of the American Planning Association (1987–1988). His most recent book is *Making Equity Planning Work* (with John Forester).

Rob Mier is a professor of urban planning and public administration at the University of Illinois at Chicago. From 1983 to 1989 he worked for the city of Chicago under Mayors Harold Washington and Eugene Sawyer where he was commissioner of economic development. He is the author of numerous scholarly publications. His most recent book is *Social Justice and Local Development Policy*.

Kari J. Moe is chief of staff for Senator Paul D. Wellstone of Minnesota. During the 1980s, she was assistant to mayors Harold Washington and Eugene Sawyer of Chicago. She has a master's degree in urban planning from the Massachusetts Institute of Technology.

Derek Shearer was appointed Ambassador to Finland in 1994. Prior to this, he was director of the International and Public Affairs Center and a professor of Public Policy at Occidental College in Los Angeles. He is the author of numerous articles on progressive urban planning and participatory democracy.

Howard Stanback is city manager for Hartford, Connecticut. Formerly, he held important positions with the city of Chicago, including acting as commissioner of aviation and deputy mayor for infrastructure. His Ph.D. is in economics from the University of Massachusetts at Amherst.

Margaret D. Strachan is a planning consultant in Portland, Oregon. She was formerly a neighborhood organizer and an elected Portland city commissioner with administrative responsibility for transportation, building, human services, and planning. For her innovative planning initiatives and work on the Central City Plan, Strachan was awarded the American Planning Association's Distinguished Leadership Award of 1988.

Arturo Vazquez is director of the Eighteenth Street Development Corporation, a neighborhood-based development group in Chicago's Pilsen area. He is a former deputy commissioner of economic development in Chicago and has a long association with Mexican American social and community development issues.